Risk Management in Dentistry

Risk Management in Dentistry

J. B. R. Matthews BDS, DGDP(UK)
Honorary Clinical Tutor, Department of Dental Services, Sheffield University School of Clinical Dentistry; Formerly Member of Dental Secretariat, Medical Defence Union Ltd

WRIGHT

Wright
An imprint of Butterworth-Heinemann Ltd
Linacre House, Jordan Hill, Oxford OX2 8DP

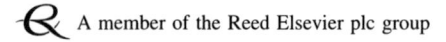

A member of the Reed Elsevier plc group

OXFORD LONDON BOSTON
MUNICH NEW DELHI SINGAPORE SYDNEY
TOKYO TORONTO WELLINGTON

First edition 1995

© Butterworth-Heinemann Ltd 1995

All rights reserved. No part of this publication
may be reproduced in any material form (including
photocopying or storing in any medium by electronic
means and whether or not transiently or incidentally
to some other use of this publication) without the
written permission of the copyright holder except
in accordance with the provisions of the Copyright,
Designs and Patents Act 1988 or under the terms of a
licence issued by the Copyright Licensing Agency Ltd,
90 Tottenham Court Road, London, England W1P 9HE.
Applications for the copyright holder's written permission
to reproduce any part of this publication should be addressed
to the publishers

British Library Cataloguing in Publication Data
Matthews, J. B. R.
    Risk Management in Dentistry
    I. Title
    617.60068

ISBN 0 7236 1011 8

Composition by Genesis Typesetting, Laser Quay, Rochester, Kent
Printed and bound in Great Britain by Biddles Ltd, Guildford and King's Lynn

Contents

Foreword vii

Preface ix

1 Introducing Risk Management 1

2 Clinical practice organization for Risk Management 15

3 Workplace and environmental risks 36

4 Medico-legal Risk Management 94

5 Risk in clinical dental practice 130

6 Risk transfer, insurance and indemnity 164

7 Professional risks 182

8 Occupational risk 212

9 Developing a Risk Management strategy 226

Appendix 246

Index 251

Foreword

During the twentieth century the practice of dentistry has developed from comparative infancy into a highly sophisticated health care specialty. As a result of this, within three generations the expectation of dental patients has changed from one of resignation to the almost inevitability of edentulousness to that of maintenance of an aesthetic natural dentition throughout life.

The increasing complexity of dental treatment, with its associated higher costs and even greater patient expectations, places an increasing demand on both the clinical and communication skills of the dentist. These factors, together with the rise of consumerism and the easier access to legal redress, have led to an escalation in patient complaints and civil claims arising from dental treatment; this is further demonstrated by the very considerable increase in the annual subscriptions payable to the defence organisations.

The desirability of reducing the likelihood of such complaints or legal action is both an obvious and ethical objective of all health care professionals. Hence the concept of Risk Management has evolved and thus this book is likewise most timely. The presentation of a comprehensive overall risk management strategy, bringing together both the clinical and non-clinical elements wil be particularly welcome to all those concerned with the provision of dental care.

The author is a general practitioner, and is also an acknowledged expert in dento-legal matters with particular expertise in dental risk management. The advice and guidance contained in this book will help those in clinical dentistry both to avoid those mishaps which are avoidable and to resolve as expeditiously as is possible those which are unavoidable, to the mutual benefit of both patient and dentist alike.

Peter Swiss BDS, LDSRCS, DGDP(UK)
Managing Director, Denplan Professional Ltd.
Formerly, Dental Secretary and Head of Dental Division,
The Medical Defence Union Ltd.

Preface

When I qualified as a dentist in 1970, dental plaque was an unfamiliar term, and fluoride toothpaste merely a future prospect. There was, however, an accelerating trend towards the recognition of 'preventive', as opposed to chiefly therapeutic dental care. Twenty years later, on taking up full-time dento-legal work, I found a parallel situation occurring with the development of 'risk management'. I hope that this book will go some way towards de-mystifying the topic, and who knows but that twenty years hence we shall not wonder how we coped without it?

Risk has much to do with the unfamiliar and the unknown. The preparation of this text would therefore itself have been an unacceptable risk without the advice, wisdom and encouragement of many colleagues. I am indebted to the Medical Defence Union for access to its unequalled computer database, and in particular to Dr Michael Saunders, General Manager, Professional Services, and Mr Peter Swiss, Dental Secretary. Invaluable help was given also by Dr Geoffrey Roberts, head of Healthcare Risk Management (now MediRisk) at the MDU, and Mrs Christine Orchard, whose computer terminal tolerated (mostly!) my investigations.

My thanks are due additionally to Mr Michael Ryan, of Hempsons solicitors, Professor Peter Rothwell, Dr Keith Hurst, of the Nuffield Institute for Health and especially to Professor David Poswillo, for their inspiration and assistance. Mr Norman Davies, Registrar of the General Dental Council provided valuable advice and information. Mrs Maureen Gibbins, of the Institute of Risk Management helped to introduce me to the wider world of risk and insurance.

In the course or research and writing, I have been helped by many experts and friends to whom, together with those who have kindly given permission to reproduce material, I again extend my thanks and appreciation. Dr Geoffrey Smaldon and Mrs Mary Seager, of Butterworth-Heinemann have been an unfailing source of encouragement.

As a devout proponent of equal opportunities, it is a matter of some regret that the use of gender-specific pronouns has been occasionally necessary solely in the pursuit of readability.

Nothing in this text is to be interpreted as other than the opinion of the author: although every reasonable care has been taken with legal and statutory information and guidance, readers should seek independent professional advice in connection with specific incidents or undertakings.

1
Introducing Risk Management

Old wine in new bottles?

Risk management is a relatively new concept in healthcare, and there will, no doubt, be doctors and dentists who will say that clinical practice can ill-afford yet another discipline to be assimilated into professional life and training. Others will say, after a cursory examination, that risk management offers nothing new to the assidious, caring and up-to-date practitioner: that it is indeed 'old wine in a new bottle'. A third group might take yet another view, asserting that the business of the health care professional ought to be devoted exclusively to patient care, and that others – be they administrators, lawyers or politicians – may address matters such as legal constraints, petty regulations and the niceties of ethics or philosophies. Such opinions have certainly greeted other 'innovations' in the past: they were appropriately acknowledged by Crocker,[1] who stated 'One man's common sense is another's novel concept, whilst it is heresy to a third and nonsense to a fourth'.

In anticipation of all these views, this introductory chapter is dedicated to all constituencies and will consider the following topic areas:

1 What is Risk Management?
2 What is its relevance in healthcare – and in dental healthcare especially?
3 How had the need for healthcare risk management come about?
4 How, in general, should risk management principles be applied in the practice of dentistry?

In reviewing these fundamental questions, it is the intention to concentrate on broad principles: more detailed considerations of their application will be found in the chapters which follow. Despite this necessarily wide approach, it is hoped that the importance and relevance of risk management in the practical everyday work of all dental professionals and their staff will become apparent.

What is Risk Management?

The Institute of Risk Management, based appropriately near the commercial hub of the City of London, defines the subject as being concerned with: '... the identification, measurement, control, financing and transfer of risks which threaten life, property and the continued viability of enterprises'.[2] It may be seen from this definition that the scope of the subject is wide. It may also be considered that whilst – thankfully – threats to 'life and property' may be considered relatively rare in dentistry, the 'continued viability' of a practice, clinic or any healthcare establishment may be endangered by an almost limitless range of adverse events. Bearing in mind that the Institute caters for specialists in both manufacturing and service industries, as well as the professions and Government, we will look, a little later, for a definition which focuses more directly on our needs as dentists. It is, however, useful to review the origins of risk management as a discipline, in order to improve understanding of the benefits it can bring.

It is self-evident that risk management is concerned with 'risk', yet although we can easily define the concept of 'risk' – the probability of a hazard occurring – both the word and the concept are relative latecomers to the English language. Giddens notes that the idea of risk as we know it today originated in the mid-seventeenth century.[3] Prior to this, hazards were chiefly regarded as either the outcome of luck or chance, or as being governed by the supernatural.

It can be scarcely coincidental that this period was also remarkable for a great upsurge in the development of commerce and international trade. Merchants were devising and organizing the basis of today's financial and commodities markets around this trade, and insurance – particularly the marine insurance of cargoes and vessels – was one service those markets could provide.[4] 'Risk' acquired, and has retained, a particular meaning in the context of the insurance contract, and as the statistical skills of the insurance industry improved, the opportunity to offer an expanding range of insurance products developed.

In commercial terms, then, risk management came to be associated with insurance. Businesses needed to insure against risks, so that the cost of a single and perhaps catastrophic event could be transformed into affordable annualized premium payments. Insurers existed, in general, to provide 'that the heavy losses of the few should fall lightly on the many'.[5] It was always in the interests of both parties that foreseeable risks should be avoided or minimized. Some commentators identify the 'Plimsoll line' (a mark which indicated how much cargo a ship could safely carry) as being a nineteenth-century example of risk management.

In more recent times, two factors have brought risk management into a more prominent role. The first has to do with the sheer pace and breadth of change which our modern society is undergoing. The second, to some extent the result of the first, is the volatility which some insurance markets have displayed. We shall examine these elements in greater detail in Section 3 of this chapter.

The relevance of risk management to healthcare

We have seen that risk management is concerned with controlling loss or damage to an undertaking. References in the healthcare literature date largely from the 1970s onwards, and are found in response to the medical malpractice crisis in the United States which arose at that time, and which resulted in an explosion of litigation and vastly increased insurance premiums.[6]

More recently, and in the dental context, Kenny and Valentino refer to risk management as concerning the 'detection, evaluation and resolution' of risks to people and property which may cause financial loss.[7] They expand on this:

> Risk management is concerned with the prevention of loss to physical and human resources, security, occupational health and safety, environmental and administrative areas. Risk management is an all-encompassing concept that not only protects the dentist from patient and staff complaints, but ensures that the office is safe for all persons by providing verification that ... regulations and prudent rules of practice are adhered to.

This description brings the reality and relevance of risk management directly into the context of clinical practice. One might at once be led to consider practical applications, such as:

1 The design of a surgery that does not leave adequate clear floor-space for cardio-pulmonary resuscitation of a collapsed patient (potential for major medico-legal action)
2 An accounting system that fails to alert a principal or manager to critical cash-flow anomalies, or which may be vulnerable to staff fraud (potential for major financial loss)
3 Inadequate employment procedures for dealing with recruitment, grievances or dismissals (potential for costly tribunal proceedings or civil action)

4   Unclear or misleading information to patients about charges for treatment (potential for civil action and professional complaints procedures)

It can be seen from these random examples that the application of risk management may extend to many areas of dental practice. In view of this broad scope, a simple definition of risk management is offered: 'The formulation and application of procedures, policies and designs intended to minimize the risk of foreseeable loss, injury or error.' By way of clarification, it is proposed to exclude from this remit the following:

(a) Speculative risks: these are defined as those risks which may leave the dentist either better or worse off than at the outset. Consideration here will be confined to pure risks, where the outcome will never be more advantageous than the status quo ante.
(b) Political risks: all businesses – and health care is no exception – may be subject to fluctuation and uncertainty as a result of Government policy and social change. Whilst the sociology of healthcare is undoubtedly of profound importance to the practising dentist, its detailed consideration is outside the scope of this work. Changing social attitudes do, however, rightly impact on professional ethics, and these will be studied in a later chapter on professional regulation and policy.

Having considered a definition and some examples, it is helpful to classify the risks which dental surgeons are – increasingly – likely to encounter during a professional lifetime. Kahn has suggested a list of risk criteria which, although originally intended for hospital settings, are equally appropriate in general practice:[8]

It is, unfortunately, probable that the practising dentist today, will at some point be faced with a potential loss from an event meeting one or more of these criteria. It will be the function of this book to examine in

Table 1.1 Criteria of risk significance – Kahn (1987)

1 Demonstrated potential for litigation
2 The possibility of erosion of reputation or of confidence
3 A breach of or threat to security of facilities, equipment, staff or premises
4 An illegal act committed on the premises
5 Significant actual or potential injury, compromise of well-being or loss of life of a patient, staff member or other
6 Minor incidents that occur in a cluster and develop significance because of such groupings or trends
7 Significant occupational health and safety hazards

detail how, in various aspects of the practice of dentistry, these criteria may be identified, assessed and dealt with.

Clearly, however, not all risks merit equal attention, and it would be profoundly wasteful of professional time to spend one's day in the constant pursuit of risk avoidance or control. Risk is present in any form of human activity. As Peter F. Drucker put it:

> To try to eliminate risk in business enterprise is futile. Risk is inherent in the commitment of present resources to future expectations. Indeed, economic progress can be defined as the ability to take greater risks. The attempt to eliminate risks, even the attempt to minimize them, can only make them irrational and unbearable. It can only result in that greatest risk of all: rigidity.[9]

Drucker was including 'speculative' risks in his definition, and clearly, without risk the entrepreneur would have no future. It is nevertheless important to retain some sense of perspective in devising a risk management strategy. A cost:benefit ratio must be kept in mind, but this can be difficult when the cost and the benefit are expressed in different currencies. To what extent, for instance, is financial constraint to be taken into account when considering, say, the implementation of cross-infection policies?

To make sense of risk management requires some understanding of risk perception, and this in turn is bound up with the challenges and complexity of modern life and healthcare.

How has the need for healthcare risk management come about?

It must be said at the outset that this brief section alone could well constitute an entire volume! The sociology of risk and its application to healthcare provision has been the subject of expert and lengthy debate in recent years. There can be little doubt that in the developed world the public is assailed each day by media news of risks and hazards of all kinds, but that risks associated with healthcare appear to be considered particularly 'newsworthy'. In the past month as this chapter is written (October 1993), UK newspapers have included reports of (allegedly): inaccurate radiotherapy dosages, incorrect pathology reports of bone cancers, and (four instances of) faulty cervical cytology technique; in the past three months, network television has featured the supposed links between cancer and water fluoridation, dental cross-infection procedures and HIV infection, and mercury toxicity from amalgam restorations.

This interest in medical risks begs a number of questions. Is healthcare becoming more risky? If not (as national morbidity and mortality data would suggest), is it simply that patients are demanding higher standards, a better guarantee of treatment outcome? Have attitudes to risks as a whole changed? Is healthcare perceived as lagging behind other aspects of modern life, or is it merely a more visible or emotive target?

The answers to these questions lie, at least in part, in the changing attitudes of society at large. In his book *The Reflective Practitioner*, Donald Schon observes how the relationships of professionals and their clients have changed since,[10] in 1963, the prestigious journal of the American Academy of Arts and Sciences could say, at the beginning of an issue devoted to extolling professional virtues: 'Everywhere in American life, the professions are triumphant'.

Schon traces the decline of this 'triumph' and the rise of the scepticism of the 1980s, and attributes it amongst other things to technological change. Change, as Drucker inferred, means uncertainty and risk. A society whose recent collective experience (at least, 'second-hand experience', courtesy of the technological advances of the media) included Three Mile Island, Bhopal, Thalidomide and Chernobyl, is unlikely ever again to place its unreserved trust in professionals.

Starr, in a seminal article in *Science* (1969),[11] is credited by many with one of the first attempts to quantify technological risks, by assessing them in terms of their economic costs. He based his calculations on the risk assessment programmes associated with the commissioning of nuclear power stations, and although later criticized, his approach signalled the beginnings of a new sensibility of risk, in a climate of rising doubts about the role of the 'professional expert'.

Giddens has noted that modern concepts of risk are tied into the modern proliferation of what he calls 'expert systems'.[3] These systems are characterized as any specialist field, the competence and authenticity of whose knowledge we are not generally in a position to exhaustively evaluate. When we interact with such a system – whether it entails getting onto an aircraft, or consulting a medical specialist, we essentially take on trust assurances that it is based on sound principles – we accept that expert systems generally work as they should.

The continued accumulation of knowledge, in all aspects of human affairs, has necessarily given the specialist an ever-narrowing field of expertise, since it is only possible for any one individual to command a finite – and itself expanding – sphere of information. On the other hand, as Crockford notes 'Corporations have become larger and more complex, and machines and industrial processes too complicated to be understood by those operating them'.[12] The same is true of today's general hospitals, and even in the microcosm of dental practice, the dentist who, forty years ago might himself replace the belt-drive or gears of a handpiece, would today be less likely to dismantle an air rotor or dental unit. Even the expert depends on other experts!

Thus as specialisms have become ever more fragmented and individual, so the potential for the malfunction of systems (composed of a number of specialisms working together) has increased. An expert in one field will not necessarily be aware of problems in a related field, and to some extent, particularly in industry, and more recently in healthcare, the role of the professional risk manager has become that of a generalist, a 'peerer over fences' who can perceive and evaluate an overall risk of which individual specialists are unaware.

If the professional risk manager is a 'professional perceiver of risk', then it must also be acknowledged that he or she should be equally concerned with the outcome of research into public perception of risk. In healthcare, consideration of this vitally important topic is increasingly required when medical or administrative errors, with a potential for litigation or loss of public confidence, come to light and a response or strategy is called for. Table 1.2 summarizes some findings of research into public perception of risks.[13]

It should be noted that observations such as these are necessarily over-simplifications of a complex and as yet inexact area of study. Douglas cites work which shows variously that: individuals are erratic

Table 1.2 Public perception of risk

1 *Involuntary risks* (e.g. environmental pollution) are more disquieting than voluntary risks
2 Risks under personal control (e.g. driving a car) are more readily accepted than those *not under personal control* (e.g. flying in an aeroplane)
3 Risks that seem 'fair' are more acceptable than those that seem '*unfair*'
4 *Catastrophic events* (i.e. simultaneous or involving groups) are more distressing than random events
5 Familiar risks (such as household accidents) are of less concern than *unfamiliar risks* (e.g. ozone depletion and skin cancers)
6 *Ethically objectionable* risks are less well tolerated than those which are not
7 Natural risks are accepted better than *man-made risks* (e.g. natural flooding as opposed to a dam collapse)
8 Naturally *memorable* or horrific events (e.g. terrorist bombings) are viewed as more risky
9 '*Dreaded*' risks are feared more, even though their probability is much lower (e.g. accidental clinical acquisition of HIV)
10 *Undetectable* hazards are more greatly feared than those which are readily visible
11 *Risks which can be scientifically explained* are less distressing than those about which scientists have to admit unceatinty

(Adapted from Baker: 'Risk Communication about environmental hazards'[13]

in their over-estimation or under-estimation of different risks; that the dangers of rare events tend to be over-estimated, whilst common risks are under-estimated; and that people tend to err on the optimistic side about hazards which flow from their own actions.[14]

In dentistry, one subject which has been for several decades a focus of public risk perception is the fluoridation of water supplies. This measure was originally proposed and encouraged with a paternalistic approach which often derided those who were opposed to it.[15] More recent authors are more careful to take account of the public's perception of risk.[16]

The two themes so far introduced in this section: increased risk as a by-product of modern technological society, and the varying perception of risk by individuals and society, suggest that possible solutions, or the most effective form of risk management, might be found in stringent regulation, and the adoption of higher levels of safety standards. These 'imposed' solutions have major drawbacks.

In the first place, regulations and safety precautions are costly. Whilst cost in itself should not be a bar to the assessment and reduction of risk, such costs will, ultimately, be borne in mind by the same society that expects to benefit from technological advance. Annual monitoring of all healthcare premises, such as dental practices, would undoubtedly contribute to safer care, but the associated costs would significantly reduce the funding available for that care. Then too, over-zealous regulation is wasteful – in that it regulates the conscientious as well as the careless or ill-informed. Such regulation may indeed be counter-productive. Who has not impatiently discarded a multi-page official circular of which nine-tenths is apparently irrelevant, and which in its entirety is badly presented and incomprehensible?

Yet in healthcare as in other industries and services, the demands and expectations of the consumer are fuelled by that very improvement in communications which publicizes risks and failures. Harvey Brooks may have been addressing engineers,[17] but they could equally have been dentists, when he wrote: 'The dilemma of the professional today lies in the fact that both ends of the gap he is expected to bridge with his profession are changing so rapidly; the body of knowledge that he must use and the expectations of the society that he must serve.'

One outcome of this dilemma has been the emergence of quality assurance, particularly in North America. In the United States and Canada, formal state regulation of healthcare institutions, both large and small, has historically been more stringent than in the United Kingdom. As a result, criteria and standards are formulated by federal agencies such as the Joint Commission on Accreditation of Healthcare Organizations (JCAHO), or by individual state or provincial authorities. These standards are formalized into quality assurance programmes. Wilson,[18] reviewing society's past and present attitudes to professional services, identifies a prime function of quality assurance as 'the promise of performance':

> Thus society, *and we are society*, says: "Before we give you our money, our trust, our bodies, our children, answer these questions: how do you know how good is the service you are offering? What evidence do you have which you can show us and which convinces you that your care, administration, service, teaching are what you say they are, and are what we want to receive? (my italics)

In the United Kingdom, where healthcare establishments have, since 1948, largely been operated by the State itself, through the Department of Health, a quite different approach has existed. Crown Immunity actually exempted NHS hospitals from many of the 'standards and criteria' which were invoked by legislation such as the Health and Safety at Work (1974) Act, and effectively insulated individual Health Authorities and healthcare workers against litigation from patients.

The Department's consultation paper 'Working For Patients', in 1989, eventually brought the issue of quality assurance to the forefront, by proposing that all clinical staff in the National Health Service should be involved in medical audit. The 1990 reforms of the NHS separated the 'purchasers' of healthcare – such as Health Authorities – from the 'providers' – hospitals, community services and so on. Contracts placed by purchasers with providers now included quality requirements, placing the onus of responsibility on individual provider units.

This was followed, in 1990 by the introduction of 'Crown Indemnity', and the cost of patient litigation was now substantially borne also at unit level. Some authorities predicted that litigation costs alone might account for 12% of the entire National Health Service budget by the mid-1990's.[19]

The relationship of risk management to quality assurance will be considered in more detail in the following chapter. Suffice to say here that whilst each is a function of the other, they are essentially complementary means to different ends: on the one hand the raising and maintenance of standards, and on the other, the avoidance of loss. Both have their roots in the changing society which healthcare must serve.

The general application of risk management principles in dentistry

Reference was made in the previous section to the 'professional' risk manager. It is not suggested that the general dental practitioner needs to become, or to acquire the services of, a full-time specialist in the field.

Whilst larger health service providers may require to appoint risk managers trained in the appropriate skills, the practitioner, working in conjunction with his existing professional advisers, will usually be in a position to apply the basic principles of risk management. As with any management function, however, there are occasions when the employment of an independent reviewer may be both cost-effective and beneficial. This aspect will be enlarged upon in a later chapter.

Crockford points out that risk management 'can be considered as simply the application to the particular problems of risk of the normal processes of management decision-making'.[1] He reminds us that these processes consist of:

(a) defining the problem
(b) evaluating possible solutions
(c) selecting and implementing the optimal solution
(d) monitoring the performance of the solution

Dentists – consciously or unconsciously – carry out these stages many times each day. Diagnosis and treatment planning are merely one obvious example. The purchase of a new item of equipment, or the appointment of new staff would be others.

In this sense, there really is nothing 'new' about risk management principles. However, as with other aspects of life, success comes not only from knowing the correct answers, but also from first asking the correct questions. In this respect, stage (a) is the most important: if one does not place one's self in a position to comprehend the risks that exist, then it is unlikely that potential solutions will be found – or possibly not until it is too late.

The adaptation of the decision-process stages to risk management is usually in the form of a cycle; this cyclic feature reflecting the fact that risk management is a continuous function. Changes in procedures, personnel or premises (internal changes), or in technology, regulations or social trends (external changes) mean that a risk management strategy is a dynamic function.

Table 1.3 shows the risk management cycle, and its similarity to the processes of management decision-making can be readily seen.

The first stage, that of risk identification, corresponds to defining the problem (or asking the right question). The identification of risks may be achieved by internal research, by discussion with staff and patients, or by external survey. Preferably – especially in larger facilities – all three techniques will be employed.

Risk assessment is an analysis of the 'raw data' identified as above. At this stage some risks may be classified as insignificant – though care must be exercised in such classification (see the sixth of Kahn's criteria in Table 1.2). It must also be borne in mind, as Douglas noted,[14] that

Table 1.3
The risk management cycle
An overview

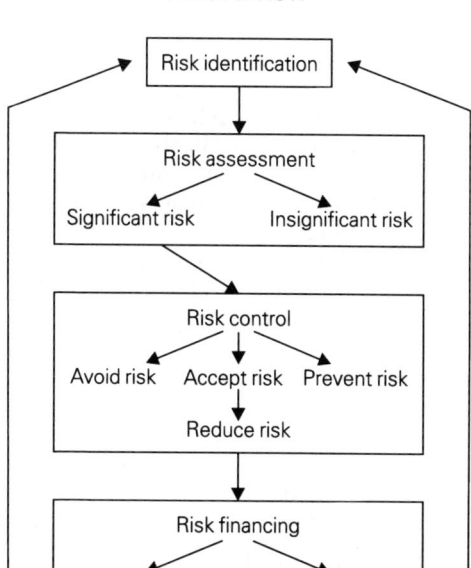

self-analysis may err on the side of optimism. Those risks which are considered of significance will required further action.

Risk control will depend on whether an individual hazard can be avoided or prevented in some way, or whether its existence is a necessary function of the institution's work. If a risk is inherent in this way, and can be neither avoided nor prevented, it is termed a 'retained' risk, and steps will subsequently be taken to reduce it to the minimum attainable level of incidence or severity.

Risks that are 'retained', albeit at a reduced level, must be catered for in some way. If the cost of the risk is low, it may be acceptable as part of the organisation's overall annual budget. If, however, the cost of the risk may be substantial, then it should be 'transferred' in some way. Insurance, by exchanging a known annual cost (the premium) for an indeterminate or possibly catastrophic loss, is the best known form of transfer.

The risk cycle is completed by a periodic review of both existing and newly identified risks, followed by a repetition of the procedure.

In brief and purely theoretical terms, this constitutes the risk management cycle. The procedure may appear to be self-evidently pedantic and time-consuming. Consider it, however, in the daily context of diagnosis and treatment planning. As a student or newly qualified professional, it is essential that these activities are carried out in accordance with a rigorous 'template': medical, social and dental histories, presenting complaints, full examinations, special tests, differential diagnoses and so on. Inevitably, as experience is gained, a dentist acquires the ability to focus on significant signs and symptoms. Indeed, patient care would grind to a halt were the full diagnostic net applied to every consultation.

In effect, dentists are not in any sense abandoning the rigours of diagnosis, and the prudent clinician appreciates that to do so would incur its own risks – those of missed or faulty diagnosis. Instead, there is acquired the ability to apply the principles without the pursuit of irrelevant or confusing detail, and it is towards the acquisition of the skill, amongst others, of determining what is or is not relevant that the lengthy path of medical training leads. In this sense, the risk management cycle is to be seen as a framework of principles which underlies everyday applications.

Conclusion: the cost of risk

It was earlier suggested that, by the mid-1990s, the cost of legal and indemnity payments to patients might amount to 12% of the total National Health Service budget in the UK. What might the cost of dental risk amount to?

1   In 1991, there were approximately 16,500 dentists on the lists of Family Health Service Authorities in England and Wales. (Source: Annual Abstract of Statistics.) On average, each of these practitioners will have paid some £300 in that year for professional indemnity 'insurance' to one of the three medical defence organizations (MDOs).[20] This total sum amounts to some £4.95 million.
2   Approximately 1,600 Community dentists and 600 hospital dentists will have paid a total of £165,000 to MDOs for advice and assistance on ethical and disciplinary matters, indemnity having that year been assumed by Health Authorities and Trusts.
3   It is estimated by MDOs that approximately one-tenth of their membership are involved in NHS, disciplinary or complaints procedures, or in proceedings preliminary to civil litigation in any one year. If it is conservatively estimated that each dentist so affected will have expended the equivalent of two working days on

correspondence, meetings or documentation, then from target average gross income figures for dentists in NHS general practice a time cost equivalent to £11.5 million is achieved.

4   In 1991, 472 formal investigations into complaints against dentists were held by Family Health Services Authorities in England alone. The administrative costs, staff time, and expenses paid to the professional and lay members of the investigating (Dental Service) Committee and witnesses are estimated at some £2,500 for each case. Additionally, an estimated 23,000 informal complaints and enquiries (at a ratio of 50:1 to formal hearings) were dealt with by the same bodies, incurring an estimated administrative cost of some £384,000.

The total costs of these four areas of expenditure amount to some £18.2 million. This figure excludes indemnity payments by Health Authorities, refunds made to patients by individual practitioners, industrial tribunal hearings, General Dental Council proceedings and a small number of criminal prosecutions.

The total cost of risk to each practising dentist in the UK would therefore approximate to one week's gross income. Whilst the application of risk management principles will not eradicate risk, it is probable that substantial savings, both to the individual dentist and to the public purse, may be made.

References

1   Crocker N. (1982) *An Introduction to Risk Management.* Woodhead-Faulkner, Cambridge
2   The Institute of Risk Management (1991) Student handbook
3   Giddens A. (1990) *The Consequences of Modernity.* Stanford University Press, Stanford, p. 30
4   Gibson-Jarvie R. (1979) *The City of London: a Financial and Commercial History.* Woodhead-Faulkner, Cambridge, p. 74 *et seq.*
5   Foresight (September 1993) *Journal of the Institute of Risk Management*
6   Hill G. (1991) What is Risk Management? *International Journal of Risk and Safety in Medicine*, **2**, 83–90
7   Kenny D.J. and Valentino C.L. (1991) Risk Management: The Clinician's Defense Against Liability. *Canadian Dental Journal*, **47**(3), 193–195
8   Kahn J. (1987) *Stepping Up to Quality Assurance.* Methuen, Toronto
9   Drucker P.F. (1973) *Management Tasks, Responsibilities and Practice.* Heinemann, New York
10 Schon D.A. (1983) *The Reflective Practitioner.* HarperCollins, New York
11 Starr C. (1969) Social Benefit versus Technological Risk. *Science*, **165**, 1232–1238
12 Crockford N. (1982) op cit, p. 2
13 Baker F. (1990) Risk Communication about Environmental Hazards. *Journal of Public Health Policy*, **11**, 341–359
14 Douglas M. (1985) *Risk: Acceptability According to the Social Sciences.* Routledge and Kegan Paul, London, p. 21

15 Douglas B.L. (1962) Dentistry and the Fluoridation Issue: The Dentist in the Social and Political Arena. *New York State Dental Journal*, **28**, 347–355
16 Christoffel C. (1992) Fluoridation; legal and political issues. *Journal of the American College of Dentists*, **59**(3), 8–13
17 Brooks H. (1967) The Dilemmas of Engineering Education. *IEEE Spectrum*, February 1967, 89
18 Wilson C.R.M. (1987) *Hospital-Wide Quality Assurance*. W.B. Saunders, Toronto, p. 2
19 Dingwall R. and Fenn P. (1991). Is Risk Management Necessary? *International Journal of Risk and Safety in Medicine*, **2**, 91–106
20 See Chapter 6 for a fuller description of the legal status of Defence Organizations

2
Clinical practice organization for Risk Management

The previous chapter defined risk management as the application of management principles to the identification, analysis, control and financing of risk. Indeed, the risk management cycle has been compared to the decision-making cycle in management theory.[1] This comparison begs the question: to what extent are dental clinicians trained in, and aware of, management skills, and what part should such training and awareness play in their professional development?

Traditionally – since the dental undergraduate curriculum was developed in the nineteenth century – the professional training of dentists has broadly followed the medical model. Schein identifies three components common to most professional training:[2]

1. A 'basic science' component, on which the profession's knowledge ultimately rests
2. An 'applied science' component which underlies the diagnosis and treatment of problems particular to the profession concerned
3. A 'skills and attitudes' component concerned with the actual performance of professional services to clients

Such features can be identified in the disciplines of medicine, law, architecture, engineering and most other modern professional training courses. In dentistry, the 'basic sciences' generally parallel similar teaching of medical undergraduates, with modifications and emphases appropriate to dental needs. 'Applied sciences' are taught in modular form alongside the 'skills' components in the clinical setting of the dental hospital. These sciences – such as pharmacology, radiology and general medicine – form the specific background against which the professional 'skills' are acquired, usually by a combination of theory and repeated practice of operative procedures.

The academic blend as described here was broadly adopted by most dental schools in the UK, and also in the United States, until the mid-1970s, and had remained essentially unchanged in format and length for half a century. The approach followed prevailing scientific doctrine: it was analytical, specialist and compartmentalized. The new dental graduate was skilled in undertaking specific procedures and in the basic elements of treatment planning, but although there were always notable exceptions both in course design and individual student abilities, the newly-qualified dentist was relatively unprepared for the synthesis of approach required after graduation. In other words, he was able in the performance, rather than the practice of his profession.

There have been innovations in the past decade – and currently continuing – which redress this balance, but management (an essentially synthetical skill) still tends to be seen as an alien concept in professional training, particularly scientific training based on the analytical model of technical rationality.[3] It is perhaps this fundamental dichotomy, rather than the traditional 'taint of commercialism' which has relegated the teaching of management skills to a low priority in dental undergraduate curricula.

Wilkinson defines management simply as;[4] 'the art of organizing people and events in a structured way'. He suggests three stages in the management process:

1 The identification of objectives and goals
2 Deciding the best means of achieving them
3 Controlling, guiding, reviewing and adjusting

This illustrates the synthesis of management in action. A simple objective is stated, acquires detail and complexity in deciding and implementing the optimum course of action, and is then further expanded in the process of monitoring, reviewing and ultimately revising the original objective in the light of changing circumstances and ideals. This contrasts with the scientific method, characterized as it is by the analytical reduction of problems to their basic components.

Unfortunately, professional practice does not solely consist of scientific problems with clearly defined parameters – if it did, risk management (and management in general) would be infinitely simplified! Practice is complicated by people, by relationships, by external constraints and internal politics. As Ackoff observed:[5]

> Managers are not confronted with problems that are independent of each other, but with dynamic situations that consist of complex systems of changing problems that interact with each other. I call such situations *messes*. Managers do not solve problems, they manage messes.

This is not a book about management theory. It would be a mistake, however, to believe that risk management is only about hazards resulting from regulations, from litigation, from the environment, or from clinical science. It is also about communication, planning and procedures. Writing of the dental malpractice crisis in the United States, Pollack noted: 'Dentists in general became high-liability risks because claims against them are difficult to defend, often as a result of poor office practices'.[6]

Risk management in dentistry develops from sound practice organization and procedures, the setting of aims and objectives, and the regular planned review of processes and personnel. Risks can be minimized most effectively, and the consequences of inevitable mishaps best reduced, when clinical care and treatment in accordance with current teaching and practice is built on a foundation of good administration and management.

Organization and procedures

1 Aims and objectives

There are essentially two methods of learning: we can learn from our own mistakes, or we can learn from the mistakes of others. The second is usually found to be less painful and less expensive. However, the majority of procedures in the majority of organizations exist because they have 'always been done that way', and they will usually continue until one of three circumstances occurs:

(a) A change is forced by external events;
(b) The procedure proves to have serious shortcomings
(c) There is a change in personnel involved

Consider a situation where the senior receptionist of a practice or clinic controls the timing of appointments. This procedure generally operates effectively except where clinical circumstances are exceptional. Junior clinical staff are unwilling to raise the issue, whilst senior staff are more able to cope with the time pressures generated. Typical possibilities for returning control to those responsible for carrying out treatment might be:

(a) Commissioning an independent survey of service efficiency (external event)
(b) A formal complaint by a patient resulting in an overhaul of the appointment system (major shortcoming)
(c) A replacement receptionist (personnel change)

Similar scenarios can be constructed for any number of procedures, from financial planning to protection against ingested root canal instruments. Problems and responses such as these typify the process of learning from our own mistakes. There is, however, a fourth way to initiate change – by managing it.

Zaltman and Duncan suggest that different techniques may be needed to bring about change in different types of organization.[7] They suggest four principal models:

1. Re-education   This model suggests that if personnel are given rational arguments about perceived problems and possible solutions, they will be encouraged to accept change
2. Persuasion   This model depends on inspirational leadership on the part of managers in proposing that change is both necessary and possible. Problems may arise if the results do not live up to expectations
3. Facilitation   This depends on emphasizing the role of individual members of the organizational 'team'. Training in team building and group problem-solving is used to encourage a sense of belonging and interdependence which leads to examination of both means and objectives
4. Power   This alternative depends on the organization's powers of coercion. Personnel are compelled to become involved in change by the use of rewards and punishments

Whilst this last option might be regarded as the least constructive, there are arguments to be made for and against the other choices. It is for the individual manager to decide which model, or combination, to employ in given circumstances.

An intention or commitment to change can only come about when there is a strongly held sense of purpose, whether consensual (preferable) or individual. This sense of purpose is dependent, amongst other things, on the formulation of objectives or goals. It is fashionable today for organizations to embrace 'mission statements' or even 'vision statements' which are often a product of marketing strategy and expensive consultancy fees. There is, nevertheless, a sound and commercial wisdom in considering the central goal of any undertaking, however small in size or limited in resources.

The assertion that the only long-term goal of a dental practice or clinic is – 'to provide dental care and treatment' – might properly invite the queries: 'to whom?'; 'on what terms?'; 'to what standard?' and 'irrespective of cost?'.

Without a strategic aim, and medium-term objectives which strive towards it, there can be no sense of measured progress, no distinction between the personal aspirations of one professional as compared to others, and certainly no feeling of achievement. Harvey coined the term 'The Abilene Paradox' to describe a possible and common outcome of such failure.[8] He described a family outing to a restaurant (in Abilene, Texas), which involved a long, hot, tiring and uncomfortable journey. On arrival, the food was so poor that argument broke out among the group. After heated discussion, it transpired that no family member had actually wanted to make the trip, but each assumed that the others wished to go, and did not want to appear unsociable. Harvey uses this story to illustrate how a large number of organizations have arrived, by dint of prolonged and arduous endeavour, at a situation entirely different from, and even contradictory to, their original desires and aspirations. Many dentists will have experienced the Abilene Paradox, and will be aware that the current operational and management status of their workplace bears little relationship to the original, or desired goals. Moreover, if there is no effective procedure for periodically redefining goals, nor for assessing progress towards them (or deviation away), then the establishment is a vessel without a tiller, borne along on the tidal currents of external forces.

Aim: To set up a dental health education facility for patients within the practice

Objectives:

1 Agenda for staff meeting: discuss options, benefits, costs, etc.
   Time: within six weeks   Personnel: all staff

2 Detailed discussion with hygienist: explore requirements (space; equipment; fittings; materials)
   *Time: within two weeks   Personnel: Hygienist

3 Costings from builder and plumber: alterations and fittings
   *Time: four weeks   Personnel: Dentist,
                                           contractors

4 Compile list of materials, leaflets and costs from catalogues, magazines, sales staff
   *Time: four weeks   Personnel: Dentist,
                                           hygienist

5 Discuss arrangements for appointments, charges, patient circular
   *Time: six weeks   Personnel: Dentists,
                                           reception,
                                           hygienist

* Timings are cumulative

Figure 2.1 A sample aim and related objectives

The terms **aims** and **goals** are used here interchangeably to denote relatively long-term strategies. Aims are most easily accomplished by breaking them down into more accessible and measurable objectives. To use a travel analogy, my aim may be to travel to London: my objectives might be to order a taxi, book a train ticket, catch the right train, and so on.

A sample dental aim and related objectives are shown in Figure 2.1. Note that whilst the goal, although specific, is stated in general terms, the subsidiary objectives are more structured in respect of parameters of time, techniques and attainability. There is little point in a philosophy of absolute perfection, and the setting of unrealistic targets results in disappointment and loss of motivation.

The acronym 'RUMBA' is often cited as a standard for the writing of objectives:[9] that is, they should be:

Relevant: they should be clearly related to the organization's core business

Understandable: all personnel can comprehend and identify with the objective

Measurable: it must be possible objectively to show whether, and to what extent, objectives are achieved

Behavioural: objectives should relate to things people do, rather than merely what they believe

Attainable: objectives which are unrealistic tend to de-motivate and depress

For a new clinic or practice, the establishment of aims and objectives at the outset is, then, a logical extension of the business planning process which properly incorporates financial, structural and staff planning.[10] For the established unit, it will be necessary to undertake careful research before drafting objectives and then, preferably, convening a meeting of the appropriate staff to discuss, validate and agree the proposed strategy.

Setting aims and objectives is central to good management and to risk management. There are two dictionary definitions of a 'team': either – 'beasts of burden harnessed together' or – 'a group working towards a common goal'.[11] The identification of common objectives is what differentiates the two. In a managed and harmonious environment, the individual is aware of his or her purpose and the significance of the task, and takes responsibility for its completion. In these circumstances, the possibility of untoward outcomes is greatly diminished.

The suggestion is often made that dentists 'do not have time for' such activities as goal-setting. This is partly true: the majority of dentists do not set long and medium-term aims and objectives, and this suggestion is invariably made by a member of that majority. The goal-setting minority are generally rewarded by greater personal achievement and success. There is substantial evidence that goal-setting is a basic human characteristic and need without which mental and physical deterioration may result (see Chapter 8).[12] We all set goals, but if these are short-term and lack challenge and satisfaction (for example, the often-quoted 'survive until Friday' attitude), risks are increased and rewards diminished accordingly.

2 Procedure Planning

The first step in any risk management process is that of assessment, and this is possible only in an ordered environment where the management, workplace and clinical aspects are planned – as far as is possible. This is not to say that a rigid bureaucracy should exist: quite the contrary. In an efficiently managed practice, personal freedom and initiative is enhanced by the acceptance of common goals and individual responsibilities.

As has been suggested in the above section, planning flows from the setting of strategic objectives and aims. Procedures are the basis for the effective fulfilment of those objectives. If a dental practice sets as one of its objectives; '... the reception and administration staff deal with patients in a prompt, courteous and efficient manner' – such a statement implies two concepts. First that there will be agreed 'ways of dealing with patients' which correspond to the ideals aimed at, and second, that some way of measuring the achievement of this objective can be arrived at. The first defines procedures, whilst the second (dealt with later in this chapter) introduces some notion of performance measurement.

It has already been suggested that the majority of organizations, including many primary healthcare establishments, have poorly defined administrative procedures. By contrast, their clinical procedures may be highly systematized (even if not recorded). Thus the same sequence of clinical events will be followed for a full crown preparation, or the removal of an impacted lower third molar. The administrative functions of clinical practice may contribute significantly to the risk and liability of the enterprise, but the development and implementation of its procedures is usually far less controlled.

> Office procedures and policies communicate much about the organization of a dental office. Procedures for informing patients about delays, returning patients' calls, making billing arrangements and conveying the dentist's post-operative instructions ensure that the patient receives prompt attention and accurate information.[13]

Developing a procedure manual for both clinical and administrative functions may help greatly, not only in identifying and reducing risk, but also in promoting efficiency, staff motivation and standards of care.

Writing procedures can be a time-consuming process, but when set against time taken in the induction and training of staff, the penalties incurred by using inefficient methods and the difficulties which can be caused by staff members each adopting a different approach, time devoted to integration and planning is an excellent investment.

Clinical procedures can be drawn up by reference to existing dental and chairside assisting texts and training programmes, such as the British Dental Association's 'Teamwork'.[14] The latter also provides a starting point for the development of administrative procedures, and courses are currently being developed by the British Dental Association in conjunction with the Association of Medical Secretaries and Receptionists.[15]

Procedures for administrative functions might include, for instance:

Telephone techniques
New patient clerking procedure
Allocating emergency appointments
Dealing with dissatisfied patients
Cash handling
Arranging referrals
Stock ordering and management

It should not be difficult for management and staff to define the routine procedures which occupy the greater proportion of their working day, and to draft and then to agree definitive methods of work.

The practice manual

Neither the setting of objectives nor the definition of procedures is an end in itself. Additionally, these functions will need regular review and updating. Producing a practice manual, in loose-leaf format, is one way of documenting these aspects of management. Each staff member, on appointment, can then receive a personal copy which can be updated as required, which can serve as a reference source during training, and which can be maintained as a record of further training, staff meeting notes and so on. Figure 2.2 shows a suggested contents page for a dental practice manual.

It will be seen that not all sections of the manual are directly applicable to all staff members; does the receptionist need to know about cross-infection, or the hygienist about cash handling? There are good reasons for providing basic information to all personnel, however, in a small establishment, role flexibility may be essential, all staff should be aware of the job descriptions of others, which encourages mutual respect and understanding, and finally, joint discussion and

The Practice Manual

Section 0

Contents

1 Introduction
1.1 Purpose of manual
1.2 Aims and objectives of the practice
2 Staff/employment
2.1 Organization plan
2.2 Guidance on employment contracts
2.3 Disciplinary and grievance procedures
2.4 Dismissal
2.5 Job descriptions
2.6 Induction and training programmes
2.6.1 Teamwork
2.6.2 Other programmes
3 Health and safety at work
3.1 Practice health and safety policy
3.2 Fire procedure and equipment
3.3 Emergency and CPR procedure
3.4 Accidents at work
3.5 Equipment and electrical safety
3.6 Principles of cross-infection control
4 Equipment and premises
4.1 Security – general
4.2 Cleaning and maintenance procedures
4.3 Services – general information
4.3.1 Heating
4.3.2 Electrical
4.3.3 Gas
4.3.4 Water
4.4 Clinical services – air, gases, waste
4.5 Equipment – general
4.6 Equipment – instructions, faults
4.7 Equipment – maintenance

5 Surgery staff
5.1 Cross-infection procedures
5.2 Cleaning and care of equipment
5.3 Specific safety precautions
5.4 Radiation
5.5 Mercury
5.6 Sharps
5.7 Waste
5.8 Materials and drugs
5.9 Stock and ordering
6 Administration
6.1 Dealing with patients:
6.1.1 On the telephone;
6.1.2 In person.
6.2 NHS procedures
6.3 Private patients
6.4 Appointments
6.5 Clinical records
6.6 Complaints
7 Finance
7.1 Collecting money
7.2 Accounting procedures
7.3 Cash security
7.4 NHS procedures
8 Ethics
8.1 Behaviour with patients
8.2 Appearance
8.3 Confidentiality
9 General
9.1 Inventory and asset register
9.2 Personal training programme
9.3 Staff meeting notes, updates

Figure 2.2 The Practice Manual

revision of procedures is helped by a general comprehension and commitment to the undertaking as a whole.

3 Performance measurement

This is a rather formal title intended to include two separate but related functions, whose interdependence is not fully appreciated. The risk management process has been illustrated as a 'loop', following the application of risk control measures, the whole procedure must be regularly reviewed. Staff, equipment and techniques change, materials and drugs are updated, new research findings are published – all these factors require that risk management is a cyclic and continuous process. Mere repetition would be tedious and unproductive, performance measurement makes a significant difference.

To take a financial analogy, almost all enterprises, whether in private or public ownership, prepare monthly accounts or financial statements. These are aggregated into annual financial reports or accounts, which in turn are used to prepare budgets for the succeeding period. If such a procedure were to be carried out each month, or each year with no reference to past performance, or without comparison to national or professional criteria, the task would be largely pointless and inefficient. The whole objective of accounting, budgeting and planning is based on measurement and projection, increased output to be achieved at A, savings made at B or a re-allocation of resources to C.

Effective management, of which risk management forms part, operates no differently, and needs mechanisms of comparison, to enable future projection based on past experience. Two of the tools available for review and planning are Audit and Appraisal.

Audit

It has been observed that audit has a 'disquieting' and threatening aspect, carrying overtones of third party assessment of performance in a judgemental fashion.[16]

Audit need not be like that at all. In their introductory workbook,[17] the British Dental Association and the Faculty of General Dental Practitioners (UK) observe that audit is a loose term which may, at the one extreme, be used to describe an external and regulatory procedure, or at the other, a self-administered developmental and management exercise. The use of audit in a voluntary and educational sense is commended.

Audit is also a cyclic process (see Figure 2.3), involving the observation of activity, comparison of the results observed with those expected, and the subsequent modification of practice.

A simple example illustrates. Take twenty patient records from the current treatment file. Count how many include: a full initial medical history; an updated medical history note, dated, and relating to the most recent course of treatment; and a written or annotated treatment plan for the most recent course of treatment. If the score is less than 100% on all

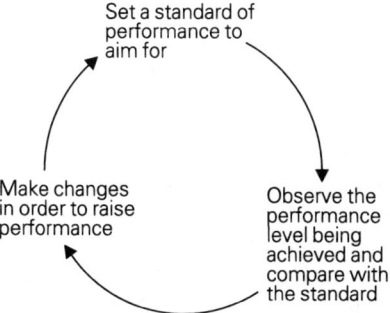

Figure 2.3 The audit cycle (adapted from *Clinical Audit – a Workbook* (1993) British Dental Association)

three counts, consider how procedures might be modified to improve performance. Finally, make a note to repeat the exercise in 12 months time (see also Chapter 4: Clinical records).

Alternative audit projects might record the number of patients waiting more than ten minutes beyond their designated appointment time (or those who arrived more than ten minutes beyond the appointment time – the choice depends on which is perceived as a greater problem); or the number of radiographs in a sample of records which were of less than optimum processing and diagnostic quality.

Audit need not be quantitative, it can also be qualitative. The use of video cameras (with consent) to record consultations can assist greatly in analysing and improving communication skills. A combination of qualitative and quantitative information may be derived from a patient questionnaire using both simple and open-ended questions. The possibilities are endless, and the first significant question is to evaluate which areas for audit will be useful, effective and (most important) relatively economical in time and cost terms. As Shaw has noted, 'Audit takes time. Busy people find it hard to pause long enough to demonstrate how effective is their activity.'[18]

Audit in the National Health Service has been fostered by the Department of Health's White Paper 'Working For Patients',[19] following its earlier commendation in the Griffiths Report on the National Health Service.[20] In primary dental care, the Department has allocated funding for peer review projects which embrace similar characteristics and intentions, but on a shared and confidential basis between practitioners. Both approaches can be used simultaneously, but audit procedures can be individually tailored to the needs of an individual practice or clinician.

Appraisal

If audit is considered as the evaluation of procedures with a view to maximizing the achievement of desired outcomes, then appraisal may be regarded as a complementary process designed to review staff performance with the intention of developing their potential both as individuals and as members of the healthcare team.

Appraisal should also be regarded as an everyday management task, an integral part of the supervising clinician's or manager's role. Staff represent a major investment of any business or undertaking; annual expenditure on staff salaries, training and recruitment is usually the greatest single overhead cost. Moreover, staff who fail to fulfil their potential are one of the greatest sources of reduced efficiency and increased workplace stress. Dissatisfied staff may be the source of future employment disputes or claims (see Chapter 3), and poor staff selection, training or task competence may lead to patient complaints or dento-legal actions (see Chapters 4, 5).

The notion of appraisal grew out of the work of Mayo in the 1930s.[21] Whilst investigating the effects of the working environment on output and efficiency, he observed that the actual process of consulting and involving staff appeared to account for more improvement in performance than any experimental changes in their surroundings or tasks. Modern approaches to appraisal take account of the fact that efficiency and effectiveness are maximized when staff and management participate jointly in setting objectives and reviewing progress.[22]

Like audit, appraisal may also have negative connotations. These may come about for a variety of reasons, including:

1. The linkage of appraisal to disciplinary procedures, criticism or conflict
2. The use of appraisal solely or principally to determine pay rises or bonuses (performance-related pay)
3. The concept of appraisal as a bureaucratic annual exercise which 'changes nothing'
4. The embarrassment of conducting interviews which analyse an employee's performance

1 Whilst appraisal *can* be used – as can audit – as an instrument of discipline and control, there is equally no reason why this should be the motive. Appraisal has been shown to be most successful when conducted in an equitable and co-operative atmosphere between appraiser and appraisee.[23] The intention of appraisal in a risk management context is to capitalize on the abilities and potential of staff members and to introduce mutually agreed preventive or controlling actions when desired or correct results are not attained.

2 The use of performance-related pay is a topic of considerable current dispute amongst management theorists. Whilst there are arguments in favour of its use in certain circumstances,[24] there are equally a number of studies which fail to show that it makes a positive contribution to output.[25] Appraisal for performance and development is better separated from pay and reward negotiation.

3 Certainly, in some large organizations, the annual round of appraisals is met by staff and management alike with scepticism. This is usually the result of appraisal procedures which are imposed, rigid, paper-generating exercises. There is also a tendency to devalue the day-to-day 'appraisal' which we all carry out on our co-workers, and which, in management, should be a developed and recognized skill.

4 Finally, in a well-prepared appraisal programme, there should be neither embarrassment nor confrontation in the appraisal interview. Instead, the emphasis should be on negotiated agreement, based on the validity of viewpoint of both the appraiser and appraisee.

The detailed design and implementation of an effective appraisal programme is beyond the scope of this book. The reader is advised to consult one of the eminently readable texts on the subject,[26] and to discuss the whole topic with staff before introducing such a project. Imposed programmes are unlikely to succeed, but once it is generally recognized that appraisal offers each individual the opportunity to contribute to the overall development of the practice, clinic or department, whilst at the same time improving personal development and relationships, the possibility exists to introduce an effective appraisal structure.

A brief example of an approach to appraisal might be as follows:

Stage 1 After discussing the general ideas and aims of appraisal, team members each prepare their own job description, detailing the principal tasks they are responsible for. In conjunction with their manager (dentist, practice administrator), each individual agrees standards for each task area (an example for a dental surgery assistant is shown at Figure 2.4). When setting standards (as in devising objectives) it is important to ensure that they are reasonable, valid, relevant and agreed. It may be tempting to propose that for instance 100% of all patient records will be available at the time of the patient's attendance, but such a standard is probably unworkable, and fails to consider that the occasional 'missing' record will turn up on the senior clinician's desk.

Stage 2 A timetable is drawn up for preparation and completion of appraisal interviews. A commitment is made to abide by this, and not to postpone or interrupt these meetings. In advance of the interview, both the manager and the appraisee will note what they consider to have been

Task area	Task description	Standard agreed	Assessment
Patient care	Greet patient by name on arrival; seat and place protective wear/glasses. Keep mouthrinse available. Overall monitoring and support of patients	Use patient name for all regular patients; all patients have appropriate protective wear/glasses. Mouthrinse and tissues always available for patient use	
Chairside assisting	Aspiration, retraction, passing instruments and materials. Mixing materials to quantities and consistency shown	Dentist can work in accessible field; appropriate instruments and materials available with minimal delay; wastage of materials minimized.	
Sterilization	Collect and sort used instruments/materials. Correctly discard disposables, sharps, clinical waste. Ultrasonic or lubricate as necessary. Autoclave instrument trays	Waste disposal correct. Use of TST strips/autoclave tape. Sterile materials flow planned to avoid delay	
Cleaning/maintenance	Carry out between-patient procedure: wipe listed surfaces and contact zones. Maintain general surgery cleanliness. Carry out end of session and weekly tasks as listed	Between-patient procedures consistently performed. Surgery in clean and orderly state	
Administration	Collect/return records and day lists. List treatments in daybook. Liaise with reception. Control laboratory dockets; check lab. work schedules. Enter chartings on records	Cards available as required. Daylists and daybook kept up to date. Lab. work returned correctly; delays notified in time to adjust appointments	
Stock control	Maintain weekly surgery order list for practice manager. Check delivered stock	Materials and supplies available when required. Over-stocking minimized.	

Figure 2.4 Tasks and standards examples for Dental Surgery Assistant

the appraisee's performance in relation to each standard agreed. The appraisee should also have the opportunity to comment on aspects of the work or establishment which are relevant to their role, and both parties should consider what future development, or training might be helpful to the appraisee.

Stage 3 At the interview, levels of performance should be freely discussed. Praise for achievement at or beyond the standards set in particular task areas is a valuable motivator (When did you last thank someone for a job well done? Can you more easily remember criticizing staff for failures?). In areas where shortfalls occur, constructive discussion might centre on possible obstacles to good performance. All too often, staff are criticized without sufficient consideration of the reasons for their 'inadequacy', which may include lack of training, supervision or direction, or a failure of facilities, time or, indeed, other staff.

Stage 4 At the conclusion of the interview, a plan for action should be agreed, indicating the precise action to be undertaken, by what date, and by whom. This action might be further training, extension or reduction of task responsibilities, or greater attention to achieving particular standards.

A review date – not necessarily one year, but it should not normally be longer than this – should be set for future appraisal. Copies of the plan should be retained by the appraiser and appraisee for future reference. Whilst in larger organizations, employees are frequently given a 'rating' following performance appraisal, there is no necessity for this to be done in a small establishment. Although some managers feel that ratings add a sense of achievement, or a goal to strive for, there is no reason why appraisal should be competitive, particularly if – as recommended – pay issues are excluded from the outcome.

Risk management and quality assurance

The use of audit and appraisal, and the concepts of objective setting and procedure planning, have become more familiar in the healthcare setting following the introduction of quality assurance techniques. The work of Donabedian in the 1960s is generally considered to have been seminal in this field,[27] and quality assurance has, since then, come to occupy a position of increasing importance in both the administrative and clinical aspects of health care.

Quality assurance and risk management share some features, and it is helpful to consider their relationship for a greater understanding of the benefits which each can confer.

Quality assurance in healthcare

The application of quality assurance to healthcare is not, in itself, new. It has been suggested that Florence Nightingale – who recommended improved education for nurses and the study of mortality rates in military hospitals – was an early proponent.[28] As the technology and organization of healthcare became more developed, its methods and procedures came increasingly into question. When the National Health Service was established in the United Kingdom in 1948, an underlying principle was that the application of increased resources for health would lead ultimately to a reduction in disease and a levelling off of healthcare expenditure.[29] That this did not happen is scarcely surprising fifty years later, but it reveals how little was understood about health and healthcare at that time.

As greater proportions of national spending – on both sides of the Atlantic – were committed to healthcare and as the professions themselves became more subject to political and public scrutiny, examination of the 'cost benefits' of healthcare assumed greater importance. Techniques of 'quality control' applied in manufacturing industry – in process engineering in particular – were employed, particularly in the United States, in order to improve efficiency, health outcomes and accountability.[30] Avedis Donabedian proposed that a cyclic or reiterative approach (similar to that of the audit cycle described above) should be used to examine what he termed the **Structure, Process** and **Outcome** aspects of healthcare.

Structural aspects are considered to refer to the buildings, facilities and established organization of the service; Process to the clinical, administrative and social aspects of the giving and receipt of health care; Outcome to the effects, both short and long-term, of the care process on patients and society.

To describe aspects of quality assurance is easier than to define the concept as a whole. Much depends on what is meant by 'quality' and what is involved in assuring it.[31] The World Health Organization has proposed that the aim of healthcare quality assurance is:

> to assure that each patient receives such a mix of diagnostic and therapeutic services as is most likely to produce the optimal achievable healthcare outcome for that patient, consistent with the state of the art of medical science... biological factors... compliance with treatment and other factors; with minimal expenditure of resources...; at the lowest level of risk... and with maximal patient satisfaction.[32]

In dentistry, quality assurance was addressed in American research from the late 1960s onwards, and Jago noted, in his review of the literature:

The current concern with quality has arisen because of the proliferation of [dental care] programs, particularly those funded by governments, that have been concerned to obtain value for the large amounts of money they have appropriated. . ..[32]

He concluded that future developments would include the refinement of standards and objective indices to assess the quality of dental care and that private practices would come under increasing pressure to assure that quality. In succeeding years, numerous dental quality assurance systems were developed[34,35,36] in the United States, most of which relied principally on outcome assessments in the form of post-treatment patient examinations, X-ray and records review.

In the UK, the 1983 Griffiths Report on NHS management recommended that greater use should be made of marketing and patient satisfaction studies,[37] together with the expansion of audit procedures. These policies were included in the government White Paper 'Working For Patients' (1989),[38] by which time medical audit had become established as a means of reviewing clinical care, following the initiatives of, amongst others, the Royal College of General Practitioners.[39] The concept of clinical audit in UK dentistry, through the use of clinical standards,[40] was introduced by the Faculty of Dental Surgery in 1990. The techniques of Peer Review and Clinical Dental Audit were also promoted in 1992 and 1993 by the British Dental Association in conjunction with the Faculty and the Department of Health.[41]

It has been noted that quality assurance in healthcare has tended to predominate more in North America, where healthcare systems are more diverse and market-led, than in the UK, where the majority of funding has been provided through the NHS.

British and International Standards for quality assurance (BS 5750/ISO 9000) have been established, originally for manufacturing and later for service industries. These standards may be applied, with modification, to the healthcare field,[42] and a small number of dental practices in the UK have achieved the Standard.[43] Formal accreditation of this kind is expensive and time-consuming: it requires intensive standard-setting and documentation of compliance in all aspects of the practice's operations, in addition to the demonstration of such compliance to the satisfaction of an independent accreditation body

Risk management and quality assurance

The traditional distinctions between risk management and quality assurance were noted by Chapman-Cliburn in 1986:

> Quality Assurance is usually a responsibility of healthcare professionals, intended to identify and resolve problems in patient care, and to

identify and take advantage of opportunities to improve patient care . . . . . Risk Management, in contrast, is usually an administrative undertaking to ensure appropriate insurance coverage, to reduce liability when adverse events occur, and to prevent events most likely to lead to liability.[44]

He argues that the preventive function of risk management coincides to some extent with the objectives of quality assurance, but notes that the two programmes remain entirely separate in the majority of institutions. This separation echoes, to some degree, an established dichotomy in health service management. On the one hand, clinicians, who are primarily concerned with patient care, undertake clinical audit, the results of which are generally confidential to the department or individual clinician concerned. On the other hand, administrators attend principally to the organizational infra-structure of healthcare and see 'utilization reviews' as their principal input to the quality assurance process. As was identified in Chapter 1, risk management straddles this divide, being concerned equally with clinical care and with auxiliary and non-clinical facilities.

Although in the past healthcare risk management methods were based on the assumption that an adverse event had already occurred, and then sought to mitigate the damages which might accrue to the patient, personnel or the institution, it can be argued that optimal quality care can only be said to exist when basic issues of patient safety have been resolved.[45] When for example, as a result of allegedly incomplete instructional material for a radiotherapy machine, several thousand patients receive inappropriate dosages and multiple negligence claims result, it is not easy to apportion liability between the 'structure' and the 'process' of care. In this context, risk management could have a clear preventive role to play in the minimization of injury to patients

Risk management has also been distinguished from quality assurance on the grounds that its aims and principles differ. (Figure 2.5). This view suggests that the legalistic and financial basis of risk management differs fundamentally from the ethical and altruistic considerations which lie at the origins of quality assurance. In practice, however, such apparent differences are less valid. Risk management does not suggest that patient care should be only at a legally acceptable standard: to do so would be to advocate defensive medicine or dentistry. Risk management is about the avoidance of litigation – not its evasion.[46] It can equally be argued that the stimulus to the development of quality assurance techniques in healthcare was provided as much by external forces - provider cost containment and public accountability – as by the search for clinical and administrative excellence.

Risk management	**Quality assurance**
Legally acceptable level of patient care	Optimal level of patient care
Identifies risk factors through specialist data collecting systems	Identifies problems through medical audit/peer review activities
Focused on reducing organization's expenditure on legal costs and settlements	Focused on improving patient care
Concentrates on claims prevention and management	Possible reduction in claims incidental

Figure 2.5 Contrasts between risk management and quality assurance (after Hill G. (1991) *International Journal of Risk and Safety in Medicine*, 2, 83–90)

The alternative view, as expressed by Land, is that risk management, peer review and quality assurance are different, but overlapping concerns of the same issue.[47] This belief is illustrated graphically in the manual: 'Risk Management in the NHS'.[48] (Figure 2.6).

In the primary healthcare field, clinical and administrative functions are more closely related and often indivisible. The dentist who carries out treatment may also be responsible for health and safety policy, for insuring the premises and for training the staff. In such circumstances, risk management gives valuable additional guidance which clinical audit alone does not provide. It may be seen as a stepping stone on the route to total quality management or may develop from a check-list of possible risks across the whole spectrum of practice management and clinical care. (See Chapter 9). It is characterized not only by such techniques as untoward incident reporting and occurrence screening, but

```
┌─────────────────────────────────────────┐
│ TOTAL QUALITY MANAGEMENT                │
│   ┌─────────────────────────────────┐   │
│   │ RISK MANAGEMENT                 │   │
│   │   ┌─────────────────────────┐   │   │
│   │   │ CLINICAL AUDIT          │   │   │
│   │   │   ┌─────────────────┐   │   │   │
│   │   │   │ MEDICAL AUDIT   │   │   │   │
│   │   │   │                 │   │   │   │
│   │   │   └─────────────────┘   │   │   │
│   │   └─────────────────────────┘   │   │
│   └─────────────────────────────────┘   │
└─────────────────────────────────────────┘
```

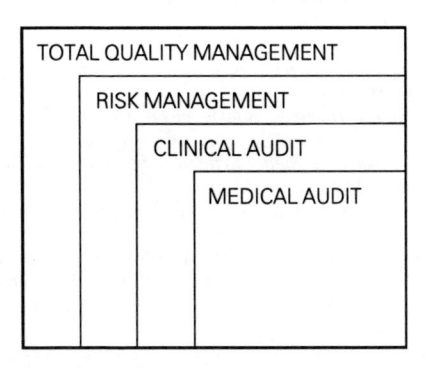

Figure 2.6 Suggested relationships of audit, risk management and quality management (from: *Risk Management in the NHS*. Department of Health 1993)

also by an approach to care which is based on an underlying knowledge of risks and the aspiration to reduce them for the benefit of patients, staff and the well-being of the enterprise.

References

1. Crockford N. (1986) *An Introduction to Risk Management.* (2nd edn). Woodhead Faulkner, Cambridge, p. 3
2. Schein E. (1973) *Professional Education.* McGraw-Hill, New York, p. 39
3. Schon D.A. (1983) The Reflective Practitioner. HarperCollins, New York, p. 40
4. Wilkinson M.D. (1990) Management Science in *Into Dental Practice* (Seward M., ed.) British Dental Association, London
5. Ackoff R. (1979) The Future of Operational Research is Past. *Journal of Operational Research Society,* **30** (2), 93–104
6. Pollack B.R. (1987) *Handbook of Dental Jurisprudence and Risk Management.* PSG Publishing Co, Littleton, Mass., p. 62
7. Zaltman G. and Duncan R. (1977) *Strategies for Planned Change.* Wiley, New York
8. Harvey J. (1974) The Abilene Paradox: The Management of Agreement. *Organisational Dynamics* **3**(1): 274–283
9. Hurst K. (1992) Specifying quality in health and social care. *Quality Assurance in Health Care,* **4,** 3: 193–197
10. Williams S. (1993) *The Lloyd's Bank Small Business Guide* (7th edn). Penguin, Harmondsworth, p. 68 *et seq*
11. *The Concise Oxford Dictionary* (4th edn) (1960) The University Press, Oxford
12. Maltz M. (1970) *Psycho-Cybernetics.* Grosset and Dunlap, New York
13. Brown J.L. (1992) Communicating to avoid liability. *Journal of the California Dental Association,* **20**,(3), 57–60
14. British Dental Association (1989) *Teamwork: a Distance-Learning Package for Dental Surgery Assistants.* British Dental Association, London
15. Details of the BDA/AMSPAR Dental Receptionist programmes are available from the British Dental Association or Radcliffe Medical Press, Oxford
16. Grace M. (1993) Fun with audit. (Editorial) *British Dental Journal* **174**, (8), 261
17. British Dental Association and Faculty of General Dental Practitioners (UK) (1993) *Clinical Audit – A Workbook.* British Dental Association, London
18. Shaw C.D. (1986) Introducing Quality Assurance. King's Fund project Paper No. 64. King Edward's Hospital Fund for London
19. Department of Health (1989) *Working For Patients.* (Cmnd 555) HMSO, London
20. Department of Health and Social Security (1983) *NHS Management Inquiry* (R. Griffiths). DHSS, London
21. Mayo G.E. (1933) *The Human Problems of an Industrial Civilisation.* Macmillan, New York
22. Fletcher C. (1993) *Appraisal: Routes to Improved Performance.* Institute of Personnel Management, London
23. Scott R. (1983) Evolution of an Appraisal Programme. *Personnel Management,* August 1983
24. Appelbaum S.H. and Shapiro B.T. (1991) Pay for Performance: Implementation of Individual and Group Plans. *Journal of Management Development,* **10**, (7), 30–40
25. Berlet K.R. and Cravens D.M. (1991) *Performance Pay as a Competitive Weapon.* Wiley and Sons, London
26. Philp T. (1990) *Appraising Performance for Results.* McGraw-Hill, London
27. Donabedian A. (1966) Evaluating the Quality of Medical Care. *Millbank Quarterly,* **44**, 166–203

28. Kenny D.J. and Valentino C.L. (1991) Quality Assurance: A Process for Continuous Improvement. *Journal of the Canadian Dental Association*, **57**, (4), 313–315
29. Hart N. (1985) *The Sociology of Health and Medicine*. Causeway Press, Ormskirk, p. 125
30. Ellis R. and Whittington D. (1993) *Quality Assurance in Health Care: a Handbook*. Edward Arnold, London. pp. 9–35
31. Little N. (1992) *The Quality Assurance – Risk Management Interface*. Emergency Medical Clinics of North America, **10**, (3), 573–581
32. World Health Organization (1985) The principles of quality assurance. Report on working group meeting convened by Regional office for Europe (Copenhagen) in Barcelona. p. 5
33. Jago J.D. (1974) Issues in Assurance of Quality Dental Care. *Journal of the American Dental Association*, **89**, (10), 854–865
34. Demby N.A., Rosenthal M., Angello M. *et al.* (1985) *A Comprehensive Quality Assurance System for Practicing Dentists*. Dental Clinics of North America, **29**,(3), 545–556
35. Morris A.L., Bentley J.M., Vito A.A. *et al.* (1988) Assessment of Private Dental Practice; Report of a study. *Journal of the American Dental Association*, **117**, 153–162
36. Schoen M.H. (1989) A Quality Assessment System: the Search for Validity. *Journal of Dental Education*, **53**, 658–661
37. Department of Health and Social Security (1983) National Health Service Management Enquiry: the Griffiths Report. HMSO, London
38. Departments of Health (1989) *Working For Patients*. (Cmnd 555), HMSO, London
39. Royal College of General Practitioners (1985) *Assessing Quality of Care in General Practice*. Royal College of General Practitioners, London
40. Advisory Board in General Dental Practice (1990) *Self Assessment Manual and Standards* (Grace M. ed.). Faculty of Dental Surgery, Royal College of Surgeons, London
41. British Dental Association (1993) *Clinical Audit: a Workbook*. British Dental Association, London
42. Rooney E.M. (1988) A proposed quality system specification for the National Health Service. *Quality Assurance*, **14**,(2), 45–53
43. Davies L. (1993) What is BS 5750? *British Dental Journal*, **174**, (8), 289–290
44. Chapman-Cliburn G. (1986) *Quality Assurance and Risk Management: Issues and Interactions*. (Foreword). Joint Commission on Accreditation of Hospitals, Chicago, p. 5
45. Little N. (1992) *The Quality Assurance – Risk Management Interface*. Emergency Medicine Clinics of North America, **10**, (3), 573–581
46. Clements R. (1992) Defensive medicine – is this where risk management leads? *Health Service Journal*, **102**, No 5298, 2(supp)
47. Land D. (1991) What do Indicators Indicate? *QRC Advisor*, **7**, (4), 1–6
48. NHS Management Executive (1993) *Risk Management in the NHS*. Department of Health, London, p. 125

3
Workplace and environmental risks

Introduction

At one time, healthcare risk management tended to concentrate on professional negligence claims and on the limitation of damage once iatrogenic injury to a patient had been established or alleged.[1] This approach now finds less favour, and the growth in legislation and in the potential cost of claims from patients, staff and others in matters not directly related to treatment now requires a wider remit.

Professional associations and indemnity organizations receive large numbers of enquiries relating to the management of non-clinical risks in dental practice. The majority of these concern Health and Safety aspects, employment matters, and contractual relationships with professional colleagues.

The British Dental Association and other bodies publish leaflets and handbooks on these matters (see Figure 3.1). Despite this fact, individual dentists, dental healthcare Trusts and other establishments continue to experience losses, inconvenience and, on occasions, legal and statutory proceedings resulting from difficulties in these areas.

One reason advanced for the occurrence of such problems is similar to that given in the previous chapter on management: namely that a fundamental and co-ordinated understanding of employment law, health and safety requirements and related subjects has not traditionally been provided during professional training. Additionally, the pace of change and the development of regulations, statutes and case law in these subjects has increased markedly in the past decade

Scope

The layout of this chapter is given in Figure 3.2. It can be seen from this that a considerable breadth of subject-matter is included, and it is not

A Practice management

- A1 Planning permission
- A2 Buying and selling a practice
- A3 Health and safety law for dental practice
- A4 Independent practice
- A5 Fee assignments
- A6 Promoting your practice
- A7 Associateship agreements
- A8 Employing an assistant in general practice
- A9 Expense sharing agreements
- A10 Partnership agreements
- A11 Radiation in dentistry
- A12 Control of cross-infection in dentistry
- A13 Locumships in general dental practice
- A14 Dentists' maternity arrangements and pay
- A15 Computers in dental practice

B Ethical and legal

- B1 Ethical and legal obligations of dental practitioners
- B2 Data protection
- B3 Giving evidence
- B4 What to do when a practitioner dies
- B5 Service Committees
- B6 Consent to treatment
- B7 Practice inspections
- B8 Did you know? Essential legislation for general practitioners
- B9 Prescribing in general dental practice

C Financial

- C1 Sickness and accident insurance
- C2 Collecting money from patients

D Employing staff

- D1 Contracts of employment
- D2 Conditions of employment for dental surgery assistants
- D3 The employment of dental hygienists
- D4 Conditions of employment for dental technicians
- D5 Advice on the direction of dental therapists
- D6 Pay for dental surgery assistants in general practice
- D7 Pay for dental hygienists in general practice
- D8 Pay for dental technicians in general practice
- D9 Employees' maternity rights
- D10 Redundancy
- D11 Dismissal
- D12 Staff recruitment

E Miscellaneous

- E1 Practising dentistry in the EC
- E2 Questions and answers
- E3 Vocational training in general dental practice

S Students

- S1 Help with overseas electives
- S2 Successful interviews
- S3 Getting an interview

Figure 3.1 Advice sheets produced for members by the British Dental Association

Workplace and environmental risks

```
                    ┌─────────────────────────────────────┐
                    │ Workplace and environmental risks   │
                    └─────────────────────────────────────┘
                                    │
                    ┌───────────────┴─────────────┐
                    │ Health and safety            │
                    │ General policy               │
                    └──────────────────────────────┘
```

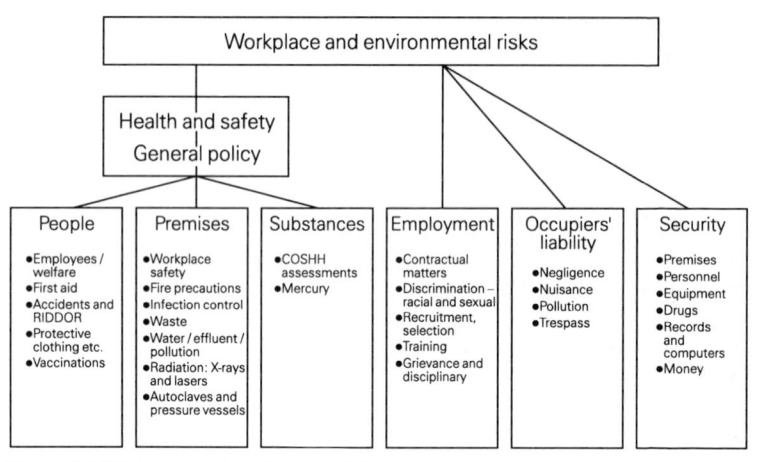

People	Premises	Substances	Employment	Occupiers' liability	Security
•Employees / welfare •First aid •Accidents and RIDDOR •Protective clothing etc. •Vaccinations	•Workplace safety •Fire precautions •Infection control •Waste •Water / effluent / pollution •Radiation: X-rays and lasers •Autoclaves and pressure vessels	•COSHH assessments •Mercury	•Contractual matters •Discrimination – racial and sexual •Recruitment, selection •Training •Grievance and disciplinary	•Negligence •Nuisance •Pollution •Trespass	•Premises •Personnel •Equipment •Drugs •Records and computers •Money

Figure 3.2 Workplace and environmental risks

intended that an in-depth treatment of every topic listed can be achieved. Where possible, suggestions for further reading are included, and in view of the rapid changes in this field, it is essential that dentists remain aware, through professional journals and the services of dental associations and medical indemnity organizations, of current developments. Awareness by itself is however insufficient: time must be set aside to obtain and to read current publications.

The intention here is to provide a broad overview, and to encourage safe and prudent practice which should promote the avoidance or reduction of risk, where however a specific problem or untoward incident arises, it is essential that expert advice be sought at the earliest opportunity.

In the first section, Health and Safety risks are divided, for ease of classification, into those aspects which are primarily concerned with 'People', be they employees, patients or others. Risks relating to 'Premises' include also equipment and power sources. The third category of risk is that relating to 'Substances' used in dentistry.

Because current legislation requires an overview of Health and Safety – that is, a systems approach rather than piecemeal compliance, this section is prefaced by a consideration of what is required in developing a satisfactory policy, and the procedures to be adopted in carrying out a risk assessment in a healthcare setting.

The remaining sections of the chapter are devoted respectively to: the main provisions and requirements of Employment law; the legal responsibilities placed upon the occupiers of property and finally a consideration of the various aspects of security involved in the management of dental practice

Health and safety

Development of the systems approach

Throughout this text, certain themes recur. One of these themes is Systems Theory. This approach emphasizes the consideration of complex organizations as a whole,[2] acknowledging that each part of the system is dependent on other components for its optimum function. Health and Safety legislation has, particularly over the past two decades, undergone a revision of approach from a relatively 'piecemeal' application to a more comprehensive 'systems' strategy.

The growth of industrialization in the nineteenth century was accompanied by an increase in law-suits brought by workers as a result of accidents and injuries sustained in employment. Although these early Actions were through the civil courts, legislation was gradually introduced to protect the workforce, and a body of Statute grew up which controlled different aspects of the safety and welfare of employees.

This accumulation of Acts and Regulations affecting Shops, Railways, Docks, Factories and many other workplaces continued, but inevitably gaps in the legislation existed – and were exploited. Although it was established that an employer owed a common law duty of care to his employees,[3] and strict liability applied in some circumstances,[4] essentially the onus remained on the worker to show that negligence had occurred. The Factories Act (1961), and the Offices, Shops and Railway Premises Act (1963) provided a stronger framework for promoting Health and Safety, but it was the report of Lord Robens' Committee on Health and Safety at Work which produced, in the Health and Safety at Work etc., Act 1974 what has been described as; '... providing for one comprehensive and integrated system of law dealing with the health, safety and welfare of workpeople and the health and safety of the public as affected by work activities'.[5]

Even the title of the Act is significant. As Crockford[6] notes, 'it is the first time that "etc." has featured in the name of an Act of Parliament. This inclusion, which is meant to imply that the scope of the Act extends beyond workers and their workplace, to include liabilities to the public and others, may in itself be seen as a step towards a systems approach in Health and Safety Law.

The Health and Safety at Work etc., Act is chiefly an enabling Act; it opens the way for Regulations to be laid by (chiefly) the Secretary of

State for Trade and Industry. Examples of these Regulations as they affect dentists include:

The Ionising Radiation Regulations (1985);
The Control of Substances Hazardous to Health Regulations (1988);
The Electricity at Work Regulations (1988);
The Pressure Systems and Transportable Gas Containers Regulations (1989);
The Health and Safety (First-Aid) Regulations (1981).

Section 2 of the Act places the following clear and comprehensive responsibilities on every employer, including (so far as is reasonably practicable):

– to ensure the health, safety and welfare at work of all his employees
– to provide and maintain plant and systems of work that are safe and without risk to health
– to make arrangements to ensure that the use, storage, handling and transport of articles and substances is safe and without risk to health
– to provide instruction and training which ensures the health and safety at work of employees
– to maintain the workplace and its access in a safe condition
– to provide a written statement of health and safety policy

Additionally, employers must conduct their businesses in such a way as to ensure (again, so far as is reasonably practicable) that persons not in their employment, but who may be affected by the business, are not exposed to health and safety risks.

The Act modifies previous legislation, such as the Factories Act and the Offices, Shops and Railway Premises Act so that they take effect within its framework. Although the Fire Precautions Act (1971) is still enforced by the Home Office and fire brigades, the Health and Safety Executive (who are responsible for enforcing Health and Safety legislation) also have powers in this area (see below).

By forming an 'umbrella' of legislation, the Health and Safety at Work etc., Act has adopted more than just a multi-disciplinary approach to Health and Safety; it has become a discipline in its own right. Breaches of the Act are a criminal offence; however conviction does not in any way preclude the civil law rights of individuals in taking action against employers or business owners.

The most recent development in Health and Safety Law has come about as a result of the so-called 'harmonization' between member countries of the European Union. Six directives were issued in 1989 and

1990,[7] which, in the United Kingdom, were introduced on 1 January 1993 as individual Regulations under the Health and Safety at Work etc., Act 1974. These Regulations – which became popularly known as the 'six-pack' – were as follows:

1 The Management of Health and Safety at Work Regulations 1992 (The Framework Regulations)
2 The Personal Protective Equipment at Work Regulations (1992)
3 The Provision and Use of Work Equipment Regulations (1992)
4 The Health and Safety (Display Screen Equipment) Regulations (1992)
5 The Manual Handling Operations Regulations (1992)
6 The Workplace (Health Safety and Welfare) Regulations (1992)

Although these appear, at first sight, to be a formidable array, the pre-existence of the 1974 Act in the United Kingdom has drawn much of their sting. The fine detail of the Regulations should not hold enormous difficulty in compliance for most dental surgeons who have already complied with the requirements of the 1974 Act and the subsequent Regulations made under it. The principle of the 1992 Regulations is to further encourage a systems – that is to say, a holistic - approach to Health and Safety policy

Health and safety – general policy

There are currently two requirements which call for an employer to consider Health and Safety in general terms. Section 2 of the Health and Safety at Work etc., Act (1974) (quoted above) sets out general duties for employers, and in Section 2(3); 'Except in such cases as may be prescribed, it shall be the duty of every employer to prepare a written statement of his general policy with regard to the health and safety at work of his employees.'

Examples of model statements may be found in Health and Safety Executive publications (see Appendix for details), or in British Dental Association Advice sheet A3. A further example is shown in Figure 3.3.

Additionally, the Management of Health and Safety at Work Regulations (1992) (The Framework Regulations) require (Regulation 3) that:

Every employer shall make a suitable and sufficient assessment of:

(a) the risks to health and safety of his employees . . .whilst they are at work; and
(b) the risks to the health and safety of persons not in his employment arising out of or in connection with his undertaking

42 Workplace and environmental risks

ANYWHERE DENTAL PRACTICE
HEALTH AND SAFETY POLICY

It is the policy of this practice to provide and maintain a safe and healthy work environment, equipment and working procedures for all employees. Training, information and supervision will be provided, updated and recorded to comply with this policy. The premises, equipment and procedures will be maintained so as to ensure, so far as is possible, that the health and safety of employees, patients and others affected is not compromised. The practice will comply with all appropriate legislation and codes of practice. Employees have a responsibility to take reasonable care of their own health and safety and that of others.

ACCOUNTABILITY
The practice principal is responsible for health and safety in the practice. All accidents and spillages should be reported to him at once. Any queries or problems should be raised with him.

GENERAL SAFETY
Employees should not act in a manner which may put themselves or others at risk.

The practice operates a no-smoking policy.

Do not eat, drink or apply cosmetics in clinical areas.

ACCIDENTS AND EMERGENCIES
All accidents must be reported. Training in emergency drills will be provided regularly. The practice first-aid kit is located ....
Emergency drugs are located ....
Oxygen and resuscitation equipment is located ....

FIRE
The fire procedure is posted in each room. Fire extinguishers are located ....

The procedure and equipment are regularly tested.

CROSS-INFECTION
All staff must follow personal hygiene requirements. All equipment used for clinical treatment must be sterilized as instructed. Regard all used or non-sterile clinical equipment as contaminated. Disposable items will be discarded after single use. Hands must be washed thoroughly before and after each patient, and gloves worn for all clinical procedures or instrument handling. Work surfaces will be disinfected as instructed.

PROTECTIVE EQUIPMENT
All protective equipment provided for staff and patients must be used as instructed.

Heavy duty gloves are to be worn when cleaning sharp instruments and when using hazardous chemicals.

MERCURY
The practice guidlines for handling and using mercury will be followed. No eating, drinking or applying cosmetics in clinical areas.

X-RAYS
The practice conforms to the requirements of the Ionizing Radiation (protections of persons undergoing medical examination or treatment) Regulations 1988. The Radiation Protection Adviser is the practice principal. The practice local rules will be followed.

EQUIPMENT
Only operate equipment when you have been trained in its use, and only in the approved manner shown. Never dismantle equipment: inform the practice principal at once of any failure or malfunction. Do not handle electrical equipment, plugs, etc. with wet hands. Switch off and unplug equipment before carrying out maintenance and at the end of each day.

PRESSURE VESSELS
The autoclave and compressor are correctly maintained and certificated. All pressure vessels pose a potential hazard and their use and operation require particular care.

REVIEW
This policy will be reviewed no less than annually, and immediately if circumstances change.

Signed (Employer) ....

Signed (Employee) ....

Date ....

Figure 3.3 Health and safety policy

for the purpose of identifying the measures he needs to take to comply with the requirements and prohibitions imposed upon him by the relevant statutory provisions.

Regulation 3(4) requires the results of such a risk assessment to be recorded where five or more employees are employed. This 'small businesses' exemption should be regarded with caution, since part-time cleaners and gardeners, and also self-employed associates and hygienists may be regarded as 'employees' in this context.

A risk assessment should include five components:

1 Identification   Potential hazards need to be itemized
2 Evaluation   The likelihood of an accident or injury occurring should be evaluated.
3 Consequences   The extent and severity of possible damage or injury which may result.
4 Information   Sources of advice which have been consulted on the hazard.
5 Risk Reduction   The measures which will be taken to minimize or respond to the hazard

A typical risk assessment is recorded at Figure 3.4.

It is interesting to compare Figure 3.3 (Health and Safety Policy) with this Risk Assessment. Note that the Assessment shown relates only to a clinical area; further assessments would be needed for, say, waiting/reception, laboratory and so on. Neither is it suggested that the Assessment shown would be complete or appropriate in every instance.

The Health and Safety Policy is essentially a statement of intent. It takes as a normative state a workplace which is safe and healthy, and proposes general measures which will keep it so. The Risk Assessment, on the other hand, is concerned with actual hazards and risks which may be present, evaluates and quantifies them, and proposes measures, taken in the knowledge of stated information, to reduce them.

The 1992 Framework Regulations therefore may be interpreted as a more focused and active response to workplace risk. Moreover, they encourage an approach which is more in keeping with the Risk Management cycle proposed in Chapter 1: risks are identified, analysed and reduced or transferred.

The risk analysis presented in the Assessment is not intended to be an exact quantification. Some indication of whom may be affected, is called for together with an evaluation of the frequency and severity of the risk: in dental practice terms, only a simple breakdown is called for. An appreciation of the consequences of an untoward incident occurring

44   Workplace and environmental risks

ANYWHERE DENTAL PRACTICE
RISK ASSESSMENT – CLINICAL AREA

Hazard	Who?	RF*	RS**	Consequences	Information sources	Risk reduction measures
Cross-infection	Pt	Low	High	Mild to severe infection	BDA Advice sheet A12 and Glenwright and Martin 'Infection Control in Dentistry'	1 Staff training 2 Adherence to strict cross-infection guidelines (q.v.)
Cross-infection	Staff	Low	High	Mild to severe infection	– as above –	1 Cross-infection guidelines 2 Vaccination programme 3 Personal protective equipment
Mercury poisoning	Staff	Low	High	Neurotoxicity – chronic effects to acute poisoning	BDA Advice sheet A3: Health and Safety	1 Mercury handling procedure (q.v.) 2 Regular urinalysis (chairside staff)
Needlestick/sharps injury	Staff/Pt	Med	High	Skin puncture/incapacity/infection	Scully Cawson & Griffiths 'Occupational Hazards to Dental Staff'	1 Training – needlestick routine (q.v.) 2 Protective equipment 3 Waste disposal guidelines (q.v.)
Hazardous substances	Staff/Pt	Low	Med	Toxic effects of chemicals	BDA Advice sheet A3. HSE COSHH booklet	1 As per COSHH assessment (q.v.) 2 Staff training
Anaesthetic gases	Staff	Low	High	Miscarriage, toxicity	BDA Advice sheet A3, Scully Cawson and Griffiths	1 Staff training 2 Active scavenging system 3 Mechanical ventilation to surgery 4 Well-fitting facemask
Ionizing radiation	Staff/Pt	Low	High	Mutagenicity, radiation toxicity	BDA Advice sheet A11, SDAC booklet, Mason 'Guide to Dental Radiography'	1 Staff training, local rules (q.v.) 2 Annual NRPB certification 3 Equipment maintenance contract
Visual display equipment	Staff	Low	Low/Med	Eyestrain, muscular pain, fatigue	HSE VDU guidelines, BDA Advice sheet A3	1 Staff training, information 2 Workstation assessment 3 Availability of eye testing
Electrical equipment	Staff	Low	High	Electrocution, shock, burns	BDA Advice sheet A3	1 Staff training 2 Periodic check by electrician 3 Regular visual monitoring
Minor cuts and injuries	Staff/Pt	Med	Low	Minor cuts, abrasions	St John Ambulance First Aid	1 First Aid training kit 2 Regular checks of workplace

* RF = Risk frequency; ** RS = Risk severity

Figure 3.4 Risk assessment – clinical area

helps not only in assessing severity, but is a useful staff training aid – as indeed is the Assessment as a whole.

Case:

A dental receptionist suffered back and leg injuries when the chair on which she was standing in order to close a window collapsed. It is likely that she would succeed in a civil claim against her Employer since, although it could be argued that her action in climbing on the chair was itself risky, its unsound condition had been previously reported to the Employer, who had taken no action to repair or replace it.

Under current Health and Safety law, the dentist might also come under scrutiny for failing to maintain a safe workplace: the chair was faulty; the window could not be safely closed without risk, and no general instructions to staff about safe practice had been given.

One of the most significant aspects of the risk management of workplace health and safety is adequate and appropriate insurance. This will be dealt with in more detail below in the sections on 'Health and Safety – people' and 'Occupier's liability'. Suffice it to say here that separate cover is required to satisfy the requirements of the Employers' Liability (Compulsory Insurance) Act (1969), and to indemnify against liability under the Occupiers' Liability Act (1984) and other statutes.

Health and safety – people

It will be apparent from the preceding section that the adoption of a 'systems' approach to health and safety requires a general overview of all aspects of a business enterprise such as dentistry. Such a view dictates, nevertheless, that there is detailed awareness of the various statutory and common law obligations placed on an employer.

In this section aspects of health and safety applying directly to the health, safety and welfare of employees will be considered. The section must be read in conjunction with the immediately following topics of 'Premises' and 'Substances'.

The welfare of employees
The general liability of an employer towards his employees arises from three sources:

1   In contract (see section on 'Employment' below, p. 77)
2   At common law, and
3   By statute

The common law duty of an employer has been defined as follows:

> It is the duty of an employer, acting personally or through his servants or agents, to take reasonable care for the safety of his workmen and other employees in the course of their employment. This duty extends in particular to the safety of the place of work, the plant and machinery, and the method and conduct of the work: but it is not restricted to these matters.[8]

Where an injury occurs to an employee through the negligence of an employer – that is to say, where there is a failure of the duty of care, and harm results – an employee may sue for damages in negligence. Thus in the Case noted in the section above, an employer may find himself in 'double jeopardy', since an action may arise both in the civil court and under the Health and Safety criminal legislation.

Cassidy considers that this common law liability falls into the following categories:[9]

1. Safe place of work
2. Safe plant and machinery
3. Safe system of work
4. Competent and suitable fellow employees
5. Employer's own actions

Categories 1 to 3 may be considered to be parallel liabilities to the statutory requirements of health and safety law. The fourth category is interesting, since it has been established that an employer has a duty to ensure that fellow employees are suitably qualified and trained, and injury or damage to an employee due to the acts or omissions of another employee may, if the employer has failed in this duty, result in a successful claim against him. Naturally, direct actions or failure to act by the employer himself may also be found negligent.

Under statute, the general welfare of employees is now protected and codified by the Workplace (Health, Safety and Welfare) Regulations (1992). The requirements of these Regulations are briefly given here; readers are referred to the Health and Safety Executive's Approved Code of Practice (ACOP) for detailed provisions.

> Reg. 5 Maintenance – the workplace, equipment and systems must be kept in efficient order and good repair
> Reg. 6 Ventilation – all indoor workplaces must be sufficiently ventilated. Recirculated air must be properly filtered
> Reg. 7 Temperature – a reasonable or comfortable temperature must be maintained (16°C for sedentary workers)
> Reg. 8 Lighting – shall permit safe movement and avoid eyestrain

Reg. 9 Cleanliness and waste – All floors, walls and ceilings shall be capable of being kept clean
Reg. 10 Space and dimensions – minimum room sizes and heights are recommended
Reg. 11 Seating and workstations – shall be suitable for the procedures carried out
Reg. 12 Traffic routes – i.e. corridors, doorways, shall be even, lit, safe and free from obstruction
Reg. 13 Falls – measures shall be taken to avoid falls by persons, or objects falling on them
Reg. 14 Windows and doors – glazing in windows and partitions below waist height, and glazing in doors below shoulder height must be of a safety type
Reg. 15 Windows and ventilators – must be able to be operated safely
Reg. 16 Windows – must be capable of being cleaned in safety
Reg. 17 Traffic flow – both people and vehicles must be able to circulate safely
Reg. 18 Doors and gates – must operate safely (e.g. swinging doors should have a transparent panel)
Reg. 20 Toilets – there must be an adequate number,[10] they must be clean, and adequately ventilated and lit
Reg. 21 Washbasins – must be sufficient and accessible, clean, have soap, towels and running hot and cold water
Reg. 22 Drinking water – must be an accessible and signed supply
Reg. 23 Clothing – there must be accommodation for employees clothing not worn during working hours
Reg. 24 Changing – there must be suitable changing room for employees
Reg. 25 Rest and eating facilities – must be provided, with non-smoking provision

Although these regulations may seem over-prescriptive, there can be little doubt that they are mostly either 'common sense' or 'good housekeeping', and that in the majority of dental practices or clinics little difficulty will be experienced in complying.

First aid
Under Section 2 of the Health and Safety at Work etc. Act (1974), an employer is required to make all necessary provision for the safety and health of his workforce: this requirement was inclusive of the earlier duties, under the Factories Act 1961, to provide suitable and sufficient first aid equipment.

As with other aspects of health and safety, regulations made under, and subsequent to the 1974 Act, specified the requirements more exactly: in this case, the Health and Safety (First-Aid) Regulations (1981). These make employers liable to provide: suitable and sufficient first-aid equipment (and to maintain it); instruction and training for staff; the services of a qualified first-aider, and (in larger firms) a first-aid room.

In dental practice, the presence of a suitably qualified dental surgeon exempts the business from needing a qualified first-aider, but as there may be occasions when no dentist is present, it is prudent (and only proper in a healthcare establishment) to provide first-aid courses for staff.

Additionally, the General Dental Council state in their guidance to dentists;[11] 'Dentists should . . . ensure that all members of their staff are properly trained and prepared to deal with an emergency should one arise.'

The basic principles of first-aid fall well within this requirement, and the provision of training in first-aid and cardio-pulmonary resuscitation for all staff (including non-clinical staff) is therefore essential. Family Health Service Authorities and Health Boards are taking steps in many areas to facilitate such training, and following the publication of the Poswillo Report,[12] some have appointed facilitators to advise dentists and organise suitable courses. In the absence of such assistance, courses are run in many areas by the St John Ambulance Society and the Red Cross (see Appendix for addresses). Help may also be available from Health Authorities. First-aid training should be documented, preferably in a practice training manual.

Standard first-aid kits are commercially available and should indicate that they conform to the regulations according to the number of employees present. First-aid kits should not contain any medications. Their location must be known by all staff members, and they should be inspected periodically by a named responsible person (an adhesive label on the box with space for date and initials is the simplest way). A simple first-aid manual (for example 'Practical First-Aid' published by the Red Cross Society) should be kept with the kit. Emergency telephone numbers should be listed with the kit, and in a prominent place near to the telephone(s).

Accidents, injuries and their reporting
The Reporting of Accidents Act (1894) first placed a general requirement on employers to notify the authorities of workplace injuries. Current legislation is again to be found in Regulations laid under the Health and Safety at Work etc Act 1974. These are the Health

and Safety (Reporting of Injuries, Diseases and Dangerous Occurrences) Regulations 1985, or RIDDOR.

To comply with the regulations, employers must:

1 Notify the Health and Safety Executive of serious accidents (i.e. those causing death or serious injury) or dangerous occurrences
2 Confirm notification in writing on the official form (F2508)
3 Keep a written record of all notified events
4 Notify HSE of relevant diseases (see below) on form F2508A

One important exemption in dental practice is accidents occurring to patients in the course of treatment. Other serious accidents or occurrences affecting staff or patients must be notified. The appropriate forms are available from HMSO bookshops, or from HSE Books and Publications (addresses in Appendix).

Accidents and occurrences of the type which would require notification are specified in the regulations, and include:

- explosion bursting or collapse of any pressure vessel which might cause major injury or significant damage
- fire or explosion resulting from electrical short-circuit or overload
- explosion or fire which prevented normal work for more than 24 hours occurring as a result of process materials, by-products or finished product
- uncontrolled release or escape of any substance in circumstances which might cause damage to health or injury
- inhalation, ingestion or other absorption of any substance, or lack of oxygen, requiring medical treatment
- acute illness resulting from occupational exposure to pathogens or infected material
- fracture of skull, spine, pelvis, arm or leg
- accidents resulting in 3 or more days work lost by an employee

Examples of incidents in dental practice have included:

- the explosion of a poorly-maintained autoclave causing structural damage
- major spillage of metallic mercury resulting in contamination of a surgery and drainage plumbing
- fire damage to a surgery caused by faulty wiring
- Hepatitis B infection contracted by an oral surgeon
- patient fainting on a staircase and suffering concussion
- malfunction of an X-ray machine resulting in the continuous discharge of radiation

Additionally, where ten or more persons are employed, an Accident Book must be kept in which a written record of all accidents and occurrences, however seemingly minor, should be noted both to satisfy the general requirements of Section 2 of the Health and Safety at Work etc. Act, and for use in the event of claims by employees or others for Industrial Injury Benefit or other cause. Appropriate accident books are available from HMSO bookshops or the HSE.

Personal protective equipment (PPE)
Protective clothing, gloves, masks, etc. is now generally covered under the Health and Safety (Personal Protective Equipment) Regulations (1992). Detailed requirements already exist for hazardous industries such as nuclear installations and pathology laboratories, and the regulations make clear that they do not supersede these. They call instead for every employer to assess the risks to which his workforce (and himself, as a self-employed person) are exposed, and to provide suitable and sufficient protection against those risks which remain when all other risk reduction measures have been applied.

The regulations are fulfilled by:

1   Assessing what PPE should be provided (Reg. 6)
2   Providing the appropriate PPE (Reg. 4)
3   Instructing and training staff in its use and maintenance (Reg. 9)
4   Ensuring that it is used as instructed (Reg. 10)
5   Maintaining and replacing the equipment as necessary (Reg. 7)

The necessary assessment will normally be implicit in the general risk assessment carried out under the Framework Regulations: a straightforward list will suffice in the normal circumstances of dental practice – see Figure 3.5.

Provision of PPE – including clothing where appropriate (e.g. clinical staff) is the responsibility of the employer. Suitability must also be considered; for example, eye protection for child patients may not be satisfactorily achieved by the use of adult-sized equipment, and clinical overalls should be made of a fabric which will not be harmed by laundering at 80°C.

Staff must be adequately instructed and trained in the use of PPE, and, whilst they have a general responsibility under the 1974 Act and a specific responsibility under these regulations to use the equipment provided and to protect their own safety and that of others, the employer is equally charged with ensuring that equipment is used or worn as directed.

The prudent employer will therefore include this subject in staff training, and document the fact. He will write PPE guidance into the Health and Safety Contract (as in the example given previously), and include the correct use of PPE in disciplinary procedures (see 'Employment', below).

ANYWHERE DENTAL PRACTICE
PERSONAL PROTECTIVE EQUIPMENT

For protection of:	Procedure	Equipment	Specification	Notes
Patient	Clinical treatment	Eye protection Bib Airway protection	To BS 2092/2 Impermeable, absorbent Rubber dam (pref); sponge pack	Child/adult sizes required For endodontics/composites
	Radiography	Lead apron Film holder	To BS 5783	
Clinical staff	Clinical treatment	Eye protection Face mask Gloves – latex Clothing Filter/shield Needle guard	To BS 2092/2 High filtration To DoH spec. hypoallergenic Washable at 80°C Effective below 500 nm	Change when moist Vionyl as alternative Pref. synthetic For curing light Avoid re-sheathing where possible
	Radiography – developing	PVC gloves Plastic apron	BS 1651	When handling concentrated chemicals, cleaning processing tanks
	Instrument cleaning	PVC gloves Eye protection Apron	BS 1651	
	Disinfection	Nitrile gloves		
Cleaning staff	General cleaning	PVC gloves Apron		Test household-type gloves by rolling up, not by inflation!

Figure 3.5 Personal protective equipment

	Route	Length of protection
Tetanus	I.M.	5 years
Poliomyelitis	Oral	5 years
Hepatitis B	I.M. 0, 1, 6 months	3 years*
Tuberculosis	Subdermal	Test if no Mantoux or BCG was done in childhood

* Or less if post-vaccination titre suggests that this is necessary.

Figure 3.6 Vaccination schedule for dental personnel (from Glenwright H.D., Martin M.V. (1993) Infection Control in Dentistry: A practitioner's guide, *British Dental Journal*, **175**, (1), supp.)

Vaccination and Health
The Health and Safety at Work etc. Act (1974) and the Control of Substances Hazardous to Health Regulations (1988) (COSHH) call for employers to take steps to ensure that the health of staff is not compromised by exposure to harmful substances or pathogens. (See also Section 1.4 below).

It has been recommended that dentists and other clinical staff should be vaccinated against Hepatitis B and other infections (see Figure 3.6),[13] and that a record of vaccinations should be kept. Staff who decline to receive this protection should sign a statement to this effect and employers should consider whether such refusal enables them to comply fully with Health and Safety Law. Professional advice on this point should be sought.

Additionally, staff should be advised to report any illness or condition which may be related to their work, such as hand dermatitis arising from contact with cleansers, gloves or other substances.

Mercury screening for clinical staff who handle or work with amalgam alloys has also been recommended, and is covered in Section 1.4.

Advice to employers concerning occupational health is available from the Employment Medical Advisory Service (addresses in Appendix) and dentists may also be able to obtain information from the Occupational Health department of their Health Authority.

Health and safety – premises

Workplace safety
Some reference has been made in the preceding section to general workplace safety. Aspects which have not been addressed are now considered, with particular reference to equipment and machinery,

computer display screens, and work procedures such as lifting, storage, etc.

The Provision and Use of Work Equipment Regulations (1992) cover all types of equipment. In the dental context this would extend from major items such as dental chairs and suction systems to individual hand instruments. These regulations principally require that equipment shall be suitable and properly maintained; that appropriate written information and training is available to staff on its use (taking into account their experience and the complexity or otherwise of the equipment), and that equipment can be safely operated.

Whilst none of these requirements should be difficult in dental practice, employers are again advised to assess any particular risks which may arise, and take steps to avoid them. It is, for instance, well recognized that open-flame bunsens present a fire and injury hazard to clinical staff wearing latex gloves. The external surfaces of some equipment, such as autoclaves, can become dangerously hot in use, and it would be expected that staff should receive the appropriate training and warnings. Instances have arisen where a child has trapped its fingers in the articulating parts of a dental chair arm, or where a wall-mounted X-ray machine fell on to a patient whilst in use. These examples emphasize the need for a constant vigilance, since the likelihood of report and prosecution must be considered high.

The increasing use of computer display screens in dental practice means that the provisions of the Health and Safety (Display Screen Equipment) Regulations (1992) now apply to a significant number of premises. The Dental Practice Board estimate that the proportion of practices using computers rose from 15% in 1989 to over 70% in 1992.[14]

These regulations – known as the VDU regulations – cover work which was not, until January 1993, specifically controlled. They apply to any person, employee or self-employed, who habitually uses a display screen for a significant part of their work. Strict definitions of 'habitual' or 'significant' are not offered. However, a dental chairside assistant who enters and reads data for charting or fee assessment, but is primarily engaged in clinical assisting would probably not be included, whereas a receptionist or administrator who spends the majority of their time using a computer for making appointments or assembling data probably would qualify as a VDU 'user'.

Employers are required to ensure that any risks involved in the user's work are assessed: this might include screen glare from poorly sited equipment, postural problems due to inappropriate seating or ergonomic difficulties arising from, say, the lack of a document holder. The views of the users themselves should also be sought, and any necessary corrections made.

Additionally, users should be given breaks and some variety of task. Again, these provisions are not further defined, but short frequent rests are generally accepted as being preferable to longer, infrequent breaks.

Finally, VDU users are entitled to eye and eyesight tests at intervals if they so require. Any corrective glasses needed specifically for VDU use must be provided by the employer, but not, obviously, if these are required for existing eyesight problems in other circumstances.

General work procedures are regulated by the Manual Handling Operations Regulations (1992). After falls, the next most frequent types of workplace accidents are those which occur as a result of 'manual handling', that is, lifting, moving or using items or equipment. Although it is recognized that dentistry is not, in the ordinary sense, a hazardous occupation, staff must be aware of the various injuries which can occur, for example:

- lifting down a case of paper towel rolls from a high stock-room shelf (move heavy objects to lower shelves, or break down into smaller components);
- dropping sharp and possibly contaminated instruments (use trays, rationalise movements, avoid open-topped footwear);
- twisting to reach an item from the chairside (improve seating and storage arrangements).

All of the above have resulted in injury or absence from work in dental sites.

Whether in the overall risk assessment covered in Section 1.2 above, or as a separate exercise, dentists should consider the work processes which occur in their premises, and use reasonable foresight in instructing, training and monitoring hazardous procedures.

Fire precautions
The Fire Precautions Act (1971) places responsibility for the inspection and certification of premises on the Home Office, through the agency of local fire services. Where new premises are constructed, or existing premises materially altered, local planning authorities will often advise whether certification may be required, but in all circumstances, the decision of the local fire precautions officer will be required. Factors which will affect the need for certification will include the layout and location of premises, the number of occupants (staff, patients and others), which floors of buildings are occupied and the number and accessibility of escape routes. It is not possible, without professional advice, to determine whether certification is required, and inspection is therefore always advised.

Where premises are certificated, the fire officer will specify the appropriate equipment and its siting, necessary signing, and the designation (and where appropriate the construction or modification) of escape routes. Reviews will normally be carried out at regular intervals to ensure that all directions are being complied with. Failure to obtain certification or to maintain safe precautions may result in prosecution, or, in serious cases, in an order closing the premises.

More important, however, is the potential risk to persons and to a business, arising from a fire. There is a general requirement in all policies of insurance that the insured will take reasonable care to protect premises and items insured, and failure to obtain certification or to maintain adequate or required precautions may invalidate all or part of the insurance cover. Additionally, under Section 2(1) of the Occupier's Liability Act (1957); 'An occupier of premises owes the same duty, the common duty of care, to all his visitors except in so far as he is free to and does extend, restrict, modify or exclude his duty to any visitor or visitors by agreement or otherwise.'

Patients, staff and others are therefore entitled to expect that a dentist or Health Authority will be liable in the event of injury or loss sustained.

Even in non-certificated premises, therefore, there is a responsibility to have a Fire Procedure, and it is suggested that the points indicated in Figure 3.7 should form the basis – modified, of course, by any statutory requirements in force.

Fire procedure notices should be displayed in each room of the premises, and staff should be trained in their allocated duties. Responsibility for control of evacuation, and for summoning emergency services should be clearly defined, and the procedure tested by fire drill. Advice on the appropriate extinguishers can be obtained from fire protection officers, but it is equally important that equipment is correctly serviced and maintained. A recent fire on healthcare premises resulted in fatalities because, in the presence of smoke, a staff member was unable to operate an extinguisher; she was unable to see that the plastic safety cap was still in place over the operating knob and sustained serious injury herself in attempting to activate the striker. This underlines the point that for any emergency procedure to be effective, it must be tested.

Cross-infection control

Perhaps in no other area of contemporary dental practice has the changing **perception** of risk had such an impact as in the area of infection control. It is not so many years since the boiling-water sterilizer (which often neither boiled nor sterilized), the re-usable needle

FIRE PROCEDURE
BASIC ELEMENTS

1. Post Fire Procedure Notice in every room (see example below)
2. Install smoke detectors: test weekly, clean and replace battery annually
3. Install suitable fire extinguishers: check regularly, arrange annual inspection
4. Train all staff in fire procedure and use of equipment. Document training
5. Sign fire exits and fire escape routes. Keep free of obstructions
6. Ensure flammable materials are kept in minimum quantity and correctly stored
7. Detail evacuation arrangements and responsibilities, including calling emergency services, assembly point(s) and roll call
8. Ensure electrical appliances and wiring are inspected
9. Fit self-closers to internal doors – ensure they are not wedged open
10. Ensure gas fires, etc. are adequately guarded

ANYWHERE DENTAL PRACTICE
FIRE PROCEDURE
ON DISCOVERING A FIRE:

1. Alert reception: state location
2. Commence evacuation: staff in surgery 2 will check the first floor
   staff in surgery 1 will check the ground floor
   reception staff will remove the appointment book
3. Assess whether local measures will extinguish the fire. If not:

DIAL 999
ASK FOR FIRE BRIGADE
STATE LOCATION
Anywhere Dental Practice
47 High Street, Anytown

4. Leave the building, do not wait to collect personal belongings
5. All personnel will assemble in the car park for roll call

Figure 3.7 Fire procedure

and stylet, and the ungloved hand were normal aspects of dental care. Yet, as Cottone *et al.* have pointed out, recognition of the hazards is not new; 'In 1881, Miller recommended that microbiology be made an integral part of dental curricula and, in 1884, Koch demonstrated that tuberculosis could be transmitted by airborne droplets from the mouth . . ..'[15]

By the 1920s, it was also recognized that possible dental vectors of infection included aerosols, needlesticks and direct transfer by contaminated instruments and hands. However, infection control in dentistry, and particularly in general practice, was relatively unregulated until the mid-1980s. Certain reasons behind this situation may be identified:

1 **Knowledge** It can be argued that not until recently were the risks, infective agents and modes of transmission of – particularly – viral infections adequately understood.
2 **Materials** Although such items as surgical gloves, steam autoclaves and disposable needles had been in medical or hospital use for a considerable time, their relatively economic adaptation to the specific requirements of general dentistry has evolved only gradually.
3 **Risk Perception** It is only with the advent of a wide public perception of the risks of viral diseases such as herpes, hepatitis B (HBV) and most notably Human Immunodeficiency Virus (HIV), that a combination of professional regulation and public demand has acted as a spur to improved infection control in dentistry.

It is not proposed here to investigate in detail the many aspects of infection control which are considered applicable in dental practices under different jurisdictions. Guidelines and statutory requirements are in a state of continual evolution, and the clinician must remain constantly aware of current policy. Risk management of infection control requires however that a broad approach to the identification, assessment and reduction of infection risk should underlie clinicians' strategies in this field. Additionally, the concept of risk perception, by the public, the media and professional regulatory bodies has been highlighted in the area of infection control to a greater extent than in any other aspect of dental practice, and this factor must be considered. The speciality of 'risk communication' has been introduced to examine this concept.[16]

Research conducted by Scully, Porter and Epstein showed that in a dental teaching hospital environment presumably less subject to the time and economic pressures of general practice, 31% of glove-wearing clinicians failed to either change or wash their gloves between patients.[17] In a questionnaire distributed to general dental practitioners,

58 Workplace and environmental risks

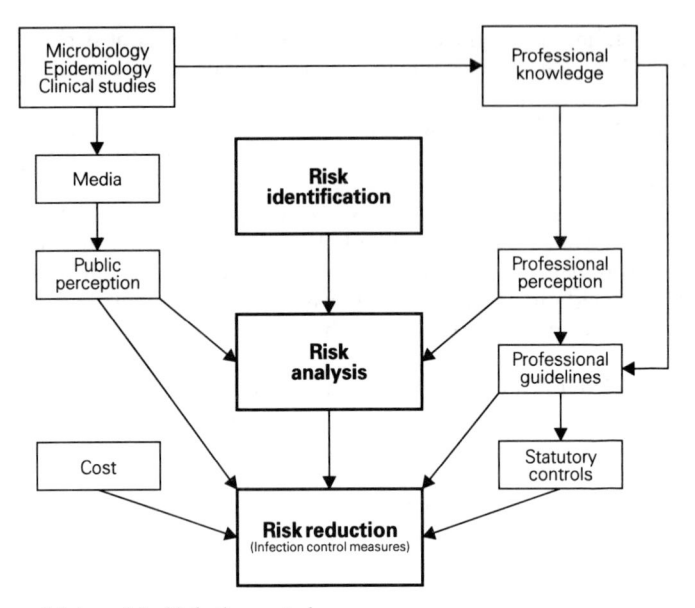

Figure 3.8 A model of infection control measures

Burke, Wilson and Wastell found that 23% of respondents wore gloves only for selected procedures or selected patients.[18] Both of these findings suggest either a misunderstanding of the basis of cross-infection precautions, a misperception of risk or conceivably a conscious or unconscious disregard for recommended procedures.

Cross-infection precautions as they are actually implemented in dental practice are therefore necessarily affected by objective scientific findings, by clinicians' perceptions of risk, by public perceptions of risk, and by professional compliance with recommendations and requirements in force. A model of these inter-relationships is shown in Figure 3.8.

The interactive nature of this model goes some way towards explaining the many apparent inconsistencies and anomalies which are revealed by research, such as those instanced above. This is a field in which there are few absolutes, and the concept of the elimination of risk is even further from reach than in other aspects of dental practice. There can be little doubt, moreover, that in an age when the trends in medical care have been towards the vanquishing of the threat of infection, the emergence of an agent – HIV – which is not only (so far as can be determined by present knowledge) fatal and currently incurable, but could conceivably be acquired through medical care itself, has dramatically altered the nature of clinical practice.

Risk identification
Considering first the 'objective' evidence offered by microbiological and epidemiological studies, there is little support for the suggestion that the risk of HIV transmission in clinical practice is numerically significant. Siew *et al.* rank selected risks from healthcare activities as follows:[19]

	Risk/million
HBV seroconversion after needlestick exposure to HbeAG+ blood	300,000
HIV seroconversion after needlestick	3,000
Anaesthesia-related mortality	100
Death from penicillin anaphylaxis	10–20
HIV seroconversion after transfusion of screened blood	6.7–2.5
HIV seroconversion after invasive procedure by HIV+ surgeon	2.4–24
Death due to HBV infection after invasive procedure by HBeAG+ surgeon	0.7–13.2
HIV seroconversion after invasive procedure by HIV+ dentist	0.0038–0.038

Considering the relative risks of HIV and HBV, Cottone illustrates the point:

> One milliliter of blood from a hepatitis B carrrier diluted in a 24,000 gallon swimming pool could still result in infection if one milliliter of that swimming pool water were injected into a susceptible individual. In contrast, one milliliter of blood from a patient with AIDS diluted in one quart of water would result in a viral concentration which would not transmit HIV infection[15] (p. 211).

Additionally, dentists had been implicated in nine out of twenty 'cluster' outbreaks of Hepatitis B reported in the United States up to 1987,[20] one of which involved 55 patients.[21] HBV was a condition whose infectivity, morbidity and mortality had been recognized for some time, yet 'because there was no real way to avoid it, everyone just took their chances with little worry'[15] (p. 18). As an estimated 50–80% of all hepatitis infections are thought to be subclinical, and the incidence of asymptomatic carriers of Hepatitis B varies from 0.1–0.5% in Western Europe and North America (up to 40% in some equatorial countries),[22] this approach illustrates the perceptual changes which have taken place in little over a decade. In the United Kingdom, cases of acute hepatitis amongst dentists were about two or three per year until the mid-1980s,[23] when the uptake of newly available vaccines began to increase, and it is possible that the prolonged incubation period of the illness reduced the likelihood of 'cluster' outbreaks amongst dental patients being identified.

Other infective agents whose risks of transmission in the dental clinical setting have been examined include herpes viruses and *Mycobacterium tuberculosis*. Some 75% of the population over the age of 30 are seropositive to herpes simplex antibodies, and the incidence of digital infection ('Herpetic whitlow') has been a known and unpleasant occupational disease of dentists. Recent reports from North America indicate a notable increase in reported cases of pulmonary tuberculosis, attributed to an ageing population, an increase in medically compromised patients, social deprivation and substance abuse.[24]

Additional factors in the identification of risk include the efficiency of transmission of infective agents by various means in the clinical setting. The Centers for Disease Control have suggested that the behaviour of the hepatitis B virus is a suitable model for the design of infection control procedures, and lists, in descending order, the most likely vectors:

1 Direct or percutaneous transmission by a contaminated needle or sharp object;
2 Non-needle percutaneous inoculation (scratches, burns, dermatitis);
3 Infected blood or serum on mucosal surfaces;
4 Other infectious secretion (saliva) on to mucosal surfaces;
5 Indirect transfer of infected serum via environmental surfaces;
6 Aerosol spatter of infected serum (theoretical).[25]

Figure 3.9 lists infections of significance for dental staff and patients.

Risk analysis
In undertaking risk analysis, the microbiologist and the clinician will need to consider the various infectious agents identified, the epidemiological data and the known vectors of transmission in the clinical setting, and to consider the probability and consequences of such transmission occurring.

Infections may be transmitted in three ways; patient to patient, patient to dental staff, or dental staff to patient (Figure 3.10), and different pathways will be involved in each case. Additionally, not all routes will be the same for different pathogens; respiratory infections are more likely to involve droplet spread, whereas HBV is most likely to transmit by needlestick or puncture wounds. The consequences of infection will

INFECTION HAZARDS IN DENTISTRY

(Arising from pathogens whose presence in the mouth, in oral lesions or secretions has been identified)

Bacterial

Whooping cough
Diptheria
Tuberculosis
Syphilis
Gonorrhoea
Pneumonias

Conjunctivitis
Endocarditis
Meningitis
Otitis
Bacteraemias

Viral

HIV
Hepatitis A, B, D, non-A, non-B
Hand, foot and mouth disease
Herpes virus infections
Infectious mononucleosis
Measles

Rubella
Mumps
Poliomyelitis
Chicken pox
Influenza, respiratory infections

Fungal

Candidosis

Figure 3.9 Infection hazards in dentistry

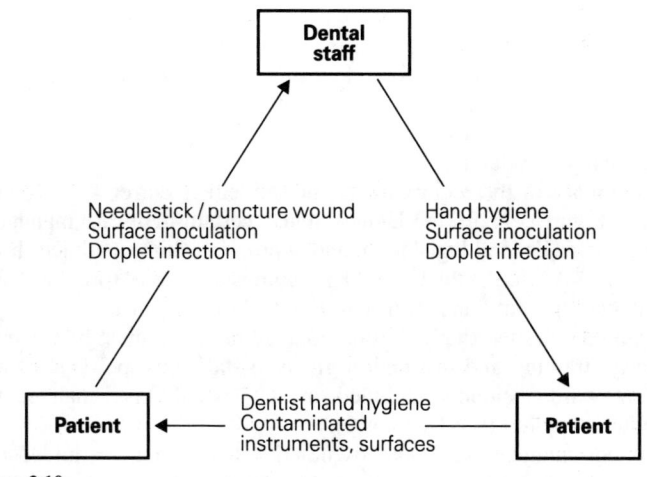

```
                    ┌──────────┐
                    │  Dental  │
                    │   staff  │
                    └──────────┘
                   ↗            ↘
   Needlestick / puncture wound    Hand hygiene
   Surface inoculation             Surface inoculation
   Droplet infection               Droplet infection

  ┌─────────┐                            ┌─────────┐
  │ Patient │ ←── Dentist hand hygiene ──│ Patient │
  └─────────┘     Contaminated           └─────────┘
                  instruments, surfaces
```

Figure 3.10

also vary according to the severity of the agent and the susceptibility of the recipient. Thus whilst at one extreme, the transmission of HIV would be invariably grave, the significance of rubella would depend on specific factors such as pregnancy and antibody status.

Recognition of the complexity of possible pathways, agents and susceptibilities, together with imponderable factors such as the actual patient/dentist infective state (medical history notwithstanding) has led to the development of so-called 'universal precautions' which are designed to minimize all and any transmission risk.

It is essential, however, to regard such precautions not as a 'shopping list', of individual items to be checked, but as an overriding approach to clinical care of the patient. Thus, where possible, infection control should be considered at the outset of surgery design and construction, and its principles built in to all procedures undertaken.

Risk control

With regard to the foregoing sections, risk control must be considered in relation to the concept of 'universal precautions', to statutory requirements and guidelines and to public perception.

Universal precautions, or the single-tier approach, require that all patients be treated as though they were a potential source of infective pathogens. A common misperception is that past guidelines have suggested that known carriers of, for example, HBV or HIV, are treated exceptionally (either in designated treatment areas or with additional precautions). It is notable that in current publications, such references are absent. The concept of 'risk' as applied to patients is now superseded by the notion of 'risk' applying to procedures. Thus, whilst it is sensible and prudent to defer procedures, such as soft tissue and bony surgery, which may involve increased spatter, to the end of a list, when time is available for cleansing the increased number of instruments, or remote surfaces, the routine treatment of HBV or HIV seropositive patients who are otherwise well is considered appropriate and ethically mandatory.[26,27,28]

A summary of the requirements and guidelines currently in force is given in Figure 3.11. In the United States, certain items are mandatory under State or Federal legislation, and appropriate current advice should be sought.[29] Advice in the United Kingdom is available from the British Dental Association[26] and from UK Health Departments.[30]

It should be noted that infection control measures must be reviewed regularly: training and instruction given to staff must be documented, and untoward incidents included in the overall risk management procedures applied (see Chapter 9).

Risk communication, as already noted, refers to policies intended to improve patient and public perception of risk reduction programmes.

Item	Monitors
Surgery design (cleanable surfaces, foot controls, etc.)	Vaccination register
Vaccination programme for clinical staff	
Full medical history and updates, every patient	Records review
Pre-treatment antiseptic mouthrinse, patient	
Pre-gloving handwash	
Disposable latex gloves	
Protective eyewear, staff and patient	
Disposable face mask	
Appropriate clinical clothing	
Rubber dam where possible	
Sharps handling/disposal system	Clinical waste monitoring
Sterilizable handpieces	
Instrument tray system	
Ultrasonic and autoclaving, all non-disposable instruments	Autoclave test strips, spore tests
Surface cleaner and surface disinfectant	Clinical protocols
Disposable 3 in 1 tip, aspirator tip	
Covered glutaraldehyde bath for non-autoclavable, non-disposable items	
Surface covers (switches, etc.)	
Protocol for laboratory work, equipment repairs, etc.	Records, pro-forma
Regulated clinical waste disposal	Transfer contract

Figure 3.11

Banting and Robertson summarize:

> Dentists, as health professionals, are responsible for synthesizing and presenting accurate information to their patients from an informed and unbiased perspective. When the magnitude of the risk is uncertain, it is important to keep an open mind and avoid focusing too narrowly. The public's heightened awareness of the environment and elevated health consciousness are laudatory and to be encouraged, but conclusions about risks must be based on facts from reliable and credible sources.[31]

It is not acceptable for dentists to distance themselves from public and media speculation regarding infection control. Where coverage is sensationalized, as in recent reports of the single – and thus far unexplained – episode of HIV transmission by a Florida dentist,[32] there is a responsibility to reassure and to place things in perspective, whilst at the same time realizing that the concept of informed consent requires that information provided is correct and authoritative. Some evidence has been presented to suggest that patients whose attention is drawn to infection control procedures have a heightened concern about risks,[33] but this finding was dependent on the timing of the information. Earlier work by Worthington *et al.* suggested that patients were,[34] on the contrary, supportive of measures taken for their welfare. In the wake of press reports that the Florida outbreak was due to failure of practice infection procedures (apparently without foundation),[35] it has been suggested that dentists should take the initiative in informing their patients fully about the precautions taken; 'Presenting your current office procedures to patients as part of an evolutionary process will help offset negative reactions and position dentistry as a caring profession with an excellent track record on safety.'[36]

Additional public concern has arisen from reports of HIV seropositive healthcare workers: the Centers for Disease Control has studied 23 dentists in this context.[37] Although the risks to patients are considered (see above) to be extremely slight, and the ethical and legal implications are considerable.[38] The current position is that such individuals must report their status to their employers (or in the case of general practitioners in the UK to their FHSA) and take medical advice if they are, or have been, involved in invasive procedures,[39] and should discontinue such procedures pending review.

Waste disposal
Waste arising from dental clinical premises is of two kinds: that designated as 'clinical waste', and other waste. Clinical waste includes all material generated directly from the diagnosis or treatment of patients such as dressings, cotton wool rolls, tissue, items containing secretions, used instruments and sharps. Other waste may include office waste, and domestic type waste from staff rooms, etc.

Waste from clinical premises is controlled in the UK by the Health and Safety at Work etc. Act, and by the Environmental Protection Act (1990). Requirements are that waste must be segregated and identifiable; clinical waste is placed in sturdy, impermeable plastic sacks coloured yellow. 'Other' waste may be disposed of – provided local by-laws permit – by means of the usual domestic waste system. Any materials containing patient information must, however, be obliterated before consigning, since the professional duty of confidentiality still applies once such material leaves the premises. Shredding, or incinerating should be used in this case.

The principle and procedures for the segregation of clinical waste must be made known to all relevant staff.

Bags must not be overfilled and must be securely closed before collection. Sharps and glass should be immediately disposed of into a suitable puncture-proof container constructed to BS 7320, and these containers should be filled only to the extent specified by the maker. Recent problems have occurred where containers of cardboard construction have become damp, allowing sharps to project. Care must be taken with siting and storage. Sharps containers for disposal should not be placed inside other containers or sacks.

Waste may be stored outside the premises so long as it is secure from weather and animal or human disturbance. Action has been brought against a clinician when children gained access to sharps containers stored outside and were subsequently found playing with contaminated syringes.

Clinical waste may only be disposed of by incineration, and by an authorized person, who will carry a certificate of registration. In the UK, all transfers of waste must be documented by a transfer note which specifies the parties involved, and the physical description and appearance of the waste. Repeated transfers of similar waste may be covered by a single note for up to one year. Transfer records must be retained for at least two years.[40]

In many cases, local authorities or health authorities will make the necessary arrangements for disposing of dental clinical waste. One or two points should not be overlooked; waste amalgam and other materials such as crowns and inlays are clinical waste, and must be disposed of, with a transfer note, to an authorized collector. Additionally, clinical waste generated during house calls is the responsibility of the clinician, and must be wrapped appropriately and removed for disposal in the correct manner.

Water, effluent and pollution

Public water undertakings in the UK jealously guard the purity and freedom from contamination of their supplies. The Back-Siphonage Regulations 1981 were superseded and supplemented by new water supply by-laws which took effect in 1987.[41] Considerably more stringent requirements include the provision of a Type–A air gap in circumstances where a Class 1 risk of mains contamination exists. This would include dental units, spitoons and ultrasonic units, and may include surgery sinks and wash hand basins. Some dental equipment has been engineered to avoid such problems, but it is imperative that advice from the local water undertaking, or from a reputable plumber with local knowledge be sought. Where a sufficient 'head' can be established, it may be possible to supply the surgery by an indirect system served by a storage tank. Some local by-laws require that sufficient water to serve the establishment for 24 hours be maintained. Again, early advice is imperative.

There has been some investigation of the contamination of dental unit water supplies by bacteria,[42] particularly *Pseudomonas* species, and it has been suggested that a captive water system, or a reservoir of antimicrobial agent,[43] should be used. A Californian dentist has been sued for allegedly cross-infecting a patient due to dental unit water supply contamination.

Waste effluent in liquid form, and gaseous waste from dental premises are theoretically sources of litigation, being subject to Health and Safety, and Pollution, legislation. Additionally, unpleasant waste effluent may form the basis for an action in nuisance. The general requirement is to exercise reasonable care, and to ensure, for instance, that surgery exhaust ventilation, or dry-line suction apparatus does not discharge into a confined or populated adjacent space.

Radiation – X-rays and lasers
The use of ionizing radiation for medical care in the UK is strictly controlled under the Ionizing Radiation Regulations 1985 and the Ionizing Radiation (Protection of Persons Undergoing Medical Examination and Treatment) Regulations 1988 (POPUMET). These regulations expand and identify the requirements of the Health and Safety at Work etc. Act in relation to X-ray machinery, its operation and the processing of films.

Notification to the Health and Safety Executive must be given of all premises where X-rays are being, or will be, used. It is sufficient to identify the type of use and the number of machines. Dental practices are, in the majority of cases (but see below) exempt from the most stringent requirements of the regulations, including the need to appoint a qualified medical physicist as a designated Radiation Protection Adviser, but only if certain conditions are met.

For detailed advice, dentists are referred to the Standing Dental Advisory Committee's booklet 'Radiation Protection in Dental Practice',[44] available from Health Authorities or FHSAs. The advice of the National Radiological Protection Board (NRPB) (see Appendix) is also available for guidance on matters pertaining to radiography, as well as providing a monitoring service for radiographic safety which assists dentists in fulfilling their legal obligations under the regulations.

In brief, the principal exempting requirements set out in regulations are:

1. Minimal usage and dosage There is no dose of X-radiation which is so low as to have no malignancy-inducing potential in human tissue. The need to justify every exposure and to take all steps necessary to minimize the dosage is therefore self-evident and

paramount. Patients should be protected from scattered radiation by adherence to correct procedure and the fastest film speed yielding satisfactory images should be employed. Failure to secure clinically adequate films could render the dentist liable to civil action, to prosecution or to professional proceedings.

2 Controlled zone No-one, other than the patient shall enter the controlled zone around the X-ray tubehead during exposure. This zone should extend for 2 metres in every direction unless adequate absorption by structural walls or other shielding is demonstrated. Doorways and occupied areas within the zone should be suitably protected by notices, warnings or shielding.

3 Every person who clinically or physically directs X-ray exposures shall be adequately trained in a 'core of knowledge' laid down in regulations. It is the responsibility of the practice principal or senior clinician to ensure that all staff are adequately trained and supervised. The General Dental Council has taken action against UK dentists who have permitted (knowingly or otherwise) untrained staff to make exposures.

4 A Radiation Protection Supervisor, who is trained and has the 'core of knowledge' must be designated to oversee radiography in the practice. Legal responsibility rests, however, with the principal or senior dentist.

5 Local Rules must be drawn up to cover radiographic procedures. These must be specific to the site. A 'machine malfunction' procedure must be available in the event of untoward occurrences.

6 X-ray sets must be 'critically examined' before first use and after repair. This examination must be carried out by a designated Radiation Protection Adviser; usually a trained and certificated engineer from the dental equipment supplier/manufacturer. Additionally, machines must be tested and certificated at three-yearly intervals, regularly inspected and maintained according to the manufacturer's specification.

In some circumstances, the type, physical layout or volume of radiographic procedures in a practice will require additional precautions, or the appointment of a Radiation Protection Adviser. These may include: the use of cephalometry, the presence of two or more X-ray machines in the same area, or dosage rates to individual staff members exceeding that which would accrue from taking 150 intra-oral or 50 panoral films per week. Further advice from the NRPB should be sought in such cases.

Risks from radiography in dental practice may arise from a number of sources. Machine malfunctions, resulting in the exposure of staff to excessive radiation, have occurred. Where personal injury has been a possibility, reporting of the incident to the Health and Safety Executive under RIDDOR requirements is mandatory. Inadequate attenuation of radiation by screen walls may lead to accidental exposure of persons in adjacent rooms, and surveys reveal that some dentists still hold films in place with their fingers.[45]

A more insidious risk is that faulty technique and/or film processing may require the repetition of exposures, and it is recommended that a periodic audit of diagnostic quality is carried out, with a record of repeat exposures needed. In medico-legal cases, a successful defence will frequently rely on the timeliness and quality of X-rays taken during treatment, and as such matters may not come to light for many years, audit of the archival permanence of films is also indicated. Careful storage and mounting, as well as good fixation and washing, is essential.

A review of nearly 1,500 assessments carried out by the Dental Monitoring Service of the NRPB in 1986/87 revealed that 25% of machines were more than 15 years old; 2% were over 25 years old. The incidence of deficiencies increased with age. Only one-fifth of sets operated at sufficient tubehead voltage (60–70kV) to obtain optimum diagnostic information: the actual kilovoltage was not always that specified by the manufacturer. Some timers are not calibrated for the low exposure times suitable for high speed film, and beam filtration could usefully be increased in these cases. It was also noted that processing was rarely to optimal standards, despite the increased use of automatic developers.[46]

Lasers

The use of lasers in dentistry is a relatively recent development. Registration of laser use by dentists is required by the Nursing Homes (Laser) Regulations (1984), which direct that the local Health Authority shall be advised, and will supervise necessary health and safety requirements. A Laser Protection Adviser must be appointed, and a controlled area, with warning notices, designated. All staff concerned with laser use must be adequately trained, and such training documented.

Three laser types are currently in use in dentistry, and specific safety procedures will vary. Reflective surfaces (mirrors, instruments and restorations) have the potential to redirect laser beams: non-reflective instruments have been advised, with the use of protective glasses for patients and staff. Additional moist cotton gauze for eye and mucosal protection of the patient is recommended for carbon dioxide laser use. The laser 'plume' resulting from application is to be considered infectious, and adequate evacuation and ventilation are needed. Lasers should be used with extreme caution in the presence of volatile or explosive materials or gases.[47]

Autoclaves and pressure vessels
Autoclaves and pressure vessels are regulated by the Factories Act (1971) and by the Health and Safety at Work etc. Act (1974). Additionally, compliance with the Pressure Systems and Transportable Gas Containers Regulations (1989) is mandatory.

Dental practices contain numerous pressure vessels and systems, ranging from pressure flasks for acrylic curing, fire extinguishers and medical gas cylinders to air compressor receiving tanks and autoclaves. Small pressure vessels are exempt from the 1989 Regulations, but subject to the general requirements of safety such as maintenance and compliance with manufacturers' instructions. In most dental situations, the 1989 Regulations will apply fully only to autoclaves and to compressor air receiver tanks.

In essence, the Regulations require that such pressure vessels and systems shall be:

1 Designed and constructed for safe use and inspection
2 Supplied with full, correct and safe information for use, and marked with the designed operating temperature and pressure
3 Installed and commissioned safely and appropriately
4 Operated correctly by staff trained in its use and in malfunction procedures
5 Inspected and certificated periodically by a 'competent person'
6 Correctly maintained, and records of maintenance kept[48]

These regulations apply from July 1994, and in the majority of cases, suppliers and manufacturers will take care of points 1–3 above. A scheme of inspection will generally be available from manufacturers for current models. In other cases, the 'competent person' who certificates the equipment will also draw up the scheme.

The Factories Act prescribed periods of inspection of no more than 14 months for autoclaves and 26 months for air compressors. These periods are now set by the individual certifying engineer, but will not, in general, be more frequent except where special considerations apply. Inspection can normally be arranged through insurance brokers experienced in dental premises cover, or through one of the certification bodies (addresses in Appendix). Health authorities may have appropriately qualified staff who comply with the requirements of the Code of Practice.

Risks arising from pressure vessels are primarily those of explosive or sudden decompression. Instances have arisen where structural damage and personal injury have occurred as a result of poor maintenance and, occasionally, poor design. Clinical staff have suffered scalds and burns from hot autoclave surfaces or faulty door seals: the doors themselves are heavy and may cause injury. Other risks may arise from failure to check consistent sterilizing performance of autoclaves, and the use of chemical and biological tests is recommended. It is advised that each autoclave should have its own record book to document test dates and results, as well as maintenance and certification visits.

Air compressors should be checked regularly; air line leakage, if undetected, may lead to additional load and premature failure of compressor units, whilst inadequate air filtration may pose infection and oil contamination risks. The means of isolating all pressure systems from electrical supply should be accessible.

Electricity at work
Electrocution, burns and fire arising from electrical appliances are consistently prominent in Health and Safety statistics. Failure to inspect and maintain wiring and installations may invalidate insurance cover. The Electricity at Work Regulations (1989) are applicable in dental practices and clinics.

All mains electrical wiring, fuseways or circuit breakers and distribution boards should be inspected by an electrician accredited by the National Inspection Council for Electrical Installation Contracting (NICEIC). Review at periods advised should be carried out. Additionally, all portable and fixed appliances should be checked by a 'competent person' (normally an electrician) and a record of this kept. Appliances and equipment must be in safe working order at all times, although the regulations make no specific recommendations about the frequency of testing. Appropriate guidance is available from the Health and Safety Executive.[49]

Particular points which are relevant to risks in dental practice would include:

(a) Never handle electrical equipment with wet hands
(b) Always disconnect appliances at the plug before moving, maintaining or dismantling
(c) Switch off and unplug all non-essential appliances at the end of each day
(d) Ensure that flexible connectors for surgery appliances do not permit them to fall into sinks
(e) Avoid trailing flexes which may be tripped over
(f) Take extreme care with appliances, switching etc. in the presence of volatile or explosive agents such as acrylic monomer, anaesthetic gases

Health and safety – substances

The Control of Substances Hazardous to Health (COSHH)
The Control of Substances Hazardous to Health Regulations (1988) were implemented in October 1989 in the UK and are broadly comparable with the Hazard Communications Standard applicable in the US from 1986. The intention is that all substances which may be potentially hazardous in the workplace are itemized, their specific risks to health identified, and all steps taken to minimize these risks specified.

These regulations, as with most health and safety legislation, have been drawn up to cover a wide spectrum of workplaces and industries. The precise method of carrying out the assessment and the form of recording it is not specified. The position is further complicated by the designation of certain substances in Regulation 2(1)(a) as 'toxic, very toxic, corrosive . . .' etc., and of substances in Regulations 7(4) and 7(5) which are subject either to Maximum Exposure Limits (MELs) or Ocupational Exposure Standards (OESs). Some of these designated substances are in use in dentistry.

Dental professional organizations give detailed advice on compliance, and a general approach and overview is presented here. Useful information may also be obtained from Health and Safety Executive publications[50] and from the Health Departments.[51]

There are six stages in COSHH assessment:

1 Assemble information on substances, work practices and personnel;
2 Evaluate the health risks present;
3 Consider control measures;
4 Make a record of the assessment;
5 Implement the recommended control measures;
6 Review the assessment as required.

The amount of time taken will, of course, depend on the substances and the workplace. 'It might take one person 2 minutes to assess the risks from using correction fluid in the office. It could take a multidisciplinary team weeks to assess the risk in the factory where it is made'.[48]

1 Information gathering At this stage it is best to include all substances which pose a hazard, even if it is slight. This is most easily done by a site check in the practice or clinic. Work procedures, and the staff members concerned, which involve these substances should be listed. For each substance, using the labels, manufacturer's data sheet, or details provided by professional associations or official Health and Safety lists,[52] note the hazards

	Long-term exposure limit 8 hr reference period		Short-term exposure limit 10 min reference period	
	ppm	mgm−3	ppm	mgm−3
Acetic acid (X-ray stop bath)	10	25	15	37
Chromium (chromic acid) (MEL)		0.05		
Dibenzoyl peroxide		5		
Ethanol	1000	1900		
Formaldehyde (MEL)	2	2.5	2	2.5
Glutaraldehyde			0.2	0.7
Halothane	10	18		
n-Hexane	500	1800	1000	3600
Hydrogen peroxide	1	1.5	2	3
Iodine			0.1	1
Iodoform	0.6	10	1	20
Isopropyl alcohol	400	980	500	1225 Sk
Methyl methacrylate	100	410	125	510
Nitrous oxide	100	180		
Phenol	5	19	10	38 Sk
Trichloroacetic acid	5	40	5	40
Trichloroethylene (Trilene) (MEL)	100	535	150	802 Sk

Sk = absorbed through skin. MEL = maximum exposure limit (all other figures are occupational exposure standards (OES))

Figure 3.12 Exposure limits for substances found in dentistry (examples only – not an exhaustive list) (from *EH40/94 Occupational exposure limits 1994*. HMSO, London)

associated with use. In dentistry, human tissue or secretions should also be included as posing a risk of infection.

2 Evaluation It is unlikely that in clincal practice, exposures to harmful agents will approach, let alone exceed, recommended limits. The use of glutaraldehyde as a surface disinfectant has been discontinued, and Figure 3.12 lists the current values for most materials encountered in practice.

3 Control measures These will include staff training in the use and storage of substances, and may also involve: amending procedures; use of mechanical ventilation; health surveillance (see mercury, below); emergency procedures and personal protective equipment (PPE).

4 Records The assessment should be written and in a form which will make it available to all who might need to refer to it, including employees.

5 Implementation The control measures decided on should be implemented, and a record made of the fact. This could simply be done by adding an 'initials' and 'date' column to the assessment.
6 Review The regulations require the assessment to be repeated at once if there is any material change in the workplace, or substances used. It is advisable to formally review the assessment at intervals no longer than a year.

The risks posed by hazardous materials in dentistry may rarely come to professional attention, but the consequences can be severe. Cases of patient burns to the skin, mucosa or conjunctiva from ortho-phosphoric acid are not rare. Cleaners have been injured by combining bleach and oxidizing cleaning agents. Hypochlorites may cause severe symptoms, particularly in asthmatic staff. Chronic mercury poisoning has been reported in clinical staff.[53] Increased rates of miscarriage have been reported among staff with prolonged exposure to nitrous oxide.[54] As discussed in a previous section, the possibility of infection from contaminated tissue or secretions is an ever-present hazard.

Increased awareness of the potential hazards of chronic exposure to hazardous substances are a significant cause of worldwide concern, not only to environmentalists, but to insurance companies. So called 'latent risks' such as those attributable to asbestos, coal dust and radon gas will have consequences for many years. The reasoning behind hazardous substances control: that we are presently unaware of future outcomes, leads to the conclusion that reasonable reduction of exposure is prudent.

Mercury

Mercury has been in regular dental use since at least the 1840s, and its potential toxicity to those such as clinical dental staff who are exposed to metallic and vaporized mercury is well established (Scully, Cawson and Griffiths, pp. 84–89).[23] However, a recent review[55] has failed to show any toxic effects on patients with amalgam restorations.

Risks from mercury are of three types; direct absorption of mercury through intact or damaged skin; uptake of mercury by inhalation of vapour and contamination of the environment.

Procedures should be designed so that mercury and waste amalgam is not handled. Capsules or automatic trituration are now in common use. Mercury vapour is more insidious, since it may be given off at various stages: vaporization is more likely at raised temperatures, therefore good, externally vented aspiration is necessary when grinding or removing amalgam restorations, and steam from autoclaves should be extracted by mechanical surgery ventilation. Avoid breathing steam/air when opening autoclaves. Facemasks alone probably absorb little mercury vapour. Mercury may also vaporize slowly when spilled globules evaporate at room temperature. Worktops should therefore be smooth and sealed to walls; carpet and flooring joins should be avoided in surgeries – scuffed accumulations of mercury are otherwise circulated into the air. Conventional vacuum cleaners should be avoided in the surgery for the same reason.

Minute spillages may be absorbed on to X-ray backing film or aluminium foil; triturators should stand on a shallow-lipped tray lined with foil. Small spillages should be conjoined into globules with foil and drawn up into a plastic syringe. Any sizeable spillages may be covered with a paste of flowers of sulphur and water and carefully swept into a sealed, labelled plastic bag kept in a sealed plastic container for disposal. Any spillage which is not accessible (e.g. behind fixed units or into waste plumbing) should be notified to the Health and Safety Executive for advice.

Waste amalgam should be stored under used X-ray fixer in a sealed, labelled container, and disposed of to an authorized collector.

If amalgam usage is particularly heavy, or there is reason to suppose that any staff have been exposed to significant concentrations of vapour, mercury analysis from urine, hair or nail samples may be taken. Addresses of UK agencies for mercury analysis are included in the Appendix.

Summary: Health and safety risks
Studies by F.E. Bird in the 1960s,[56] based on analysis of nearly two million work-related incidents of damage or injury in 300 companies, revealed a 'pyramid'-like distribution (Figure 3.13). As is usual in risk

Serious or disabling injuries — 1

Minor injuries
(any reported injury less than serious) — 10

Property damage accidents
(All types) — 30

Accidents with no visible
injury or damage
(Critical incidents) — 600

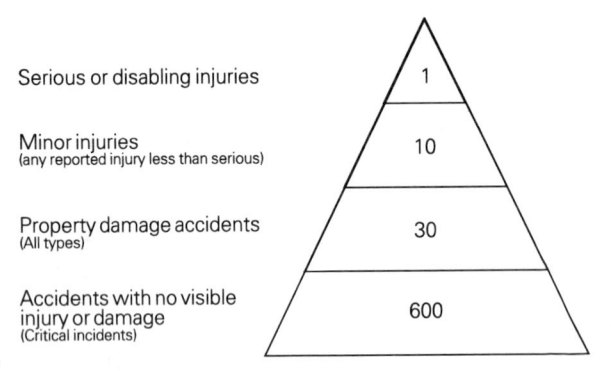

Figure 3.13 The risk pyramid. The incidence and severity of accidents reported by F.E. Bird (1969) (from Bamber L. (1993) Accident costing. *Journal of the Institute of Risk Management*, October 1993, 15–20)

analysis exercises, it was found that low-severity claims were associated with high incidence, and that conversely, high-severity claims occurred infrequently. A ratio of 1:600 was noted between serious claims and those in which no visible injury occurred. The avoidance of small incidents may therefore be related to a corresponding reduction in serious injury accidents; moreover, the cost saving to any small business which may accrue from timely health and safety measures may be significant.

UK Health and Safety statistics attest to the fact that, whilst fatal accidents in healthcare premises are below those for service industries generally, the risk of less severe accidents, but still involving the loss of three or more days absence from work, is above the service industry average.[57] It is estimated, moreover, that 70% of reportable occurrences are not notified, and steps are in hand to correct this situation (see Figure 3.14).

Even when adequate insurance is carried, the expense of time and disruption of productive process can far outweigh the costs of investment in prudent planning. A safe and ordered work environment is less stressful and more conducive to co-operative effort on the part of all staff.

Employment

If the many requirements of Health and Safety law appear to constitute an obstacle course over which the clinical manager must struggle, then Employment law, by analogy, may resemble a minefield! This metaphor is not entirely frivolous; the majority of risks which arise as a result of employment – or self-employment – in small businesses are due to inadequate planning and forethought.

A recent case will illustrate this point:

A dentist contacted his professional indemnity organization for advice. A young dental surgery assistant had gradually, and increasingly, taken short periods of sick leave, ranging from one day

	Fatal	*Major*	*3-day**	*Total*
All service industries	0.5	47.8	461.2	509.5
Healthcare	0.1	42.5	639.0	681.6
All industries	1.2	77.1	671.7	750.0

* Injuries involving an absence from work of 3 days or more

Figure 3.14 Accident rates per 100,000 employees in 1991–2 (from *Health and safety in service industries 1991–2 (1993)* HMSO, London)

to a week, for a variety of minor ailments. On review, it became apparent that she had had some 50 days of absence in her first year, and 80 days in the second year. She had now informed her employer that she was pregnant, and wished to take maternity leave. He had realized that she would have been with the practice for two years in about a fortnight's time. She had no written Contract of Employment. Her frequent absences had placed an increasing strain on other staff in a small practice. Could he now dismiss her?

Such an enquiry is neither rare nor untypical and suggests both poor knowledge and inadequate planning and management. Failure to provide a written contract now means that many aspects of the employment will, by default, be statutorily determined, whilst others (in the absence of agreement between the parties) can only be decided on the basis of what an Industrial Tribunal deems 'reasonable'.

In the above case, failure to address, or to have policies for, the management of sickness absence has resulted in an unsatisfactory situation becoming intolerable for the business, with no clear indication of what is acceptable performance by employees. Absence of a grievance and disciplinary procedure will now make decisive action difficult. Finally, the two-year qualifying period which entitles some employees to additional protection against 'unfair' dismissal does not apply to discrimination on the grounds of sex, and the employee's pregnancy may now be seen as the deciding factor if dismissal occurs.

The costs of employment mal-performance and disputes, including absenteeism, tribunal awards, case preparation, pay in lieu of notice, reduced efficiency, staff dissatisfaction and stress, can only be guessed at, but will probably impact, at one time or another, on every practice or organization. Good management can effect significant reductions in such risks.

Employment law changes constantly. It is imperative that the general advice contained in this section is checked by reference to professional associations,[58] current texts,[59] and by taking individual legal guidance before proceeding with any action or documentation.

Recruitment

Staff recruitment and selection is the art not merely of fitting the person to the job, but of matching their skills and attitudes to the needs and objectives of an organization. Whereas larger health bodies may be able to call on trained human resources managers for assistance in this task, many dentists will have to assume this role, sometimes with reluctance.

Recruitment should commence with the preparation of a job specification. It is difficult to understand why this task is so often omitted. The job specification should contain not only a description of the tasks and duties of the new staff member (the job description), but also preferred characteristics. This document will assist in focusing attention on the essential requirements, whilst also giving an 'ideal template' against which applicants' qualities and abilities can be measured. To avoid interviewing unsuitable or unqualified candidates, it is a good idea to send the job description itself to all short-listed applicants.

An organized approach to interviews is similarly important, although it is not suggested that the procedure should be over-elaborate. Many clinicians find the interviewing task difficult, and a pre-prepared checklist of relevant topics should be prepared, and a copy attached to each interviewee's application. This ensures that there is some measure of comparability between interviews, and provides somewhere to make notes for later evaluation (and memory refreshment). Care must be taken not to ask questions which could be interpreted as discriminatory under the Sex Discrimination Acts 1975 and 1986. Enquiries about marital status or arrangements for childcare could come into this category. Employers should also be aware of the risks of entering into a verbal, but binding, contract at an interview. Written notes or the presence of a second interviewer may help to guard against this risk.

Contracts of employment

The Employment Protection (Consolidation) Act (1978) – which has since been amended, most recently by the Trades Union Reform and Employment Rights Act (1992) – established the right of employees to receive a written 'statement of terms of employment'. If this is not provided as specified, then certain aspects of the employment would be held, in law, to be implied. For example, if no terms of notice of termination of the employment were set down, then the minimum terms laid down in the Act would apply: that is: 1 week after 1 month's employment, 2 weeks after 2 years, and then an additional week each year up to 12 years.

The Statement of Terms and Conditions must include at least:

1. Names of the parties
2. Date of commencement (or continuation) of employment
3. Job title
4. Pay details
5. Hours of work
6. Holiday and holiday pay provisions
7. Sick pay provisions

8 Pension rights, if applicable
9 Period of notice
and, for employment commencing after 1 July 1992:
10 Location(s) of employment.

A grievance procedure must also be provided where the number of employees exceeds 20. Other provisions of the Act include an employee's right not to be 'unfairly dismissed', that is, dismissal for reasons other than clearly inadequate performance or some other substantial reason (see Section 2.4. below).

Since July 1992, employees regularly working more than sixteen hours per week (or eight hours if there are more than twenty employees) are entitled to a statement of terms and conditions of employment, which must be supplied within eight weeks of commencement of employment.

It is strongly advised that all employees receive such a statement, and that careful consideration is given to all the above, and any additional, terms which may apply. In a clinical environment, these may include; general demeanour, attention to health and safety and cross-infection codes, and confidentiality. In a small practice, the timing of holidays is a frequent cause of friction, and the practice policy may be included (if this is restrictive, then the matter should certainly be raised at interview or even beforehand). The job description, and statements regarding grievance and disciplinary procedures (see 'Training' below) may be attached to the contract. Both parties should sign and retain a copy of the documents.

There is a belief that written contracts, especially those which are detailed, may cause future difficulties if, for some reason, the employer wishes to amend them at some time. This argument is not tenable, since provision for future consultation and review can be written into the contract, and unreasonable change can never be imposed in any event. To attempt to do so in the absence of a written contract (or a minimally drafted one) would invite litigation and possible compensation for unfair or constructive dismissal (constructive dismissal being the *de facto* termination of employment by an employee by reason of the employer's acts or omissions).

Matters of dispute in employment are dealt with by Industrial Tribunals or through the Advisory, Conciliation and Arbitration Service (ACAS). Tribunals have the powers of a court of law, and may subpoena witnesses. Whilst employers may represent themselves, costs are borne, in most circumstances, by each party, and the time involved in preparation and attendance may be considerable. Tribunals have the power to award compensation up to £11,000 in normal circumstances. Further information is given in 'Grievance and disciplinary procedures' below.

Training

The provision of adequate training for the safe conduct of an employee's duties is a requirement of the Health and Safety at Work etc. Act (1974). Over and above this basic requirement, however, should come the objectives of increased efficiency and quality of work, improved flexibility of roles, raised self-confidence and self-esteem and reduced supervision. In larger organizations the opportunity for promotion and the acquisition of new skills may apply, but in every truly successful business, opportunities for personal development exist and are exploited at every level.

Staff training begins when the new employee enters the premises for the first time. This is usually 9 a.m. on a Monday morning, which is frequently the least auspicious time to conduct an organized and comprehensive introduction! A planned induction programme, devised for all new employees, might commence at a slightly later time, when a senior staff member can be designated for this purpose. A documented induction could include:

- Programme of induction procedure
- Premises layout
- List of names and roles of personnel
- General background to the organization
- Timetable of routine activities (meal breaks, meetings, etc)
- Name of person to whom responsible
- Fire precautions

Using the organization's procedure manual (see Chapter 2) and the job description as a guide, an induction and training programme for each staff role can be developed. It is essential that all training received by all staff should be documented, and a check list for each person should be included, either in the procedure manual or in the health and safety documentation as appropriate.

In matters relating to the care and well-being of patients, the requirement to provide adequate training for staff in roles ancillary to clinical dentistry is generally an ethical responsibility of dentists in most professional jurisdictions. Professional disciplinary action, or criminal charges, may follow on the actions of untrained staff. Areas of risk include, but are not confined to; the taking of radiographs by inadequately qualified staff, illegal practice of dentistry by technicians or chairside assistants, failure to follow cross-infection control measures by clinical ancillaries, breach of confidentiality by administrative staff.

Additionally, the legal principle of vicarious liability – responsibility for the acts or omissions of another – may apply where a person suffers loss or damage as a result of an employee's failure of the duty of care. Clinical circumstances will be addressed in Chapter 5, but, for instance, the cleaner who leaves a bucket where a patient can fall over it, or the receptionist who loses a denture handed in for repair, may both look to their employer to assume liability. In this sense, the provision of training and the monitoring of good practice are clearly risk reduction measures.

Grievance and disciplinary procedures

Where less than 20 staff are employed, current employment law in the United Kingdom does not require that grievance and disciplinary procedures are set out in writing to employees. It is, however, sensible to have set procedures, first to ensure equitable treatment of all employees, second to protect the business against claims of unfair treatment or dismissal and third to protect employees against arbitrary or unreasonable action.

Procedures need not be over-elaborate, especially in small organizations, so long as they are clear to all parties in advance, reasonable, equitable and impartial.

Grievance procedure, when an employee is dissatisfied with some aspect of his or her employment, would normally involve first raising the matter verbally with a senior staff member. Complaints should be dealt with promptly, and not allowed to 'smoulder'; nothing is better calculated to undermine good working relationships. All complaints should be heard sympathetically, and an opportunity taken to seek other informal views where appropriate, or to obtain impartial advice. The reasoning used to arrive at a decision should be given to the employee, and a note made of the matter. An employee who remains dissatisfied may be given the opportunity to appeal against the decision (in writing if specified), and in larger practices or organizations, the matter may be referred to senior management – a partner or personnel officer – for review. It would be unreasonable to refuse an employee's request to take their own advice (from a recognized trade union, or workplace representative) at this stage. It is essential to keep records of grievances which pass on to a formal review stage, since in the event of a later claim for constructive dismissal, contemporary written evidence may be helpful in avoiding or winning a case before a tribunal.

Disciplinary procedures should also be simple, fair and incremental. Minor infringements of practice policy or small failures in performance should be dealt with promptly, informally and privately. An informal note of such matters may be kept, but should not form part of an employee's permanent personnel record.

More serious breaches (but still falling short of gross misconduct, which would lead to summary dismissal), should be treated formally. The employee should be given a written statement of the matter leading to disciplinary action, written factually and impartially. He/she should be advised that they will have an opportunity to state their case, and the right, if requested, to be accompanied by another employee or trade union representative. Sufficient time should be given for them to make arrangements in this regard.

Whilst it is reasonable – and should be indicated – that disciplinary action may take account of an employee's performance as a whole, care must be taken to avoid victimization or unfair treatment. If it is considered that disciplinary action is warranted, after hearing an employee's submission, then it is accepted procedure for first an oral warning, followed by a first and then a final written warning to be given on successive occasions. Oral and first written warnings should be recorded in the employee's personal file, but should be removed after a set period of time, if subsequent performance is satisfactory. Periods of six and twelve months respectively are usual.

A final written warning would normally be followed by a probationary period, of discretionary length, and further failures within such a period will result in dismissal, with the contracted notice, or payment in lieu.

It is, unfortunately, not uncommon for employers in smaller businesses to regard themselves as exempted from the requirements of employment law. The experience of professional associations and advisers is that this approach is unwise, and may lead to disproportionate costs in the longer term.

Dismissal

Reference was made above to reasons for 'fair' dismissal. These include gross misconduct, failure to respond to a final written warning or genuine redundancy. Whilst there are other reasons which tribunals have accepted, professional advice should be sought in cases which do not fall into the above categories.

By contrast, examples of 'unfair' dismissal (as determined by a tribunal) have included:

1 Where an employee has been absent for frequent short periods due to health reasons (but no warnings, or inadequate warnings were given by the employer)
2 Where, during a heated exchange, the employer has told the employee to 'make up your mind whether you wish to continue working here'

3   Where an employer has refused to renew a fixed term contract of employment without adequate reason
4   Where an employee has become pregnant and complications led to additional sickness absence

Naturally, such instances cannot be viewed in isolation from the detailed facts of each case. The general point is, however, that although only a minority of 'unfair dismissal' claims lead to tribunal hearings, and a minority of those lead to awards, the consequences may be serious financially. Prudence dictates that adequate, reasonable and written procedures should be followed.

Gross misconduct is generally defined as any act or omission which is of sufficient gravity as to lead to summary dismissal (i.e. without notice). In dental practice, examples might include:

1   Theft or fraud involving practice or patients belongings, records or money
2   Breach of confidentiality
3   Failure to follow Health and Safety or infection control procedures
4   Assault or attempted assault
5   Inability to work due to alcohol or drugs
6   Reckless actions which endanger people or property

There may be other legitimate additions to this list, but the essence must be that the offence is generally recognizable as serious, dangerous or liable to bring the business or profession into public disrepute.

Employees who have worked for an employer for an average of 16 hours a week or more are not entitled to protection against unfair dismissal unless they have been employed for two years (or five years if they have worked for more than eight hours a week). The two year time limit does not, however, apply to employees who are dismissed for reasons connected with pregnancy. The law relating to sexual discrimination, pregnancy and maternity leave is complex. Advice should be sought in case of uncertainty, either from professional associations or from the appropriate government department.

Occupier's liability

Negligence

The then Lord Chancellor, in 1967, observed that:

> Occupation of premises is a ground for liability and not a ground for exemption from liability. It ... gives some control over and some knowledge of the state of premises ... it is natural and right that an

occupier should have some degree of responsibility for the safety of persons entering his premises.[60]

This view summarizes the general attitude taken in law to occupiers, and forms the basis on which actions in negligence may be brought against them by legitimate visitors to their premises.

The tort, or civil wrong, of negligence, involves three necessary components:

1 It must be shown that the defendant owes a duty of care to the plaintiff
2 There must be demonstrated failure of that duty, and
3 There must be consequent injury, loss or damage to the plaintiff

Lord Gardner's opinion confirms that a duty of care exists to legitimate 'visitors' (for trespassers, see below). Thus, reasonable attention must be paid to the maintenance and arrangement of all aspects of the premises – including external paths, car parks, etc. – which might result in injury.

This general duty of care is confirmed and given some specific direction by the provisions of the Occupier's Liability Act (1957). Amongst other provisions, Section 2(3) notes that; '(a) An occupier must be prepared for children to be less careful than adults;' although – '(b) An occupier may expect that a person, in the exercise of his calling, will appreciate and guard against any risks ordinarily incidental to it.'

(a) would imply that particular precautions should be taken where children are involved. For instance, if a waiting area has a 'play corner', electric sockets should be protected, and extra care taken with radiators, windows and so on.

On the other hand (b) reduces liability in respect of, say, electricians or maintenance engineers, who may be considered to be aware of any special risks inherent in their work, so long as the occupier fulfils his basic duty of care. Additionally, if an independent contractor working on the premises himself negligently causes injury to another visitor, the occupier would not be held vicariously liable. This does suggest that it would be advisable to employ only reputable contractors, or to check that they carry their own liability insurance.

What, then, if the damage done by contractors injures the dentist's practice? The dentist may then be in the position of plaintiff. In one such instance, contractors working on water mains applied pressure to a supply pipe, fracturing it. Failure of supply disrupted the practice, damaged a central suction pump, and necessitated excavation to discover the fracture. Damages were recovered for the cost of digging and repair, and for the broken pump, but not for the interference with business; loss of this kind is not generally recoverable in negligence actions.

Trespass

Trespassers – those who are present on land or property without invitation, and who are either unknown to the occupier, or, if known, are unwelcome – are not owed the same duty of care as legitimate visitors.[61] However, the Occupiers' Liability Act (1984) has amended the common law position of trespassers. An occupier who is aware of the possible presence of trespassers where there is danger, is obliged to take reasonable precautions to alert them. Thus a trespasser who fell into an unmarked trench in a private car park might have a legitimate cause of action. It has always been unlawful to set traps for trespassers, or to intentionally cause them harm. Security should be defensive and not unreasonably aggressive (see 'Security', below).

Nuisance

Nuisance has two distinct legal applications. Public nuisance, which is a criminal offence, has little application here. Private nuisance, however, is a tort which may occasionally affect dental practice. Private nuisance may be alleged when an occupier of premises interferes, over a period of time, with the use or enjoyment of neighbouring property. Relevant examples might include noise, traffic movement or use of premises at unsociable hours.

Whilst legal advice is essential, general points of concern would include the following:

1. The alleged disturbance must be shown to have occurred over a 'substantial' period of time; courts are generally unwilling to grant an injunction against a short-term nuisance, since damages (see Chapter 4) are regarded as the appropriate remedy.
2. The degree of disturbance is related to the neighbourhood; what may constitute a nuisance in a quiet suburban street may not necessarily do so in a shopping centre.
3. It is not an adequate defence to show that the neighbour was aware of the disturbance before he occupied the adjacent premises.
4. A 'prescriptive right' may be acquired after 20 years; thus an established business may successfully defend its practices.
5. There is no need to show 'negligence'; an action in nuisance may succeed despite the defendant's best endeavours to limit the disturbance.

Pollution

The control of pollution is covered by several statutes, including the Control of Pollution Act (1974) and the Environmental Protection Act

(1989). Pollution may also constitute a nuisance, and there are legal precedents in common law relating to the escape of dangerous substances stored on a person's land. The Health and Safety at Work etc. Act (1974) may also apply.

Common pollutants in dental care might include mercury and clinical waste, and exhaust fumes from suction systems or surgeries. Clinical waste, the requirements of the Environmental Protection Act, and mercury have been covered earlier in this chapter.

There have been recent cases where *Legionella* organisms have originated from air-conditioning towers, but this will only apply to large institutions generally. Advice may be obtained from environmental protection agencies. Exhaust from central suction units may be required, under by-laws, to discharge directly into mains sewerage systems. It would also be unwise to vent surgery air extractors, say, at head height onto a busy pavement area.

Summary

Occupier's liability risks are normally covered by risk transfer – in this instance by the maintenance of a satisfactory third party or public liability insurance policy. Typical cover will be granted against all accidental injury or damage, generally excluding specific risks, such as motor vehicle and employer's liability which are covered elsewhere.

Policies should be carefully reviewed to ensure that required cover is available (e.g. explosion of autoclave, compressor or boiler) and the terms on which it is granted (inspection, maintenance, certification). Some policies not tailored to individual business requirements may exclude, for instance, property left for repair (e.g. dentures). As with all such policies (see Chapter 6), the wording should be either clear or explained to the policyholder.

Security

Crimes of theft, criminal damage, burglary and housebreaking have risen steadily in recent times. Assaults against healthcare personnel are also reported to have increased. Risks encountered in the dental environment include; theft of cash and possessions, theft of employees' or patients' property, burglary, deception, forgery, assault.

Surprisingly, the 'it won't happen to me' approach is still widespread, and it is convenient to avoid carrying out a cost:benefit analysis in the matter of security on the basis that insurance will absorb any losses. As most policyholders will be aware, however, insurance premiums in this area have escalated in proportion to insurers' liabilities, and annually increasing costs and 'excesses' (the amount payable by the insured in respect of a claim before liability is assumed by the insurer) are the norm.

The purpose of this section is to provide broad preventive advice to enable a sensible balance to be taken between the costs and inconvenience of security measures on the one hand and the cost of insurance and losses on the other.

Premises

All police forces employ crime prevention officers, whose advice and assistance is generally available without charge. An inspection by an impartial expert should generally be the first priority when considering security of premises. Knowledge of local crime rates and types is essential, and on many occasions business owners have fallen prey to the persuasive sales techniques of security company representatives resulting in expenditure which is either excessive, inapplicable, or worse, ineffective.

Crime sometimes runs in cycles, and local publicity given to a particular offence may give rise to 'copycat' incidents. Burglary of dental premises has been known to follow this trend.

Opportunist theft is usually concentrated on cash and easily-disposable items of value, such as computers, radios and administrative office equipment. Deterrence may be achieved by the sensible use of approved and reputable door and window locks, external lighting and a visible alarm system. Claims for theft under many office insurance policies are dependent on the fitting of, for example, mortice deadlocks and striker plates to BS3621:1980 on all external doors, and key-operated locks to all ground floor or accessible opening windows. Attention to relatively inexpensive methods, such as the use of non-drying 'anti-climb' paint, the avoidance of screening, such as planting or fencing, around doors or accessible windows, and cultivating the vigilance of neighbours, should not be overlooked.

If an alarm system is used, particularly in commercial areas, a telephone alert system to police or a security firm is recommended as premises alarms may be disabled or, commonly, ignored by neighbours or passers-by. It is strongly recommended that reputable suppliers, who are members of BSIA (British Security Industry Association) are employed; this organization maintains an arbitration and assessment scheme. Quality certification (BS 5750/ISO 9000) through NACOSS (National Approval Council for Security Systems) is desirable. An unreliable, poorly commissioned or inadequately maintained system will lead to 'false alarms' which may result in charges being levied, or disconnection, by police authorities.

Daytime theft, or housebreaking, is not uncommon in a busy practice, particularly where reception staff do not have a view of patients entering, or occupying waiting areas. Access to staff rest-rooms or cloakroom areas should be lockable if not monitored. Lockable internal doors are probably best left unlocked at night, since they are easily broken through by an intruder once initial access is gained.

Insurance companies may be willing to offer discounted premiums where specified anti-theft measures are taken, and should be consulted before installation to ensure compliance, since any savings made may affect the choice of system or approach taken.

Personnel

Fortunately there would appear to be little evidence of any substantial risk to dental personnel. A recent 'hostage taking' incident was newsworthy because of its very rarity.[62] Nevertheless, when increased amounts of money may be taken in dental practices, reception staff particularly may feel exposed. The design of reception areas, especially in new premises or during refurbishment, should be carefully considered. Counter tops should be of such a height and depth as to minimize 'snatch' attempts. The entrances to reception areas should be so designed as to deter unauthorized entry. If an alarm system is installed, it is not too expensive to add a 'panic button' to the reception area. Staff should always be advised, however, to offer no resistance if theft is attempted, since personal safety must be paramount.

Equipment

Loss of equipment due to theft is most likely, as suggested above, in the administrative area. Risk management measures are usually limited to the purchase of appropriate insurance. There are additional measures which can be taken, either to deter theft or to minimize the inevitable delays which may follow a claim.

An asset register, or inventory of equipment, is a usual record in larger organizations, where keeping an account of capital assets is of importance. The maintenance of such a register is advised in all businesses, recording the equipment type and serial number, date and place of purchase, cost, and any modifications or particular characteristics. A colour photograph of the more expensive items may be of assistance to police. Equipment can also be marked, preferably in an inconspicuous place with an identification name or number. Pens which leave little visible mark but fluoresce under ultra-violet light can be purchased for this purpose. A note of the location and nature of the marking should be kept in the register. It is also possible to purchase physical deterrents such as clamping bolts to secure costly items such as computers, copiers, etc, but there is the possibility that their use may only delay removal, and cause incidental damage to other fixtures.

Care should be taken with insurance, to confirm that the cover provided is adequate. Are claims for one particular item limited to a percentage of the total sum insured? Is payment on the basis of indemnity (restoring the status quo, and taking account of depreciation of the item), or 'new for old', permitting the current replacement cost to be claimed? And is the insurance up to date? If the total amount insured is less than the current contents value, the insurer may apply 'average' and reduce payment on even a small claim by the proportion of total under-insurance. Many insurers will refuse to cover certain items such as illuminated signs, and exclusions should also be studied. In general, insurers are willing to negotiate additional cover, provided an equitable premium can be agreed, and an experienced broker will be able to advise. Reputable insurers, who are satisfied that the insured has taken reasonable precautions and acts honestly, are more likely, when notified of a claim, to respond helpfully and speedily. However, it is always essential to notify the insurer, preferably in writing, before undertaking any replacement purchases.

Drugs

In dental practice there are unlikely, in normal circumstances, to be drugs which are subject to the Misuse of Drugs Act (1971) or the schedules to the subsequent regulations. In any event (but as a matter of statutory requirement if scheduled drugs are kept), locked storage should be provided for all drugs, and a register kept so that any losses can be immediately quantified and reported. It is not unknown for capsules of, say antibiotic, to be re-filled with other substances after a theft. Intravenous sedative agents, oral hypnotics and local anaesthetic capsules (again, refilled) have all figured in substance abuse.

Inhalational anaesthetics are of less significance in theft, but occasional cases of abuse within clinical environments are reported – including, in the past, some deaths. Reasonable precautions should therefore be taken regarding the storage of, and access to, substances and equipment and any unexplained use followed up.

Concern for security of drugs and equipment should not be allowed to impede necessary instant access to the small quantities required to deal with emergencies arising in the practice. Availability of these items is the over-riding priority.

Records and computer data

One of the most difficult and harrowing losses is that of records – primarily clinical, but also financial and administrative. A dentist once reported that the snatching, on impulse, by a dissatisfied patient, of his appointment book from the reception desk, caused in an instant more than three months disruption.

Paper clinical records destroyed by fire or lost by theft are literally irreplaceable. Insurance cover for compensation of consequential loss may be arranged, but adequate protection is also advisable. Metal filing cabinets give greater protection than open shelving, but the latter may also be covered by metal roller-type shutters affording some fire-resistance. Open storage in areas where patients may have access is unethical, and may lead to charges of breach of professional confidentiality. At night, appointment books and current financial records should be placed in a secure metal container or cabinet. Non-current records should be stored off the premises or in a fireproof location.

Computer records should be backed up on a daily basis, using at least two independent sets of back-up records on a 'father/grandfather' system. Under this technique, alternate back-up sets are used on alternate days. Back-ups should be securely stored, preferably off the premises. The more sophisticated and comprehensive the software data, the more secure and disaster-proof should be the back-up. It is also imperative that software and hardware suppliers should have speedy and available on-line and on-site maintenance services. In the case of complex software, the existence of a 'source-code escrow' scheme should be confirmed, whereby the machine code basis of the program is deposited with a bank or solicitor in the event of the company ceasing to trade or suffering its own disaster.

In the UK, the Data Protection Act requires that sensitive personal data – such as medical or clinical information – should be accessed only with a password. This should be regularly changed, and always following a change of staff.

Money

Care should be taken that cash kept on the premises does not exceed the amount insured against theft. It is preferable to bank cash more frequently than to rely on a – usually inadequate – safe or other hiding place on the premises. Even opportunist thieves are generally able to locate hidden money, whilst a locked till or cash drawer invites the use of unreasonable force and consequent damage. An open drawer containing a small sum is probably the wiser option. If substantial sums are to be banked, prudence dictates that the staff member or dentist concerned is aware of the risks and takes reasonable precautions against theft and injury. A cloth cash bag, and a regular route, day and time invite unwelcome attention.

Internal security is also appropriate as often the first intimation of 'shrinkage' occurs only after an employee has been dismissed. It would undoubtedly be more pleasant to work in an atmosphere of trust, but this commodity can unfortunately be misplaced! For this reason, daily cash balances are to be encouraged, and the use of electronic tills is an advantage. If a manual system is used, then the issue of a receipt for every transaction is mandatory, and all receipts should be serially numbered. A daily journal should record cash takings against each patient and identify cheques, credit cards, etc. Petty cash should be kept separately from takings, and receipts routinely required. Whilst no system is ultimately proof against the determined fraudster, these procedures will minimize the risks.

Despite the technological advances in banknote design and manufacture, forgery is also an occasional hazard. Cheque and credit card fraud are well known. Whilst it is unlikely that dental care would be a priority route for most criminals, high denomination notes should be routinely scrutinized, preferably by two individuals, and a record kept of serial numbers and tenderer's identity if suspicions are aroused. As a forgery is valueless once accepted, the only hope of recovery is through positive and confirmed identification of the profferer (who may, of course, himself be the innocent previous recipient). Banks and credit card companies will provide routine advice on these matters.

References

1. Little N. (1992) *The Quality Assurance – Risk Management Interface.* Emergency Medicine Clinics of North America. **10** (3), 573–581
2. Miller J.G. (1978) *Living Systems*, McGraw Hill, New York
3. See, for example, *Cole v De Trafford* (No. 2) 1918, 2 KGB 523
4. Casssidy D. (1989) *Liability Exposures*, Witherby & Co, London, p. 27
5. *Halsbury's Statutes*, **19**, 381
6. Crockford N. (1986) *An Introduction to Risk Management*, Woodhead-Faulkner, Cambridge, p. 90
7. Council of the European Union (1989, 1990) Directives 89/391, 89/654, 89/655, 89/656, 90/269 and 90/270
8. Munkman J. (1985) *Employers' Liability*, Butterworths, London
9. Cassidy D. (1989) *Liability Exposures*, Witherby & Co, London
10. Number of toilets and wash hand basins required by the *Workplace (Health Safety and Welfare) Regulations* (1992):
1–5 employees	1 toilet	1 washbasin
6–25 employees	2 toilets	2 washbasins
26–50 employees	3 toilets	3 washbasins
11. General Dental Council (1993) *Professional Conduct and Fitness to Practise*, GDC, London

12. Standing Dental Advisory Committee (1990) *General Anaesthesia, Sedation and Resuscitation in Dentistry – Report of an Expert Working Party*, Department of Health, London
13. Glenwright H.D. and Martin M.V. (1993) Infection Control in Dentistry. *British Dental Journal*, **175** (1), Supplement
14. Dental Practice Board (1992) *What Computers Can Do For Your Practice*, Dental Practice Board, Eastbourne
15. Cottone J.A., Terezhalmy G.T. and Molinari J.A. (1991) *Practical Infection Control In Dentistry.* Lea and Febiger, Philadelphia, p. 3
16. Plough A. and Krimsky S. (1987) Emergency of Risk Communication Studies: Social and Political Context. *Science and Technology and Human Values*, **2**, 4–10
17. Scully C., Porter S.R. and Epstein J. (1992) Compliance with Infection Control Procedures in a Dental Hospital Clinic. *British Dental Journal*, **173**, (1), 20–23
18. Burke F.J.T., Wilson N.H.F. and Wastell D.G. (1991) Glove Use in Clinical Practice: a survey of 2,000 Dentists in England and Wales. *British Dental Journal*, **171**, (5), 128–132
19. Siew C., Chang S., Gruninger S.E. *et al.* (1992) Self-Reported Percutaneous Injuries in Dentists: Implications for HBV, HIV Transmission Risk. *Journal of American Dental Association*, **123** (7), 37–44
20. Centers for Disease Control (1991) Recommendations for preventing transmissions of HIV and HBV to patients during exposure-prone invasive procedures. *Mortality and Morbidity Weekly Report*, 1991: 40 (RR-8)
21. Rimland D., Parkin W. E., Miller G.B. and Schrack W.D. (1977) Hepatitis B outbreak traced to an oral surgeon. *New England Journal of Medicine*, **296**, (17), 953–958
22. Mori M. (1984) Status of viral hepatitis in the world community: its incidence among dentists and other dental personnel. *International Dental Journal*, **34**, 115–121
23. Scully C., Cawson R.A. and Griffiths M. (1990) *Occupational Hazards to Dental Staff.* British Dental Journal Books, London, p. 151
24. Faechner R.S., Thomas J.E. and Bender B.S. (1993) Tuberculosis: A growing concern for dentistry. *Journal of American Dental Association*, **124**, (1), 94–104
25. Bond W. (1986) Modes of transmission of infectious diseases. *Proceedings of the National Symposium on Infection Control in Dentistry, May 1986*, Chicago. US Department of Health and Human Resources, Atlanta
26. British Dental Association (1991) *The Control of Cross-Infection in Dentistry.* Advice Sheet A12. British Dental Association, London
27. ADA Councils on Dental Materials, Instruments and Equipment; Dental practice; Dental Research; Dental Therapeutics (1992) Infection control recommendations for the dental office and dental laboratory. *Journal of the American Dental Association*, **123**, Supplement, S246
28. General Dental Council (1993) *Professional Conduct and Fitness to Practice.* Para 29. General Dental Council, London
29. Department of Labor, Occupational Safety and Health Administration. 29 CFR Part 1910.1030, Occupational Exposure to Bloodborne pathogens; final rule. *Fed. Reg. (1991)*: **56**, 64004–182
30. Advisory Committee on Dangerous Pathogens (1990) *HIV – the causative agent of AIDS and related conditions.* Department of Health, London
31. Banting D.W. and Robertson J.M. (1991) Dealing with risks in the dental office. *Journal of the American Dental Association*, **122**, (8), 16–17
32. Centers for Disease Control, Update (1991) Transmission of HIV infection during an invasive dental procedure – Florida. *Morbidity and Mortality Weekly Report*: **40**, 21–7; 33
33. Humphris G.M., Morrison T. and Horne L. (1993) Perception of risk of HIV infection from regular attenders to an industrial dental service. *British Dental Journal*, **174** (10), 371–378

34. Worthington L.S., Rothwell P.S. and Banks N. (1988) Cross infection control in dental practice. (2) A dental surgery planned with cross-infection control as the design priority. *British Dental Journal*, **165**, 226–228
35. Robinson P. and Challacombe S. (1993) Transmission of HIV in a dental practice – the facts. *British Dental Journal*, **175**, (10), 383–384
36. Runnells R.R. (1993) Countering the Concerns: how to reinforce dental practice safety. *Journal of the American Dental Association*, **124**, 65–73
37. Centers for Disease Control, Update (1993) Investigations of persons treated by HIV-infected health care workers – United States. *Morbidity and Mortality Weekly Report*, **42**, 329–337
38. Glantz L.H., Mariner W.K. and Annas G.J. (1992) Risky business: setting public health policy for HIV-infected health care professionals. *The Millbank Quarterly*, **70**, (1), 43–79
39. Saramanayake L.P. and Scully C. (1993) Revised guidelines for HIV-infected health care workers. *British Dental Journal*, **175**, (1), 2
40. Department of the Environment (1991) *Waste Management – The Duty of Care, A Code of Practice*. HMSO, London
41. White S.F. and Mays G.D. (1989) *Water Supply Byelaws Guide* (2nd edn). Ellis Horwood, Chichester
42. Martin M.V. (1987) The significance of the bacterial contamination of dental unit water systems. *British Dental Journal*, **163**, (4), 152–4
43. Douglas C.W.I. and van Noort R. (1993) Control of bacteria in dental water supplies. *British Dental Journal*, **174**, (5), 167–174
44. Standing Dental Advisory Committee (1988) *Radiation Protection in Dental Practice*. Department of Health, London
45. Monsour P.A., Kruger B.J., Barnes A. and Sainsbury A. (1988) Measures taken to reduce X-ray exposure to the patient, operator and staff. *Australian Dental Journal*, **33**, 181–192
46. Hewitt J.M., Shuttleworth P.G., Nelthorpe P.A. and Hudson A.P. (1989) Improving Protection Standards in Dental Radiography. Paper presented to 4th International Symposium on Radiation Protection, June 1989
47. Miller M. and Truhe T. (1993) Lasers in Dentistry: an Overview. *Journal of the American Dental Association*, **124**, 32–35
48. Health and Safety Commission (1990) *Safety of Pressure Systems: Approved Code of Practice*: COP37. HMSO, London
49. Health and Safety Executive (1990) *The safe use of portable electrical apparatus (electrical safety)*. HMSO, London
50. Health and Safety Executive (1993) *A Step by Step Guide to COSHH Assessment*, HS(G)97. HMSO, London
51. Department of Health (1992) *The Control of Substances Hazardous to Health: Guidance for the Initial Assessment in Hospitals*. HMSO, London
52. Health and Safety Executive (1994) *Occupational Exposure Limits*, 1994, EH40/94. HMSO, London
53. Cook T. A. and Yates P.O. (1969) Fatal mercury intoxication in a dental surgery assistant. *British Dental Journal*, **127**, 553
54. Spence A.A. (1987) Environmental pollution by inhalation anaesthetics. *British Journal of Anaesthetics*, **59**, 96–103
55. Eley B.M. and Cox S.W. (1993) The release, absorption and possible health effects of mercury from dental amalgam: a review of recent findings. *British Dental Journal*, **175**, (10), 355–362
56. Bamber L. (1993) Accident Costing. Foresight *Journal of the Institute of Risk Management*, October 1993; 15–20
57. Health and Safety Executive (1993) *Health and Safety in Service Industries, 1991–92*. HMSO, London

58. *British Dental Association Advice Sheets, 'D' series.* British Dental Association, London
59. Ellis N. (1990) *Employing Staff.* (3rd edn). British Medical Journal Books, London
60. *Commissioner for Railways* v. *McDermott* (1967) 1 AC 169: per Gardner L. C.
61. *Addie v Dumbreck,* 1929 A C 358
62. Anon. (1994) Hygienist overpowers gunman after 14-hour surgery siege. *The Probe,* **36**,(1), 1

4
Medico-legal risk management

The professional relationship – communication and trust

Good communication is fundamental to good clinical practice. Accurate diagnosis and successful treatment depend upon the art of listening and speaking to patients. A poor relationship with patients can result in misunderstandings, complaints and even litigation. Correlation has been demonstrated between poor communication and dental litigation.[1]

This passage introduces an advice booklet to dentists from the Medical Defence Union. It might be expected that an examination of medico-legal risk management in dentistry might commence with the hazards of the unprotected airway, the risks attendant on third molar extractions, or the need for good clinical notes and radiographs. However, if any common strand can be identified amongst the claims and complaints pursued against dentists, or indeed medical practitioners, it is that of the failure of communication.

Localio and co-workers reviewed the medical records of a random sample of 31,429 patients hospitalized in New York State in 1984,[2] and concluded that of an estimated 280 patients suffering adverse events identified as indicative of negligence, only 8 resulted in malpractice claims. The authors speculate that whilst legal costs, lawyers' disinclination to accept cases that are not 'clear cut', and the availability of disability insurance may dissuade many patients from pursuing a claim, a reluctance to 'spoil long-standing physician – patient relationships' is a significant factor.

A recent editorial in the Journal of the Medical Defence Union reports: 'A truism of case work is that once communication between a doctor or dentist and a patient breaks down, it is far more likely that the patient will contemplate making a complaint to a health authority or an FHSA or even suing the practitioner.'[3]

Moreover, Brown,[4] reporting the findings of a major US dental insurance company, comments:

> 75% of all liability claims to date have involved nothing more serious than a patient's minor discomfort . . . anecdotal evidence suggests that most patients who sue dentists do so for reasons other than significant injury.

He concludes:

> Effective communication is inseparable from technical competence. Patients who have reason to question a dentist's commitment to their care, whose expectations are unrealistic or who feel excluded from treatment decisions, have little reason to give the dentist the benefit of the doubt when complications or a less-than-perfect result occur.

If the importance of communication between dentist and patient is central to effective risk management, as these examples would imply, it is appropriate to consider further:

1. How is effective communication defined?
2. How is effective communication achieved?
3. How are breakdowns in communication to be avoided or minimized?

It is not the intention here to explore deeply the theories and development of communications studies, but primarily to examine the more obvious relevances and conclusions as they apply to clinical practice. Readers are referred to authoritative texts for further study, and for detailed guidance.[5,6,7]

How is effective communication defined?

As Cherry has pointed out,[8] the verb 'to communicate' means 'to share'. When we think of communication, however, we tend to think most often of *sending* messages, of speaking, writing or creating pictures. Janner corrects this misconception when he states that 'the most important organ of communication is the ear'.[9] He sees communication in terms of forming relationships and breaking down barriers between individuals, and effective listening is certainly as important as the origination of messages.

Communication then, is more than the mere imparting of information. Successful communication requires that the sender of the message, and its receiver, shall both participate. The message must have interest and meaning for both parties. In the special case of the professional-patient relationship, communication is ideally two-way: the 'communication' which occurs between a television newsreader and his audience, and that between a dentist and a patient are quite obviously different. Research has supported the view that patients are more likely to comply with health advice and instructions,[10] and to express satisfaction with dental treatment,[11] when there is mutually successful communication.

Communication with patients is not, of course, confined to face to face conversation. Even on the telephone, it has been suggested that attitude and mood can be interpreted. As the telephone may be the patient's primary point of contact with the practice and the method of choice in emergency, good telephone procedures are an integral part of patient care. In the clinical situation, the verbal message is modified further by the appearance and attitude of the participants – so-called 'body language'. Studies suggest, indeed, that this latter component is the most significant, intonation the next most significant and the actual words spoken the least significant factor in effective communication. One well-quoted study concluded that, in a presentation to a group, 55% of the speaker's message was conveyed by non-verbal means, 38% by the manner of speaking, and only 7% by the content itself.[12]

Patients will therefore judge and react to a clinician's mood, posture and relative positioning when speaking or listening, and these components will have a considerable impact on the effectiveness of the transaction between them. Equally, most dentists can readily identify patients who are withdrawn, over-excited, angry or uncooperative without there being any necessity for verbal exchanges. Effective training techniques for dealing with these situations are available, and it is never safe to assume that skills cannot be improved.

Kent and Blinkhorn[13] have reviewed this subject comprehensively, noting that the physical proximity of dentist and patient is far closer during actual treatment than most people in our society are accustomed to, other than in the most intimate relationships. Most dentists will have had the experience of standing in a crowded bus or subway train, where the effect of forced close proximity encourages a studied ignorance of the strangers next to them. Just as in a heated argument, where one protagonist pushes his face close to the other, the effect of 'invading personal space' is decidedly threatening.

Although dentists and doctors have come to occupy a special place in social exchanges, whereby such physical closeness is tolerated, many patients and especially children, need time to become accustomed to the situation; some indeed may never do so. It is not difficult to understand, in these terms, why the stereotypical image of dentists is perceived as authoritarian and controlling.

Where problems in treatment procedures or outcomes arise – as they may do in any undertaking – the dentist may be faced with a considerable inbuilt disadvantage in restoring a relationship of mutual trust and understanding. Awareness of successful communication techniques (and conversely, of barriers to communication) are of value in reducing the likelihood of complaints and claims.

How is effective communication achieved?

Observation suggests that some individuals are naturally gifted communicators, whilst others find great difficulty in interpersonal skills. There is evidence to show that training in communication skills will bring about improvement in a clinician's abilities.[14] Post-treatment patient studies also show that compliance and general satisfaction are related directly to the possession and use of such skills.[15]

Kent *et al.* have argued that there is therefore a justification for including communication skills training in undergraduate dental curricula.[16] It has also been shown that traditional medical undergraduate training may, paradoxically, have the outcome of effectively *worsening* comprehension of patients' symptoms and needs.[17] In the majority of dental courses, lectures in communication and interviewing skills are now included, in the belief that this didactic learning, combined with the clinical observation of senior staff behaviour by students and the supervision of students by staff, will help to ensure that these skills are retained into a clinical career.

Unfortunately, Maguire and co-workers, reviewing medical students five years post-qualification, have suggested that levels of competence remain low. They note:

> Teaching students ... about communication was until recently limited to history taking. Then interest broadened to teaching interviewing skills, emphasizing the value of listening and responding as well as asking the right questions .... It has seldom extended to teaching students how to handle the second part of a consultation, when a doctor explains and discusses his findings and his plans for treatment.[18]

Arguably this extension of communication skills is relevant to the teaching of dental students also. Role playing exercises and the use of video in simulated and real clinical encounters are typical of techniques now widespread in education and their increased use in dental training should be advocated.

Direct communication between the dentist and patient is only one link in the communication chain. The dentist must also communicate effectively with his staff and with outside agencies – laboratories, specialist services, health service providers. Other chairside and reception staff will also need to communicate effectively with patients, and breakdown can occur when, for instance, a dentist's interpretation of an 'urgent' appointment is subsequently misconstrued by a receptionist.

Carrotte et al. showed that written instructions to laboratories for anterior crowns were poor in 26% of cases, requiring the technician to contact the dentist for further clarification.[19] It is the experience of most commercial dental laboratories that the overall standards of written and verbal communication are poor.

Advice given to patients regarding after-care, oral hygiene or diet must be carefully co-ordinated within the practice to avoid conflict or confusion in the patient's mind. It is extremely common for patients to acknowledge understanding of the dentist's instructions, only to query them with the surgery assistant and again with the receptionist on departing. The establishment of practice procedures is the only satisfactory way of overcoming individual variations amongst staff.

Practical experience of the above has been confirmed by Logan,[20] who has reviewed a number of studies on communication and concluded that many patients in a dental setting are unable to absorb and process information logically. Repetition of messages is important and Logan suggests that three repeats appear to be optimal. Care should be taken to personalize the information, taking particular care to use words and expressions which the patient understands. The patient who reported having 'a vasectomy of the left incisor' was perhaps telling us volumes about his previous dentist's communication skills!

Significant post-operative or home care advice to patients, which may have important consequences, should be reinforced by written instructions. Examples would include post-extraction advice, and particularly post-sedation or anaesthetic recommendations, where the patient may be confused or amnesic, and escorts may be unreliable. It is wise to repeat instructions to the escort and to ensure that they are aware of any written details and of appropriate action to be taken. All patient instructions provided, whether verbal or written, should be recorded in the clinical notes.

Doubt is often expressed about whether patients read the written information they are given. Factors include; the *targeting* of material – ensuring that patients receive information which is relevant and of concern to them, *selection* of material – avoiding overloading patients with information, and *readability* – when the national average reading age has been measured at approximately 10.5 years, information should be straightforward, clear and brief.

How are breakdowns in communication avoided or minimized?

The short answer to this question is, of course, that they must first be recognised. No clinician has an ability to 'get on with', or establish a rapport with all his patients. Wills ascribed three dimensions by which physicians judged their patients, manageability, treatability and likeability.[21] Ayer suggested that these dimensions could be interpreted in dentistry as meaning:[22]

> Manageability: the degree to which the patient is prepared to submit to professional advice and treatment
> Treatability: requiring straightforward treatment, and with good motivation
> Likeability: patients having an agreeable and pleasant character

Studies have shown that these characteristics have a bearing on the quality of treatment outcomes. Weinstein *et al.*[23] asked dentists to assess patients in relation to seven criteria, such as: 'does he/she keep appointments on time', and: 'is he/she a pleasant enjoyable person'.[23] The quality of care provided was then reviewed either by peer review or self-assessment. It was concluded that treatment quality was significantly related, in particular, to the questions; 'is the patient willing and able to pay for optimal care?' and; 'does he/she follow your instructions concerning home care or other recommendations?'

Weinstein showed that the dentists reviewed reported little or no problem relating to most patients, with some 90% seen as considerate, pleasant and prompt payers. However, about 20% presented some problems, notably failing to follow advice or healthy routines, low 'dental IQ', or presenting financial constraints. It should be said that these results offer only inferential evidence that patients whom dentists perceive as 'less motivated' receive a lower standard of care because of this perception. The study took no account of the dentists' communication skills, nor of the possibility that other factors influenced the quality of treatment observed.

Studies such as this do suggest, however, that there may be a relationship not only between effective communication and patient satisfaction, but also between dentists' perception of their relationship with a patient and the quality – measured objectively – of the care provided.

When dentists report untoward incidents or notification of impending legal or disciplinary action by patients, certain themes recur:

> Although I tried to satisfy Mrs A's dental needs, and she seemed happy when the dentures were finally fitted, she never returned to the surgery or told me about her problems until I received her letter of complaint [from the Family Health Services Authority] . . ..
> Mr B was always busy and had to be fitted in at times that were convenient to him and rushed off after the treatment. He always said that he would accept my judgement, I was the expert. He now has the cheek to say that I never warned him that the bridge would look like this!

Of course, the dentist's communication difficulty is not always confined to the patient, but may be concerned with intra-practice difficulties; a practitioner wrote to her legal adviser, following a patient's complaint; 'I sympathize with Miss P's problem. It is unfortunate that the bridge de-cemented. I have been frustrated by both my technician and the poor facilities I am expected to work with. I have done the best my capabilities and the facilities will allow'.

It is recognized that the pressures of dental practice do not always allow the time for discussion and conversation with patients that dentists would like. Clinicians are repeatedly advised that they must take more time and care with communication, on the grounds that the time and energy which may be consumed by even one patient's complaint may be inordinate in comparison with this everyday commitment. These two preceding statements are correct and justifiable, although difficult to reconcile. However, there are occasions where particular care needs to be taken, and which are often indicative of an imminent communication failure, or of harmful medico-legal consequences. Examples of such scenarios, which are recognizable from case work, include the following.

(a) Time pressures It is not uncommon for medico-legal problems to arise when diagnosis or treatment is carried out on a time scale which is more urgent than usual. Medico-legal risks can obviously occur when technical 'corners are cut', but it is sometimes apparent when reviewing cases that the technique is sound, and it is in fact communication time which is being sacrificed. Pressures can arise either from the dentist's side (inadequate appointment timing, staff absences, previous appointments over-running) or from the patient's insistence. Experienced clinicians will recognize that it is so often the restoration which is 'rushed through' in time for a patient's holiday, or a family celebration, which subsequently either fails, or fails to satisfy. In these circumstances, although the practitioner may earn the sympathy of his peers, his legal duty of care is undiminished. A frequently encountered phrase in this context is that the dentist 'bent over backwards' to fulfil the patient's requirements.

Although it would be an unfeeling clinician who was unable to modify his timetable or procedures to accommodate individual patient wishes, he should first be certain that the matter can be objectively substantiated as 'urgent'; that his proposed course of action would be accepted as reasonable in hindsight, should problems arise, and, most importantly, that time is allowed for full and clear discussion of the risks involved with the patient. This area will be discussed further in the section on 'Consent' later in this chapter. There can be little doubt that the suburban practitioner who undertook, without assistance, third molar surgery at 2 a.m., following an emergency call-out would have had some difficulty in justifying his action had complications occurred.

(b) Exaggerated behaviour patterns Clinicians will recognize that some patients exhibit behaviour which is outside the usually observed parameters. Such a patient may display profuse gratitude for quite routine care and treatment, and this may be combined with exaggerated friendliness towards the dentist. This behaviour may evoke natural feelings of appreciation in the practitioner. What is described here is not to be confused with the normal, cordial relationship which dentists enjoy with their regular patients, often of long standing, but an unusual and excessive reaction. Such patients' enthusiasm may be such that they do not initially appear to consider any limitations or difficulties inherent in their treatment, and only later does it become apparent that their expectations are unreasonable.

> A 63-year-old patient and his wife registered with a new practice for dental care. Examination of the husband revealed the need for periodontal and restorative treatment and the provision of a removable partial denture. Both patients praised the comprehensive nature of the examination, and were critical of previous dentists. The husband was particularly dissatisfied with the fit and appearance of his existing denture.
>
> The periodontal treatment and crown work was carried out, accompanied by effusive thanks and constant recommendations to friends. The prosthetic stages were equally successful, and the teeth were approved by both patients at trial fitting.
>
> The day after fitting the prosthesis, the patients returned without appointment, and were seen by another dentist. Total disgust and dissatisfaction with the treatment provided, and particularly the denture appearance, was expressed. Ulceration of cheek mucosa next to a retaining clasp was diagnosed, and straightforward local treatment advised.
>
> At a subsequent appointment, the first dentist pointed out that the trial fitting stage was the correct time for the patient to approve appearance. He noted on the record: 'What does he expect me to do now? Was happy at try in.' The patient however declined an offer to replace the anterior teeth and subsequently made a formal complaint.

A significant feature in the previous recorded dental history for this patient was that he had worn his existing denture for 15 years, despite his apparent criticism of its appearance. There was no contemporaneous written confirmation in the dentist's clinical notes that the patient had in fact approved the trial set-up. The dentist's final entry – 'What does he expect . . .' reflected his anger and confusion at the patient's sudden change of attitude.

The combination of criticism of previous work, including a denture worn for 15 years, and profuse appreciation might have cautioned the practitioner. Because treatment to date has gone well, it is unwise to assume that a patient appreciates the purpose of a trial set-up. Particular care should be taken to ensure the patient understands that this will be the finished appearance. Inclusion of the note 'patient approved appearance' in the records at the trial insertion stage would probably have halted the complaint at an early stage, and saved much subsequent time and inconvenience.

(c) Suppressed behavioural patterns Conversely to the above, some patients show very attenuated behaviour when in the clinical environment: most dentists accept this as a manifestation of anxiety. Where there appears to be an excess of caution, rather than anxiety, there may be particular need to emphasize and encourage communication. The practitioner will feel that a patient who queries every diagnosis or treatment proposal, or requests second opinions, is expressing a lack of confidence in his abilities.

Such behaviour should be directly, but sympathetically addressed. It may be that there is a previous difficulty with dental care, or with some other aspect of healthcare. To continue the provision of treatment in an atmosphere of doubt or mistrust may be discomfiting for the clinician: it has been described as 'like walking on thin ice'.

The temptation is to proceed with treatment and, if the patient expresses reservations, to allow reassurance to take on the status of a guaranteed outcome. A difficulty with all clinical care is to appreciate and understand patients' doubts and fears, and yet to avoid commitment to an assured outcome. The latter is not the standard expected by any jurisdiction, as observed by Lord Justice Nourse; 'Of all services medicine is the least exact. In my view a doctor cannot be objectively regarded as guaranteeing the result of any operation or treatment unless he says as much in clear and unequivocal terms.'[24]

(d) Manipulative behaviour patterns Some patients may appear to see clinical consultation as an adversarial contest, and to be concerned primarily with determining their own treatment objectives (often as a result of influence by a third party or media promotion of a particular treatment). Clinicians may come to feel that they are merely acting as the instrument of the patient. This state of affairs is no more satisfactory if it is the dentist who is doing the manipulating, of course.

Ayer noted that relationships between clinician and patient followed one of three models;[10] active-passive, in which the clinician takes complete control of care; guidance-cooperation, where the clinician gives advice or directions; and mutual participation, in which the patient accepts responsibility for his welfare. In diagnosis and treatment planning, dentists should aim for the second or third of these forms, and avoid the scenario of domination by either party. It is no defence to an allegation of negligently inappropriate treatment to assert that it was performed solely in accordance with the wishes of the patient. Even if such a request is in written form, it amounts to an exclusion or limitation of professional liability and as such falls within Section 2 of the Unfair Contract Terms Act (1977).

> A domineering and aggressive patient, who was known by his dentist to have a criminal record for assault, repeatedly demanded the crowning of his periodontally involved lower incisor teeth, which were misshapen and discoloured. This treatment was resisted, as the patient showed no inclination to follow home-care advice, and the teeth were anatomically unsuitable for treatment. On one occasion, he was seen by a junior dental surgeon in the practice, who reluctantly agreed to crown the teeth, provided that the patient signed a disclaimer. Within two years, all of the crowned teeth exfoliated or fractured and a civil action was brought. Counsel's advice was that the claim could not be resisted on the previous X-ray and clinical evidence, and a financial settlement was explored. The document that the patient had signed would have had no credence in any Court.

Manipulative patients must be either dissuaded or discontinued with sympathy and firmness. Advice should be sought if necessary from medical defence organizations or from colleagues. It is inadvisable to wait until a crisis point is reached, or to precipitately refuse treatment, especially if the patient has acute problems. Where a dentist feels that a particular course of treatment is inadvisable or inappropriate it is his or her professional duty to advise accordingly, and to ensure that such advice prevails

(e) Post-traumatic behavioural patterns Care should always be exercised in establishing a satisfactory clinical relationship with patients who have undergone a recent trauma, whether clinical or personal. A patient who has experienced, for instance, bereavement or divorce is in a similar position, in this respect, to one who has suffered from a treatment complication or failure (whether or not due to negligence). Such patients need, and deserve, sympathetic and understanding care. They may present as typical of some of the cases described above, which underlines the importance of a thorough social and clinical history taking.

(f) Anomalous behaviour The patient whose manner changes, whose attendance pattern alters – perhaps a regular patient who suddenly fails to keep appointments – should receive careful consideration. It is not unknown for an incident to occur elsewhere in the practice, at reception or with the hygienist for example, and for the regular clinician to be unaware of the problem. A patient of long standing who fails to pay an account should not receive an abrupt demand for payment: there is much to be said for the treating dentist to review all outstanding creditors before taking action (see the section on 'payment for treatment' below). Awareness of such possibilities forms an integral part of good patient relations.

(g) Unexpected treatment complications The effective and appropriate management of complications or untoward outcomes is perhaps the greatest test of a clinician/patient relationship. Its significance may be judged from the results of the study carried out by Localio *et al.*, reported above.[1] He showed that only a tiny proportion (1.5%) of incidents arising out of negligence resulted in claims. However, the researchers identified more than four times as many claims made under circumstances of care which could not, by their criteria, be defined as negligent. These claims will take just as much (or more) time, effort and cost to defend as those which are founded on a clear failure of care.

When patients suffer an adverse event which is not, objectively speaking, due to negligence, the quality of communication and rapport which exists between them and their carer(s) must rank as a principal factor in determining their perception of the incident. When, despite an appropriate and recognized approach, and the use of reasonable care, the tooth being extracted fractures, an apicectomy fails to save an abutment, or a denture proves uncomfortable, the nature, timeliness and adequacy of the clinician's explanation is crucial.

Certainly, factors such as the patient's personality will also have a bearing: generally these are not within the clinician's control whereas effective communication should be so.

For some years, defence organizations have suggested that there are four components which are helpful when complications or unsatisfactory outcomes occur. These are: speed, sympathy, satisfaction and 'sorry'.[25]

Timeliness is of the essence. If problems arise during treatment, this should be interrupted at the earliest opportunity. If difficulties arise after the patient has left, reception staff should be trained to bring any messages of complaint or requests for assistance to the attention of the treating dentist without delay. Even if all that can be said at that moment is that the matter will be fully investigated, or a further meeting with the patient arranged, contact by the dentist *in person* should be established as soon as possible. If a patient is aggrieved, matters seldom 'blow over' – on the contrary, attitudes harden very rapidly.

Problems during treatment usually come to the dentist's notice before the patient, and there is therefore the advantage of outlining the difficulty, listening to the patient's comments and queries, offering reassurance and leading into a shared discussion of future management. Adequate time should be allowed for each of these stages.

Where, however, patients themselves identify the problem, then they should be allowed to express their views and feelings. When patients are angry, upset or emotional, never interrupt, terminate a conversation unilaterally or compete. It has been said that there is nothing easier than to win an argument – but lose a patient (and possibly a legal case). An opportunity will – eventually – occur to enable the dentist to address the second component of management.

Sympathy is not always the easiest emotion to achieve when receiving vociferous or prolonged expressions of dissatisfaction. A reaction of indignation, impatience or anger is, in many instances, more likely. Sadly, such a response is more likely to lead to an intensification or prolonging of any dispute. In their text on business negotiation, Fisher and Ury advise: 'Focus on interests, not positions'.[26] In other words, the solution to any problem is secondary to the needs of the parties involved. From an ethical viewpoint, any healthcare recipient who feels disadvantaged is entitled to a caring and understanding response. The expression 'I can understand how you must feel . . .' is probably one of the more effective responses to any complaint; the sentiment it conveys is fundamental.

To rectify a complaint to the patient's **satisfaction** should be the aim, and whilst the performance of this may not fall wholly within the sphere of communication, the ability to express possible means of redress (where appropriate) or rectification will do so. Skills will include seeking the patient's views, offering suitable alternatives, and taking meticulous care in ensuring that the proposed course of action is made clear to other staff. Once again, good intentions can go astray if promised urgent appointments are delayed, or instructions misinterpreted by staff.

'Sorry' is a difficult word to say under conditions of stress. Nevertheless, Tarsh has suggested that the first remedy sought by a complainant patient is that someone in a position of authority should apologize.[27] For an apology to be effective, it must be meant: an empty expression designed to secure exoneration, or as a short cut to ending the conversation, is likely to be ineffective, and, possibly, harmful.

To express genuine regret, a clinician must therefore be willing, in the first place, to concede that; 'Any patient who has had the misfortune to suffer through an error of whatever nature should receive a proper expression of regret'.[28] Dentists are frequently concerned that an apology will be misinterpreted as an admission of legal liability. This belief may arise from a confusion with the requirements of insurers, or from reports arising from North American jurisdictions. Most drivers are aware that motor insurance policies advise, in the event of injury or damage, that no admission of liability must be made. Insurance cover may be voided if this occurs, since the insured may, by the admission, be committing the insurer to certain settlement, thereby undermining the whole basis of risk and probability on which the insurance contract is based.

In North America, where professional liability risks are typically insurance-based, considerable care does need to be taken. Slovenko cites several US cases where a court has accepted a clinician's apology as prima facie evidence of malpractice,[29] and notes that some American lawyers even advise medical practitioners not to attend the funerals of their patients, in case this is noted and advanced as evidence of guilt at some past error of treatment!

In the UK, professional liability is generally provided by means of non-insurance based indemnity, and, although reasonable prudence should be exercised in avoiding a frank admission of liability, a sincere expression of regret is unlikely to be viewed as evidential of negligence.[1]

> A dental practitioner was extracting a loose upper deciduous molar from an 11-year-old girl under local anaesthesia. The tooth slipped from the forceps and flew into the pharynx. After immediate attempts to retrieve it failed, the dentist gave the parents a full, honest and apologetic account of the incident. Having telephoned the local hospital, he accompanied the family there, where X-rays showed the tooth poised above the right bronchial tree. It was eventually removed by bronchoscopy, but not before the possibility of a full thoracotomy had had to be considered. The dentist remained with the family until the procedure was completed. No claim resulted, and this must be due in large part to the excellent and sympathetic care and concern shown by the dentist, and to the quality of his communication.

Consent – Communication and consensus

Consent, in the clinical scenario, could be considered as a special and formalized type of communication. It derives its importance from the legal right of each individual to self-determination and personal freedom from unlawful interference. Consent has particular significance in dental care, where there may well be a number of clinical options in the treatment of a given condition, where true 'life and death' emergencies are relatively rare, and where the technicalities of treatment and its long-term effects may not readily be appreciated by patients.

Dentistry, it might be added, is also unusual in that untold numbers of invasive, elective surgical procedures are routinely carried out without any apparent consent being either sought or given. It is entirely usual for a dental practitioner to complete a charting for a regular attender, to announce that, for instance, a 'cervical composite filling' requires replacement, to administer a local anaesthetic and finally to cut the cavity and fill the tooth without any indication from the patient that the operation has been understood, considered or agreed. It is often the rule, rather than the exception that unless the patient queries the procedure, or takes some decisive action such as leaving the chair, consent is considered to be implicit.

How is this activity to be reconciled with the doctrine of 'informed consent' currently applied in law? For it has become generally accepted that:

> ... Informed consent introduces a new element to medical treatment. It is no longer a simple matter of consent to a technical assault; consent must now be based on [the patient's] knowledge of the nature, consequences and alternatives associated with the proposed therapy.[30]

The fundamental requirements for informed consent are that the patient should be told, using words which he can understand:

1 The nature and purpose of the treatment proposed
2 Material risks associated with the treatment
3 What alternatives exist, and
4 What consequences might arise from his refusal

The law recognizes, however, that consent need not be written, or even explicitly given, in certain circumstances. Indeed the idea that a piece of paper is a consent is quite incorrect.[31] The written consent form merely provides some evidence that consent has been obtained, or, at least, discussed.

It may therefore be accepted that a patient implies consent by, for instance, sitting in a dental chair and opening his mouth. Dentists, particularly general practitioners carry out, by definition, a wide range of procedures. The risk therefore exists that a dentist may inadvertently stray over the boundary between the performance of procedures for which implied consent is adequate, and into areas where more explicit consent, either verbal or written, is advisable or required.

One useful way of clarifying this borderline is to examine in more detail the components of informed consent as outlined above.

The nature and effect of treatment

A regular patient, who has previously undergone routine restorative care (as evidenced by the state of the mouth), would not in normal circumstances need to give express consent to further care of the same type, though it is both courteous and ethical to prepare the patient for an imminent procedure by describing the intended act. However, a patient requiring, for example, a first restoration, or a patient who is new to the practitioner, would be entitled to more specific information. For instance, an attempt to administer local anaesthetic to a new patient who preferred to have treatment without it may give rise, at the least, to an indignant protest, and could be construed as an assault. (In law, the apprehension of unlawful contact constitutes an 'assault'; the contact itself being termed a 'battery').

In a similar way, where a dentist finds a non-vital pulpal exposure in the course of preparation for a restoration, it is prudent to pause and to explain the indication for endodontic treatment – and briefly its implications – before proceeding further. Successful actions have been brought where a dentist has proposed porcelain veneers on anterior teeth, and has subsequently provided jacket crowns without conferring with the patient. The fact that crowns proved to be the indicated and appropriate treatment would not be an adequate defence to a claim of battery.

Material risks

In English Law, the interpretation of a 'material risk' is derived from the case of Bolam (1957),[32] where a failure to warn a plaintiff of the slight risk of a fracture occurring during the administration of electro-convulsive therapy was considered not to have been negligent because the doctor acted in a way which accorded with the practice of his profession generally (or with a responsible body of opinion within it).

This test of negligence was held to apply to the definition of 'material risk' by the English Courts in the case of Sidaway (1985).[33] Lord Donaldson, Master of the Rolls, stated; 'What information should be disclosed, and how it should be disclosed, is very much a matter for professional judgement, to be exercised in the context of the doctor's relationship with a particular patient in particular circumstances.'

In the English jurisdiction, then, whether a risk is considered 'material', and hence should be explained to the patient, is a matter for professional consideration, primarily by reference to the usual and accepted procedures of the profession as a whole (or by a responsible body of opinion within it) and also in accordance with the practitioner's own evaluation of the particular circumstances.

Whilst this may not appear to clarify the position greatly, it stands in contrast to the development of case law in this field in the United States. Lord Donaldson, in the case of Sidaway, went on to say that he would 'reject the formulation of the duty [to disclose risks] by reference to the "prudent patient" test.' This approach is most clearly expounded in the American case of Canterbury v Spence:

> A risk is material when a reasonable person, in what the physician knows or should know to be the patient's position would be likely to attach significance to the risk or cluster of risks in deciding whether or not to forego the proposed therapy.[34]

In this particular jurisdiction – and since confirmed in other United States courts – it is for the patient to determine what constitutes a material risk. This much broader view places a more onerous duty on the clinician, since he must consider the range of risks which each patient may regard as significant.

It will be appreciated, however, that no 'hard and fast' definition of a material risk can be arrived at, even under English law. Patterns of prescribed clinical care change, and, as already suggested, individual circumstances vary. Only general guidance can therefore be given. Who, for instance, might constitute a 'respected body of opinion'? Certainly one must admit opinions and guidance proposed by the General Dental Council, the Royal Colleges or a national dental association. Papers and articles published in refereed professional journals will have been reviewed by experts in the field, and may also be regarded as authoritative. Established methods and procedures taught at Dental Schools would likewise command respect. There is, of course, no absolute requirement that there shall be only one recognized approach to diagnosis or treatment: only that the approach chosen should be justified by reference to the above criteria.

The statistical likelihood of a hazard occurring is a central concept in risk management. In the Sidaway judgement, it was held that a 10% risk (of a serious and permanent complication) was one which a prudent doctor could not ignore, whereas a 1% risk of a similar outcome would not necessarily merit disclosure. In the dental field, we do not generally deal with conditions and complications, such as spinal cord damage, which are as severe as in these well-cited cases.

Some risks attendant on dental treatment have been evaluated, however. Collins reviewed the occurrence of nerve damage following the removal of lower third molars and advised;[35] 'Because of the significant incidence of nerve paraesthesia all patients should be warned of this possibility and this warning should be recorded clearly in the clinical notes.'

Rood has suggested that labial sensory loss may occur in about 7.5% of surgical lower third molar removals,[36] and lingual sensory loss in between 5 and 13%, dependent on technique. Permanent loss of sensation may occur in up to 2% of cases.

The outcome of apical surgery has also been statistically examined for outcome. Barnes suggests an average success rate of 75%,[37] and since this procedure is frequently applied to teeth which have received previous endodontic treatment, it must be considered whether the patient should be informed of the significant possibility of failure. Clearly, a reasonable limit must be applied; to explain every consequence of every procedure would, as Calnan suggests,[38] take as long as the practitioner's training itself! Experience, however, teaches that it is indeed wise to caution against distressing, though routine, sequelae such as swelling or haematoma following surgery.

One further aspect of material risks should be mentioned. Their Lordships, in giving judgment in Sidaway, made clear that if a patient actually canvasses details of possible complications, then their reasonable questions must be truthfully answered. Whilst a practitioner may have views about over-alarming a nervous patient, reassurance should not – as discussed earlier – take on the guise of deceptive certainty.

Alternative Treatments

Where reasonable alternatives exist to a proposed treatment for a defined condition, then the patient has a right to be made aware of them. In dental care, there may be several options available, including that of not treating the condition, or reviewing it. One example would be the symptomless fracture of a cusp on a restored molar tooth. If the fracture is small, it might be considered appropriate to smooth it and keep it under observation. Presence of other weakened areas on the tooth might suggest the need for onlay or full crown preparation.

On the one hand, the patient is entitled to a brief assessment of the position and of the alternatives: the clinician may wish to recommend a particular course of action, and indeed, many patients will request and accept his evaluation. On the other hand, the 'professional test' of material risk would suggest, in the context of treatment alternatives, that the patient need not be over-burdened with technical considerations, unless specific questions are forthcoming.

The patient should be placed in a position to make an informed choice or to feel content that the discretion he gives to the clinician will be exercised in his best interests. The more complex and consequential the treatment, the more information is required. Thus, for example, orthodontic, orthognathic or extensive restorative care should receive a more detailed and critical analysis.

Financial cost may also be an important criterion in determining the patient's choice. Dentists are ethically bound to make such choices clear to patients in advance. Thus the General Dental Council advise; 'The charge for an initial examination and the probable cost of the treatment should be made clear to the patient at the outset'.[39] – whilst Pollack quotes from the American Dental Association's Principles of Ethics;[40] 'Dentists shall not represent the care being rendered to their patients or the fees being charged in a false or misleading manner.'

Dentists should be careful not to allow their own assumptions about a patient's ability or willingness to pay for treatment to over-ride their professional duty of care. Both civil actions and disciplinary complaints against practitioners have succeeded where a patient has subsequently sought a further opinion and has elected to proceed with appropriate treatment (such as the crowning of a tooth as opposed to its extraction). However, where for instance a practitioner can demonstrate from clinical records that a patient's failure to comply with reasonable oral hygiene or other recommendations precluded the provision of more extensive treatment, then this would constitute some defence against allegations of this nature.

Consequences of refusal of consent

To some extent, the explanation of possible consequences of a patient's refusal of treatment is implicit in the preceding sections, since it may well, in itself, have a bearing on the consideration of material risks, and can similarly affect the patient's assessment of the treatment options open to him.

Although severe or fatal consequences of dental care are rare, a failure to receive care may be more likely to carry serious repercussions. Odom hypothesized the situation where referral for treatment of a suspicious lip ulcer is declined by the patient on the grounds of a long-planned foreign journey.[41] Anderson highlighted the prevalence of North American claims for untreated chronic periodontal disease,[42] and noted that it is important to counsel patients about the long-term risks to their dentition inherent in the disregard of professional advice and therapy.

A dentist might be held to have acted negligently, if he did not inform a patient, therefore, of the consequences of declining any, or the proposed, treatment, particularly if those consequences were likely to be serious

The General Dental Council states that where a general anaesthetic or sedative agent is to be administered in the course of dental treatment, a formal consent must be obtained. In other circumstances, however, some written evidence of consent is strongly desirable. For instance, the General Dental Council also advise; 'Written treatment plans and estimates should always be provided for extensive or expensive courses of treatment'[39] (para 36).

As will be shown in the later section on clinical records, treatment plans and discussions with patients regarding treatment options, warnings and advice should invariably be noted.

Legal actions in consent

It will be noted that reference was made in preceding sections to the torts – civil wrongs – of battery and of negligence. An action in battery may be brought on the allegation that unlawful contact occurred. Negligence, on the other hand, is the failure of a duty of care, with resultant injury. A patient might therefore claim that, for instance, the extraction of an incorrect tooth was a battery, as it had not been consented to, or alternatively that the dentist was negligent in failing to extract the correct tooth. There are certain differences, in law, particularly relating to the assessment of damages (see Mason and McCall Smith,[30] p. 239), and the Courts have now determined that an action in battery is appropriate where no consent at all has been given,[43] but that where there has been a failure to warn or inform, then an action will lie in negligence.

Consent – Children and 'special cases'

In England, the Family Law Reform Act of 1969 effectively confirmed that a person of 16 years of age or above could give valid consent to medical examination or treatment: by implication they can also withhold their consent. (In Scotland, The Age of Legal Capacity (Scotland) Act (1991) has similar effect). Defence organizations advise,[44] however, that for major procedures on patients of 17 or 18 years, the matter should be discussed with the parents unless the patient objects.

Whilst for small children, who are not legally considered capable of understanding the nature and purpose of treatment, the consent of the patient's parent or legal guardian alone must be secured, the capacity and right to give or withhold consent for older children is less clear. The Children Act (1989), and the judgement in the Gillick case of 1985,[45] both suggest that a child who is old enough to comprehend the procedure intended is legally capable of consenting or refusing in their own right. This does not remove the practitioner's duty to seek parental authority, however, and the parent's consent should be sought if at all possible. However, where a clinician believes that, despite parental consent, a child under 16 years is exercising a knowing refusal of treatment, he should not continue with that treatment against the patient's wishes. In problematic cases, the advice of a defence organization or other authoritative source should be sought.

The treatment of patients aged over 16 years who do not have the mental capacity to give valid consent may also, on occasions, give rise to difficulty. In law, no other person has the right to give consent on their behalf. It is therefore essential to establish that the treatment is necessary and is wholly and unarguably in the best interests of the patient. Routine dental care, or the relief of dental pain will seldom cause difficulties in this respect, but particular care must be exercised. The Department of Health (HSG(92)32) has produced model consent forms for all uses, and has specifically included a format for use in these circumstances, advising *inter alia* that good practice dictates consultation with relatives and, where appropriate, with other colleagues.

The general dental practitioner is unlikely to encounter the need to provide urgent treatment for an unconscious patient, though this may certainly occur in hospital practice. All health professionals are additionally under an ethical duty to render 'Samaritan' care to any person who has suffered accident or injury or whose condition may require it. In these circumstances, necessary treatment to preserve life or health should be undertaken without waiting for formal consent. This provision was endorsed by the judgment in the case of F. v West Berkshire Health Authority, where Lord Brandon declared:

> A doctor can lawfully operate on, or give other treatment to, adult patients who are incapable . . . of consenting to his doing so, provided that the operation or other treatment concerned is in the best interests of such patients. The operation or other treatment will be in their best interests if, but only if, it is carried out in order to either save their lives or to ensure improvement in or prevent deterioration of their . . . health.[46]

The provision of emergency dental treatment for children may pose a problem. If there has been, say, an accident at school or in circumstances where a parent is not aware of the injury, the dentist should firstly make reasonable efforts to contact the child's parent or legal guardian. If these are unsuccessful, then necessary emergency care only should be undertaken and the circumstances communicated to the parents as soon as possible. Consent for any further treatment should then be sought.

The future of consent

No aspect of medical law is static; the law must reflect improvements in treatment and the changing social climate of medical care. One such change, as was highlighted in Chapter 1, is that of changing societal attitude to risk. As noted above, this has led courts in the United States to adopt the 'prudent patient' test when considering the disclosure of information to patients. Recent cases in Europe, Canada and Australia suggest that this trend is evident in other jurisdictions.[47] In the United Kingdom, Mason and McCall are of the view that:

> The professional standard is here in Britain for the foreseeable future, but not all judges are as sympathetic to the medical profession as was Lord Denning and there is evidence of its incremental erosion in favour of the rights of the patient.[48]

Before such developments are regarded as a true 'erosion' of the status of professional judgement, it may be reflected that:

> ... it is highly probable that each physician, if put in the position of the patient, would wish, or rather demand, to be totally informed of all the various factors needed to make an informed decision. Interestingly enough, studies have shown, and most attorneys acting for plaintiffs relate, that good communication between physicians and patients diminishes malpractice actions. It is the shock sustained by patients when poor results occur without their having been prepared for the possibility that sends them to lawyers.[49]

Clinical notes – communicating 'for the record'

There is an old adage in medico-legal circles which bears constant repetition: 'Poor records, poor defence; No records, no defence.' However, it is not suggested that the primary reason for clinical records is, or should be, defensive practice. McIntyre gave the view:[50]

> Records have been kept by doctors for thousands of years. The reason is clear: lawyers keep notes for the same reason. The doctor needs an *aide-memoire* to remind him of what was wrong with the patient... what his own opinions were... and what he did. This information is essential.

This may well be the prime purpose – to the clinician – of the patient's clinical notes. Every dentist who has been faced with a patient for treatment, but no notes, will bear out this fact. However, whilst there does not appear to be any general legislative requirement that records should be kept, Pollack notes that the New York Board of Regents mandate that 'clinical records shall be accurate',[51] and the NHS Terms of Service for dental practitioners state:

> A dentist shall keep a record in respect of
> (a) the care and treatment given to a patient under a continuing care or capitation arrangement and the fact of referral under such an arrangement...;

(b) treatment on referral; or
(c) occasional treatment...'[32]

It might also be expected that a Court would rule that the keeping of clinical records formed an essential part of the accepted practice of dentistry, and that to fail to do so may be indicative of a failure of the duty of care.

Defence organizations advise that records should be adequate, legible, accurate and contemporaneous. These ideal characteristics will be examined in further detail.

'Adequate' records

How much is adequate? Sufficient – as McIntyre suggests – to serve as an *aide memoire*? Copious and including all normal findings and verbatim details of conversations? The answer would appear to be somewhere between these limits, with the proviso that certain circumstances or patients may suggest a need for additional inclusions.

In a New York case of 1982, it was held that a physician's custom of recording only abnormal findings, and leaving blanks for normal results in the case history was inadequate under the State's requirement that 'records accurately reflect the evaluation and treatment of the patient'.[53] The British Dental Association advises that; 'It is essential that the practitioner keeps adequate records of all matters relating to the treatment of patients...'.[34]

The Association also recommends specifically that accurate medical histories be taken for all patients, and that these are checked and updated regularly. Individual employing NHS Authorities and Trusts may also have specific requirements in this regard.

The Advisory Board in General Dental Practice, Royal College of Surgeons of England, has suggested that a medical history form be used for all patients on their first attendance. If such a form is designed for self-completion by patients, it must be checked by the practitioner before treatment commences. It is suggested that the minimum information required is:

Is your general health good?
Have you had any serious illness in the past?
Have you been in hospital or under your doctor at home?
Have you taken or are you taking medicines or tablets on a regular basis?
Have you ever had any heart condition, rheumatic fever, diabetes, hepatitis, allergies or sensitivity to drugs?
What is the name and address of your doctor?[55]

In cases of doubt, reference should be made to the patient's general medical practitioner. It is of interest to note that in a case where a dentist took the advice of a patient's doctor, but the patient subsequently suffered a fatal haemorrhage, the court held that it was reasonable for the dentist to accept the doctor's opinion, and the dentist was not negligent in failing to detect a medical abnormality.[56] However, this English case is nearly 60 years old, and the advances in dental undergraduate training might now lead to greater expectations in diagnosis.

Significant medical history findings should be indicated on the record in such a way as to be immediately obvious to the treating clinician. A coloured external tag; 'See Medical History' – to highlight this status would be an excellent way to achieve this.[57]

Updating of medical histories at each subsequent course of treatment is essential but need not be intensive. However, a dated note indicating any changes – or none – should be included.

It is generally accepted practice that, following the medical history, note should be made of the dental and social history and the patient's presenting complaint(s), if any. Dental examination, under NHS Regulations, must include details of all work to be carried out under General Dental Services together with details of any alternative or additional treatment proposed or to be provided for NHS-registered patients under private arrangements.

A new patient's initial charting should indicate previous restorations, in addition to missing or supernumerary teeth, removable and fixed prostheses. Dento-legal claims can arise after many years, and it may be vital to demonstrate that certain treatments were pre-existent.

It is increasingly acknowledged that claims for undiagnosed or untreated periodontal disease have become more prevalent.[57,58,59] The periodontal record is therefore of importance. This should include mobility, pocketing, and the presence of debris or sites which bleed on probing, particularly in the new patient, with updates for subsequent treatments. The use of a periodontal record to display trends is an invaluable patient motivation aid, as well as being clinically useful. Patient home oral care activity and compliance (or lack of compliance) with advice should also be shown. For patients whose periodontal treatment needs are minimal or slight, such recording will not occupy much time: the use of the Community Periodontal Index of Treatment Need (CPITN) (Ainamo et al.)[60] provides a relatively rapid screening technique. Individuals whose requirements are identified as more significant will need additional documentation. Long-term prognosis for periodontal conditions is an area of developing knowledge in dentistry. Until dentists are better able to identify high-risk groups and individuals, the condition of all patients exhibiting signs of periodontal disease should be documented and they should be offered, or referred for, appropriate care.

The use of abbreviations in dental records is, unsurprisingly, widespread. It is helpful, however, if their use is co-ordinated within a practice or establishment and is limited to the more widely accepted forms. It is not uncommon for patients, solicitors or judges to seek explanation of initials or abbreviations in medical or dental notes and obscurity for its own sake – or to conceal unprofessional remarks – is not appreciated. Having to explain some abbreviations to sombre legal personnel, to complaints committees or in open court, may prove at the least embarrassing. Lewis cites HGAC (haven't got a clue); FOC (fat old cow) and SOF (silly old fool) as examples of note.[61] In similar vein, care should be taken to exclude any comments of a personal or concessionary nature. Notes should be written with the anticipation that others may well read them. Two examples from the author's experience are; 'Stupid bitch, never ever to be seen again' emblazoned on a plaintiff's record, and (written the day after fitting a particularly difficult prosthesis), 'Aaagh! Mega ease – a pity to ruin a perfectly good denture'.

Legibility

The standard of medical handwriting has long been a staple source of humour. However, where it leads, as it has in the past, to a fatal administration of an incorrect drug or the amputation of the wrong limb it is a decidedly serious matter.

In dental cases, there are many examples of incorrect extractions or restorations, inappropriate crown shades, unnecessary soft tissue surgery, or treatment of the wrong patient. In some cases it is necessary, at some time and cost to the defendant dentist, to arrange for transcription of notes in a solicitor's office in person.

When confronted by a particularly indecipherable example of their own records, dentists will often rejoin 'Well, I can read it!' This argument is not sustainable – records are not made solely for the benefit of the treating clinician at the time, who may move, retire or fall ill: on such occasions, in addition to medico-legal incidents, patients are entitled to expect that their records and care are readily intelligible to other professionals.

Apart from calligraphy, the use of some colours - especially greens – prevents adequate photocopying, whilst pencil is impermanent and faint. Blue or black waterproof ink (dental records appear to have a greater propensity for getting wet) alone should be used.

Other than in the smallest of practices, notes should always be signed, or at least initialled. Even when there are only two or three clinicians, staff turnover may mean that when an enquiry is made after several years, it can be time-consuming and difficult to trace dentists from handwriting alone. The practice of having chairside assistants write up notes is widespread. It is far better for the clinician to carry out this task, as the custom invariably gives rise to question in proceedings.

A recent comment on the quality of note-keeping from the Public Health Director of an English Regional Health Authority included the comment:

> The fact that so many operation notes could be described as 'appallingly poor' is a swingeing indictment of those concerned. ... Under the system of crown indemnity, health authorities rendered indefensible by poor record keeping on the part of clinicians could seek to mitigate their losses by suing the clinicians themselves.[62]

Particular attention must be paid to legibility where referral takes place, or where the diagnosing clinician is not also carrying out treatment. The removal of four 'b's' (first permanent molar teeth) instead of four 'C's' (deciduous canines) or four '6's' (deciduous incisors) on referral highlights the risk, and it is good practice to identify teeth in words as well as in charting symbols or numbers. The use of computers (see below) and interpretation of the FDI 'two digit' system is not infallible. An orthodontist's request to 'extract 15, 25, 45 and 63' led to the inadvertent extraction of the lower left first permanent molar by the patient's dentist.

Accuracy

The remarks in the preceding paragraphs apply equally under this heading. Notes should be checked to ensure that they are correct. The commonest error under the Palmer, or 'set square' tooth notation is a confusion of sides, so that the upper left central incisor is shown both as $\underline{|1}$ and $1\underline{|}$. The combination of this error with reverse viewing of a radiograph has led to a sizeable number of apicectomies on the wrong tooth.

If a mistake is made in a clinical record, the correct method of amendment is to cross through the error with a single line and to insert the revised entry next to it (or as near as possible) with the date of correction. The original entry should not be obliterated, either by erasing fluid or other means. To do so will severely undermine the value of a record as a valid and dependable item of evidence as any such obliteration will be viewed with suspicion.

Accuracy in records does not necessarily mean that every inconsequential or trivial occurrence must be noted. However, some examples may assist in deciding what should be included:

> Unexpected treatment outcome or finding (and fact that patient was informed)
> Instructions given to patients or parents (and compliance)
> Patient expressed preferences (shade, treatment)
> Consents given and advised treatment declined
> Appointments cancelled or failed

Unusually critical or questioning patient
Patient who criticises previous treatment/dentist

An entry should be made for each contact between the patient and the practice or establishment; it is relatively common in cases of complaint for several attempts at rectification to have been made, as for instance where a patient returns for adjustment of dentures or restorations. If each and every occasion is not recorded, subsequent proof of attendance may be impossible and the plaintiff may imply that other omissions may have occurred. As Pollack suggests, the quality of the record is often seen as indicative, to the layman, of the quality of care provided,[63] as well as the first evidence seen by advisers.

Contemporaneity

In the event of a complaint, whether disciplinary or legal, the clinical record assumes importance as an accurate reflection of events. One of its greatest strengths is that it was compiled at the time. Rules of evidence generally preclude the introduction of hearsay evidence,[64] but original records made by clinical staff with personal knowledge of the treatment are generally admissible. If a witness is unlikely to remember the full details or is untraceable, then records are again admissible. It is important, therefore, that records are written up whilst the memory is fresh, and preferably before the patient leaves the treatment area.

Any temptation to amend or re-write records at a later date must be resisted: such attempts are generally transparently obvious. 'Squeezing in' additional comments, even at the time of treatment should similarly be avoided; an orderly continuation note, correctly dated or timed is better.

It is appreciated that there may be a need, particularly with space and storage constraints, to summarize old records. Such summaries should be clearly identified, together with the date of their preparation (see 'Retention of records' below).

Computerized records

The keeping of clinical records on computer is presently confined to a minority of practices, but the trend is likely to increase. Computer records are admissible as evidence in Britain, under the Civil Evidence Act (1968), and the 1992 National Health Service Regulations specifically permit their use in general dental practice.

The Data Protection Act (1984) (see 'Access to records' below) requires all owners and users of computerized data to register with the Data Protection Registrar, and to comply with certain requirements regarding security and access. The confidential nature of clinical records means that password protection is obligatory.

Additionally, in the event of complaint or legal action, the patient or a court may need to be assured of the credibility of records held in this way. Features such as an audit trail, auto date stamping and PIN identification are desirable.[65] The audit trail automatically records the date, time and user identity of every amendment to the record. Auto date stamping inserts the current date on each line of the record, whilst PIN protection identifies the author of each entry by use of a confidential code.

Where computerised records of treatment are maintained, an orderly filing system should also be kept for the storage and retrieval of those other items, such as X-rays, pathology reports, correspondence and study models which also form part of a patient's record.

Access to records

Less than a decade ago, access to clinical records was determined almost entirely by the medical and dental professionals themselves. Patients who wished to see their records had first to convince a court that they were likely to be 'a party to proceedings in respect of personal injury': in many cases a Writ had first to be issued. The paradox facing patients was that the details of their claim – or the validity of the claim itself – might well depend on the contents of the records.

The issue hinged not only on confidentiality, but also on legal ownership of clinical notes. In private practice, these were held to be the property of the clinician; in the National Health Service, the actual record cards, sheets, etc. themselves belong to the Health Authority or Trust, whilst the information contained on them belongs to the clinician, if a general practitioner, or to the clinician's employer if in a hospital.[66]

The Data Protection Act (1984) applied only to health records which were stored on computer, but represented a major change in the law on access. Although its provisions were modified by the Subject Access Modification Order (1987), the Act provides for patients or their authorized representative to have rights of access and correction of their health records.

Following the implementation of this Act, there existed an awkward dichotomy in law; medical records on paper were treated differently from those stored electronically. Further changes were introduced in access regulation with the Access to Medical Reports Act (1988), which dealt chiefly with access to medical reports prepared for insurance companies. Finally, in July 1990, the Access to Health Records Act received Assent, and came into effect from 1 November 1991. The access rights (for patients) and responsibilities (for record holders) are now broadly similar for both computerized and paper records, and are described below.

The National Health Service guidelines on access to health records makes clear that in normal circumstances;[67] '... a patient will orally request access to the records in the course of treatment and ... the health professional responsible may wish to hand the record to the patient for inspection or go through it with him.'

Such an event will not constitute a formal application under the Act. The attitude of an ethical practitioner should therefore be, it is suggested, one of co-operation and explanation.

Where such a procedure is not forthcoming, the patient may make formal application in writing, or authorize a representative in writing to view the record. Provided the health professional is satisfied that the request clearly identifies the patient, and that the applicant is genuine, access to the record must be provided within 21 days if it is a current record which has been made or added to in the previous 40 days, or within 40 days if no such recent entry has been made. In the latter case, a fee not exceeding £10 may be charged, and necessary copying and postage may also be claimed in any event.

There are three principal exemptions to this right of access; first, if it is considered that access would cause serious harm to the patient's physical or mental well-being, second if the record identifies third parties and hence breaches confidentiality and third if the access is requested to a record made prior to 1 November 1991.

Access on behalf of adult patients with learning disabilities, or who are incapable of managing their own affairs, can only be given to a person who is authorized by a court. Children who can understand both the nature of the treatment and the request for access may refuse consent to access by a parent. These latter cases are unlikely in the dental context.

It will be apparent that the fundamental view of the law is currently that patients should not unreasonably be denied access to their health records, and that they are, in the majority of cases, legally entitled to this right. This position must be balanced, of course, against the professional – and legal – duty of confidentiality, which is addressed in the following section.

Disclosure and confidentiality

'Disclosure' of health records carries a different connotation to 'access'. It implies release to a third party and brings into play the question of confidentiality, which covers both an ethical and a legal obligation.

A clinician's ethical duty of confidentiality to his patient originated with the Hippocratic Oath. This declaration, which may or may not be formally taken by dentists, depending on their place of qualification, includes the phrase; 'All that may come to my knowledge in the exercise of my profession or outside of my profession which ought not to be spread abroad I will keep secret and will never reveal.' This is reflected also in the 'Declaration of Geneva' (1968) which states; 'I will respect the secrets which are confided in me, even after the patient has died.'

The latter obligation, it will be noted, is more stringent, and leaves no room for the clinician's judgement as to when disclosure may be appropriate.

The General Dental Council allows for some interpretation of the duty:

> Dentists who disclose to a third party, without the patient's permission, information about a patient acquired in a professional capacity, may be considered to have been guilty of an improper breach of confidence. There may, however, be circumstances in which the public interest outweighs the dentists's duty with regard to confidentiality and in which disclosure would be justified.[68]

As the Council goes on to suggest, advice in particular circumstances may be obtained from a defence organization. The General Medical Council is more specific in giving guidance on exceptional circumstances, citing;

1. Where the patient or his legal adviser gives written consent
2. Sharing information with other health professionals involved in the patient's care
3. Where on medical grounds it is undesirable to seek the patient's consent, information may sometimes be given to a close relative in confidence
4. When, in the doctor's opinion, the patient's best interests would be served by disclosure, every effort should be made to obtain the patient's consent. Only exceptionally may the doctor act without that consent
5. Where statutory requirements exist
6. Where a court orders disclosure
7. Rarely, disclosure may be justified in the public interest, such as police investigation of a grave or serious crime
8. In the course of medical research approved by a recognized ethical committee

Category 1 is straightforward – further information on solicitors' requests is given below. 2 and 8 are also self-explanatory, whilst 3 and 4 are likely to occur only in the hospital environment where conferral with medical colleagues can take place.

The principal statutory reasons for disclosure of patient information in dental care are rarities – the Prevention of Terrorism (Temporary Provisions) Act (1984), under which 'any person' is under a legal obligation to disclose relevant knowledge; and the Road Traffic Act (1988), under which, there is a similar duty to provide to the police, certain non-clinical information about a driver involved in an accident.

Courts may order the disclosure of information – by subpoena if necessary. A doctor or dentist called to give evidence under oath is bound to provide such facts as the court may require – but unless called as an 'expert' witness, is not obliged to proffer opinions. This information, given in court, is 'privileged', and a patient cannot subsequently sue for breach of confidence.

A court may also order the release of clinical records, although by the terms of the Police and Criminal Evidence Act (1984), a warrant for seizure of clinical material cannot be granted in the usual way by a magistrate; only a circuit judge is empowered to do so.

Disclosure of information or records voluntarily (point 7 above) would only be justified in the investigation of a serious crime, such as murder or rape where there is a clear need to protect the public. A school investigating truancy, for instance, would not, without the consent of the patient or parent, be entitled to know whether Johnny Smith really did have a dental appointment on such-and-such a day. The same would apply to an employer investigating absenteeism. In a recent case, involving fraudulent claims for reimbursement of dental treatment against a policeman, a senior investigating officer was persistent in his demands of a practitioner and reception staff. Faced with their refusal, the appropriate warrant was eventually obtained and served.

The belief is commonly expressed, amongst dental personnel, that such strict adherence to the ethical principles of confidentiality is somehow misplaced or exaggerated in the context of routine dental care. It must be considered whether, if the profession expect to retain and place value on the disclosure by patients of such sensitive and necessary information as HIV status, or oral contraceptive use (in view of the possible suppressive effects of some antibiotics), its standards and probity should not continue to be seen as equal to that of its sister professions.

This, then, briefly summarizes the ethical position. In law, the duty of confidentiality between healthcare professionals and their patients has been clarified by recent cases. There was, until recently, no legally defined duty particular to doctors or dentists. The Law recognized generally that the divulging of information obtained in circumstances which could be regarded as private was a breach of a common law duty, and damages could be awarded where such a breach was harmful to a party. This might occur whether or not there was a specific contractual obligation.[69] This duty would also extend to third parties, such as administrative or practice staff, who divulged information knowing it was confidential.

There is therefore no difficulty in applying this duty to a clinical situation, but what has recently been clarified is the legal position on exceptions to the rule. It would be anomalous if a clinician volunteered information which led to the conviction of a criminal, only to find himself subject to disciplinary action by his professional body. In W. v Edgell, the Court of Appeal upheld a decision that a psychiatrist had not breached his duty of confidentiality by warning the appropriate authorities of his reservations about the release of an allegedly dangerous prisoner.[70] The court found that the public interest was served both by the preservation of confidentiality between patient and clinician, and also by the disclosure of clinical information in circumstances where public safety was involved.

Requests for disclosure of clinical notes may be received from solicitors acting for a patient (not necessarily involved in an action against the dentist holding the notes), or from a dental or medical expert instructed by solicitors. Advice should always be sought from a defence organization. However, the Supreme Court Act (1981) (Sections 33 and 34) now empowers the High Court – County Courts are similarly empowered by the County Courts Act (1984) – to order the release of any documents, including medical records, on the application of; '... a person who appears to the High Court to be likely to be a party to subsequent proceedings in that Court in which a claim in respect of personal injuries to a person ... is likely to be made'. The courts are rightly cautious in permitting access to information on what they see as a 'fishing exercise', but will, on the other hand, appreciate that in medical negligence cases a clear definition of the plaintiff's complaint may not be possible until the records have been released and perused. As Lord Denning observed:

> One of the objects [of disclosure] is to enable a plaintiff to find out – before he starts proceedings – whether he has a good cause of action or not. The object would be defeated if he had to show – in advance – that he had already got a good cause of action before he saw the records.[71]

At one time, there was an established rule that clinical records would be released only to a medical expert appointed by the patient's solicitors,[23] but this has been overtaken by the 1980 Act.

If an action is intended against a patient's former or subsequent dentist, records from other practitioners may be obtained under Section 34 of the Supreme Court Act if they may have relevance to the case. In all these circumstances, costs may be awarded against a dentist who refuses to comply. It is generally advised, therefore, that disclosure is not unreasonably withheld, although as previously stated, expert professional advice must always be sought.

Occasionally, dentists are asked to disclose clinical details to assist in the forensic identification of human remains, often in the aftermath of a tragedy such as an air crash or natural disaster. On occasions such as these, it is reasonable for charting or other details to be released to the appropriate authorities, on the basis that speedy identification is in the best interests of the relatives.

Retention of Records

How long should records, X-rays, models and other patient-related data be kept? The short answer is 'never discard them'. Despite the legal requirements concerning time limits, which are often complex, requests for disclosure can come about an extremely long time after a patient's treatment, and there may be a great saving of time and stress if documentation can be produced.

At the same time, it is accepted that constraints of space may eventually limit any storage facility – unless microfilming and computer-based data is used. What is important in risk-management terms is an awareness of the relative importance of documentation and other patient records. Decisions on retention should not, therefore, be delegated to non-clinical staff.

The current Statute of Limitations sets out times by which legal actions must be commenced. For cases involving personal injury, this is three years; for cases in contract it is six years.[73] However, time does not begin to run necessarily at the point when the injury is caused; that is, the legal 'clock' may not begin to mark off the period of limitation until much later. On the other hand, the principle of limitation reflects the increasing difficulty of proof – and causation (the concept that the injury claimed actually resulted more or less directly from the cause alleged) – and there is in some cases a specific maximum limit beyond which an action may not commence.

The majority of dento-legal cases involve personal injury due to 'negligence' – the details of which are covered more fully in the next chapter. In North America, the term 'malpractice' is the equivalent. As stated above, the time limit for personal injury cases is three years – but three years from either; the date on which the 'cause of action' occurred, or the date on which the injured person became aware of the likelihood of his having a claim. This is known as the date of knowledge, whichever of these dates is the later.

If the patient is aged under 18, an action may be brought on their behalf whilst a minor, or they may bring an action on their own account, in which case the 'clock' will not start until their eighteenth birthday.

If a patient should die before the time limit, then the time begins again from the date of death, or from the date of their 'personal representative's knowledge'.

Consider a case brought in 1992. The patient developed a chronic sinus over a crowned upper central incisor. An X-ray revealed a fractured endodontic reamer in the apical third of the root canal, of which the patient was not previously aware. Apicectomy, twice performed, was unsuccessful and the tooth was extracted and a fixed bridge fitted. The patient was aggrieved that no mention of the reamer had been made, and, through his solicitor, contacted three previous dentists to obtain his records. The tooth proved to have been root treated in 1981, but the records contained no mention of the fractured instrument, nor was there a post-operative radiograph. Proceedings were accordingly commenced against the dentist concerned, who had been a young associate at the time and now practised elsewhere. Expert opinion was that at the time of operation, the taking of a post-operative X-ray would have been accepted procedure, and would have revealed the mishap (which was not in itself necessarily negligent). The case was accordingly settled some twelve years after the 'cause of action'.

Cases such as these are not rare, although records show that the majority of dental claims are brought within four years of the causative event.

Actions in contract are fairly uncommon in dentistry, but may be brought, for example, in relation to the provision of dentures, under the terms of the Supply of Goods and Services Act (1982). In the case of Gordon v Goldberg it was held that the provision of dentures implied a contract to use reasonable skill.[74] Even where the patient suffers no injury from a dentist's failure to employ reasonable skill, an action in contract may result. The time limit here is six years.

A third form of legal action may follow from obligations under the Consumer Protection Act (1987), which is concerned in part with defective products. A dentist may, for example, purchase or use equipment, materials or drugs which prove to be faulty in some way. A dentist must be able to identify the source of the faulty goods to avoid liability. It is therefore advisable to retain invoices, delivery notes, etc. and to note batch numbers of drugs and medications purchased. The time limit for actions under this heading is ten years, though if personal injury results, then the three year limit described above applies. The ten year limit derives from 'harmonized' European legislation and is the most extensive in current civil law.

In all actions other than those involving personal injury, there is an absolute restriction on the bringing of cases more than fifteen years after the events giving rise to the complaint. The courts accept that the burden of proof becomes more difficult to substantiate over time. They will, however, support the right of a patient to bring an action where, as in the 1992 case cited above, it is apparent that the professional duty of care was lacking.

What if, in that case, the records had been destroyed and the matter had come to trial? The judge would be faced with conflicting evidence on the one hand that the patient had not been informed of the mishap, and on the other that either the event had not occurred, or that the appropriate information had been given. In civil cases, a decision rests on the balance of probabilities, and, all other things being equal, the verdict could well be unfavourable to the defendant dentist. The retention of records resulted in a modest settlement; had those records indeed borne out correct practice, then it is unlikely that the patient would have persisted. In either event, the dentist was spared a stressful court appearance, and the patient benefited from a speedier result.

Records should therefore be retained wherever possible, and always reviewed individually before destruction (by shredding or incineration). Records including X-rays or involving surgery, crownwork, periodontal data or endodontics should certainly be kept indefinitely wherever possible, as should those involving any measure of difficulty, complication or dispute. Records involving the treatment of minors should be retained until ten and a half years beyond their eighteenth birthday – the extra half year over the longest period of limitation is recommended to allow for time involved in the issuing of proceedings. Retention of other records for ten and a half years is recommended.

It is frequently overlooked that documentation such as appointment books and laboratory receipts may contain valuable information. It has been possible, for instance, to show from appointment records, that patients infected with HIV following treatment from a Florida dentist were unlikely to have shared handpieces or triple syringes.[75] In less dramatic circumstances, dentists have been able to show that particular care was taken over the cosmetic appearance of a disputed anterior bridge, or that a litigious patient did not in fact attend on the days alleged.

In another case, a dentist's alleged failure to adequately plan treatment and advise a patient of likely costs was defended when an authentic, if somewhat crumpled, note written by his chairside assistant was retrieved from the records. Good records have been the saviour of many an otherwise indefensible action.

References

1. The Medical Defence Union Ltd (1992) *Talking to Patients*, MDU, London.
2. Localio A.R. *et al.* (1991) Relation between malpractice claims and adverse events due to negligence. *The New England Journal of Medicine*, **325** (4), 245–51
3. Nesbitt M-L. (1990) Failing to Communicate. *Journal of the Medical Defence Union*, **6** (4), 49
4. Brown J.L. (1992) Communicating to avoid liability. *Journal of the California Dental Association*, **20** (3), 57–60
5. Fiske J. (1990) *Introduction to Communication Studies (2nd edn)*. Routledge, London
6. Hinde R.A. (ed.) (1972) *Non-Verbal Communication*. Cambridge University Press
7. Dickson D.A. *et al.* (1989) *Communication Skills for Health Professionals*. Chapman and Hall, London
8. Cherry C. (1957) *On Human Communication*. MIT Press, Cambridge, Mass.
9. Janner G. (1988) *Janner on Communication*. Hutchinson Business Publishing, London
10. Ayer W.A. (1982) The Dentist Patient Relationship. *International Dental Journal*, **32**, 56–64
11. Ley P, (1988). *Communicating with Patients: Improving Communication, Satisfaction and Compliance*. Chapman and Hall, London

128 Medico-legal risk management

12. Mehrabian and Ferris (1967). Inference of Attitudes from Non-verbal Communication in Two Channels. *Journal of Counselling Psychology*, **31**, 248–252
13. Kent G.G. and Blinkhorn A.S. (1991) *The Psychology of Dental Care*. Butterworth-Heinemann, Oxford. p.p. 145–149
14. Bensing J.M. and Sluijs E.M. (1985) Evaluation of an Interview Training Course for General Practitioners. *Social Science and Medicine*, **20** (7), 737–744
15. Kent G. (1984). Satisfaction with Dental Care. *Medical Care*, **22**, 583–585
16. Furnham A. (1983). Social Skills and Dentistry. *British Dental Journal*, **154**, 404–408
17. Maguire P. and Rutter D. (1976) Teaching Medical Students to Communicate, in *Communication between Doctors and Patients* (Bennett A. E. ed.). Oxford University Press
18. Maguire P., Fairbairn S. and Fletcher C. (1986) Consultation Skills of Young Doctors: II – Most young doctors are bad at giving information. *British Medical Journal*, **292**, No. 6535, 1576–1578
19. Carrotte P.V., Winstanley R.B. and Green J.R. (1993). A study of the quality of impressions for anterior crowns received at a commercial laboratory. *British Dental Journal*, **174** (7), 235–240
20. Logan H.L. (1991) Communication and Persuasion: Factors Influencing a Patient's Behavior. *Journal of Dental Education*, **55** (9), 570–574
21. Wills T.A. (1978) Perception of clients by professional helpers. *Psychological Bulletin*, **85** (5), 968–1000
22. Ayer W.A. (1982) Dentist/patient relationship. *International Dental Journal*, **32**, 56–64
23. Weinstein P., Milgrom P., Ratener P., Read W. and Morrison K. (1978) Dentists' perceptions of their patients: relation to quality of care. *Journal of Public Health Dentistry*, **38** (1), 10–21
24. *Thake* v. *Maurice* 1986 QB 644
25. Medical Defence Union (1991) *Complaints about clinical care* (booklet). Medical Defence Union, London
26. Fisher R. and Ury W. (1983) *Getting to Yes*. Random Century, London
27. Tarsh M. (1993) Playing fair with plaintiff patients and hospital staff. *Health Service Journal*, **103**, No. 5361, 6–7 (supp)
28. Allsopp K.M. (1986) *Medical Defence Union Journal*, **2**, 2
29. Slovenko R. (1992) Saying You're Sorry in a Litigious Society. *Medicine and Law*, **11**, 669–671
30. Mason J.K. and McCall Smith (1991) *Law and Medical Ethics (3rd edn)*. Butterworths, London. p. 243
31. *Brazier M. (1987) Medicine, Patients and the Law*. Penguin Books, London. p. 58
32. *Bolam* v. *Friern Hospital Management Committee*. (1957) 2 All ER 118
33. *Sidaway* v. *Board of Governors of the Bethlem Royal Hospital and the Maudsley Hospital*. (1985) 1 All ER 643
34. *Canterbury* v. *Spence*. (DC 1972) 464 F 2d at 791
35. Collins M.R.N. (1988) Paraesthesia following lower wisdom tooth extraction. *Journal of the Medical Defence Union*, **4** (2), 41–2
36. Rood J.P. (1992) Permanent damage to inferior alveolar and lingual nerves during the removal of impacted mandibular third molars. Comparison of two methods of bone removal. *British Dental Journal*, **172** (3), 108–110
37. Barnes I.E. (1990) Surgical Endodontics. In *Endodontics in Clinical Practice* (Harty F.J., ed). Wright, Bristol, p. 224 et seq.
38. Calnan J. (1983) *Talking with Patients: A Guide to Good Practice*. Heinemann, London.
39. General Dental Council (1993) *Professional Conduct and Fitness to practice*. General Dental Council, London. para. 36
40. Pollack J.D. (1987) *Handbook of Dental Jurisprudence and Risk management*. PSG publishing, Littleton, Mass. p. 246
41. Odom J.G. (1985) Recognizing and resolving ethical dilemmas in dentistry. *Medicine*

and Law, **4**, 543–549
42. Anderson P.E. (1992) Are you playing Russian Roulette? *Dental Economics,* June 1992. p. 77–80
43. See *Chatterton v. Gerson* (1981) 1 All ER 257
44. Medical Defence Union (1993) *Consent To Treatment.* Medical Defence Union Ltd, London
45. *Gillick v. West Norfolk and Wisbech Area Health Authority* (1985) 3 All ER 402
46. *F v. West Berkshire Health Authority and Another* (1989) 2 All ER 545
47. Giesen D. (1993) Legal accountability for the provision of medical care: a comparative review. *Journal of the Royal Society of Medicine,* **86**, 648–652
48. Mason and McCall. op. cit. p. 251
49. Morton W.J. (1987) The Doctrine of Informed Consent. *Medicine and Law,* **6**, 117–125
50. McIntyre N. (1982) Medical Records: Computers and the patient. *Medical-legal Journal,* **4**, 159–170
51. Pollack B.R. (1987) op. cit. p. 51
52. *The National Health Service (General Dental Services) Regulations (1992)* HMSO, London, Schedule 1, para 25
53. *Schwarz v. Board of Regents of the State of New York,* 453 N Y S 2d 836 (1982)
54. British Dental Association (1993) Ethical and legal Obligations of Dental Practitioners. (Advice Sheet B1), BDA, London
55. Advisory Board in General Dental Practice, Royal College of Surgeons of England (1991) *Self Assessment Manual and Standards* (Grace M. ed.). Royal College of Surgeons, London
56. *Warren v. Greig; Warren v. White* (1935) 1 The Lancet 330
57. Bressman J.K. (1993) Risk Management for the 90s. *Journal of the American Dental Association,* **124** (3), 63–67
58. Anderson P.E. (1992) Are you playing Russian Roulette? *Dental Economics,* June 1992
59. Dunne M. and Brown J.L. (1991) Risk Management in Dentistry. *Current Opinion In Dentistry,* **1**, 668–671
60. Ainamo J., Barmes D., Beagrie G. *et al.* (1982) Development of the World Health Organization Community Periodontal Index of Treatment Needs. *International Dental Journal,* **32**, 281–291
61. Lewis C.J. (1988) *Medical Negligence – a Practical Guide.* Tolley, Croydon
62. O'Brien M. (1992) Optimistic response to NCEPOD [National Confidential Enquiry into Peri-Operative Deaths] – with provisos. (letter). *British Journal of Hospital Medicine,* **48** (3/4), 198
63. Pollack B.R. (1987) op. cit. p. 221
64. *Civil Evidence Act* (1968), sections 2(1), 4, 8
65. Norwell N. (1992) GP Computer Records – Questions Answered. *Journal of the Medical Defence Union,* **8** (2), 43–44
66. Brazier M. (1987) *Medicine, Patients and the Law.* Penguin, Harmondsworth. p. 46
67. NHS Management Executive (1991) *Access to Health Records Act (1990): a guide for the NHS,* HSG(91)6. Department of Health, London
68. General Dental Council (1993) op. cit. para 34(i)
69. Law Commission Report No. 110 (1981) *Breach of Confidence.* (Cmnd 8388). HMSO, London
70. *W v. Edgell* (1990) 1 All ER 835
71. *Dunning v. United Liverpool Hospitals' Board of Governors* AC (1973) 2 All ER 454
72. *McIvor v. Southern Health and Social Services Board (1978)* 2 All ER 625
73. *Limitation Act (1980),* Sections 5 and 11
74. *Gordon v. Goldberg* (1920) 2 The Lancet 964
75. Gooch B., Marianos D., Ciesielski C. *et al.* (1993) Lack of Evidence for patient to patient transmission of HIV in a dental practice. *Journal of the American Dental Association,* **124** (1), 38–44

5
Risk in clinical dental practice

Introduction

Having focused, in the previous chapter, on aspects of communication, consent and record keeping, this chapter is concerned primarily with clinical aspects of risk management in dentistry. First it will briefly consider the legal principles involved in the majority of actions against dentists. Second, it will review data from the United States and Britain on the prevalence of claims relating to different types of dental treatment. Finally, based on this reported prevalence, it will consider particular risks which may arise during diagnosis and treatment, suggesting appropriate risk management interventions.

Legal principles

Legal cases against doctors and dentists in the civil courts are usually brought under the torts of battery, negligence or contract. Battery has already been discussed under the topic of 'Consent' in the preceding chapter. Of the three, negligence is by far the most commonly encountered in dento-legal claims.

Negligence

The tort of negligence is the failure of a legal duty of care owed by a defendant (in this context a dentist, health authority or Trust), to a plaintiff (usually, but not always, the patient), which results in damage caused by that failure. That such a legal duty of care is owed to a patient by a medical practitioner has been recognized for many years,[1] and dentists are in a similar position in law. Health authorities, and Trusts are responsible for the acts or omissions of their employees in the course of their contracted duties and are thus usually the defendants answerable in law for injury or harm befalling their patients. As an employee has a legal duty of care towards his or her employer, it is theoretically possible, however, for an Authority to pursue a separate action against the employee. Such an action would only be taken in the most exceptional circumstances although disciplinary action might well follow (see Chapter 7).

In order to show failure of the duty of care, the plaintiff must demonstrate that the defendant fell short of the standards expected by the courts. As previously referred to, the court will have regard to the standards set out in the case of *Bolam v Friern Hospital Management Committee (1957)*, that is to say, whether the standard fell below that of the skill of an 'ordinary competent practitioner exercising and professing to have the skill which is in question'. The word 'practitioner' is here meant in the sense of 'one who practises', and the standard will be implied as that appropriate to the status of the defendant's professional position. General practitioners would thus be considered in law by the standards of their peers, as would be hospital consultants or other identifiable professional groups.[2] Moreover, a failure of treatment, or the lack of a successful outcome alone is not indicative by itself of negligence; it is the standard of care, and not the result of that care which is important.

In upholding professional standards, a dentist will be required to show that he acted in accordance with established or recognized current teaching and practice.[3] In the Bolam case, it was held that a doctor was not negligent if he; '... acted in accordance with the practice of a responsible body of medical men skilled in that particular art'.[4]

Where new or untried techniques are being used, it would be for the defendant to show that it was justified and appropriate and that the patient's informed consent had been obtained.[10]

There is also a responsibility for dentists to maintain their awareness of contemporary advances in treatment, and of newly discovered hazards and complications. Although, in 1953, Lord Denning considered it excusable for an anaesthetist to have failed to read one article (concerning injection risks), he thought disregard of a series of published warnings might be negligent.[5] Forty years later, such a view might well be thought too lenient.

It is not sufficient in negligence to show only that the required standard of care was not met – the plaintiff must have suffered damage. In the majority of dental cases this damage will be primarily physical, in the form of resulting injury, the side-effects of treatment or the need for subsequent remedial care. Psychological damage may also be demonstrated, in the form of pain, stress or apprehension. Such damage must be shown to have resulted from the act or omission complained of; 'Generally speaking, damage is recoverable if it is considered as being of a type which is reasonably foreseeable as likely to flow from the injury and which is not considered too remote.'[6]

Thus the patient whose holiday was curtailed when a recently – and unsatisfactorily – apicected tooth became acutely infected could reasonably claim for his losses, and it would be of no avail for the defendant to say that he was unaware of the forthcoming vacation. On the other hand, were the dentist able to show that the operation was carried out competently and that the subsequent infection was an occasional hazard of which either the patient had been informed, or that such an infection was sufficiently rare as not to be 'reasonably foreseeable', then there would be no negligence.

It is not sufficient for a plaintiff to show that his injuries were foreseeable. He must also show what is known as 'proximate cause'. This concept requires him to show, on balance, that the injuries derived from the defendant's failure of care. Legal arguments about the 'flow' of causation may be highly technical. Suppose a root canal treatment fails and the patient is referred for apicectomy. This too fails after a period and is repeated, with equal lack of success and the tooth is extracted. All other things being equal, it may be held that the original root canal work, if it can be shown to have been defective, was responsible for the ultimate extraction. But suppose that, following extraction the patient continues to have pain and that this is considered to be either psychogenic or due to a rare neurological complication. Is the resultant pain – possibly lifelong – due to the original event, wholly or partly? The answer will lie in the chain of probabilities which is set in motion by the original failure, and it may, ultimately, fall to the court to interpret the extent of liability.

In civil law, it is for the plaintiff to show, on a balance of probabilities, that negligence has occurred. To successfully rebut the allegation, the defendant need only satisfy the court that the plaintiff's allegations are, on the same basis, unfounded. This civil law test stands in distinction to the criminal law, where conviction requires the prosecution to establish guilt beyond any reasonable doubt. The burden of proof may, however, be shifted onto the defendant dentist if the court accepts a plea of *res ipsa loquitur* – 'the thing speaks for itself'. If the plaintiff can show that his injuries could not reasonably have resulted in the absence of negligent conduct, it is for the defendant then to show otherwise. Courts are unwilling, in medical negligence cases, to introduce this presumption unless the plaintiff is unable to prove what caused the accident or injury. When a patient inhaled a throat pack during an extraction under general anaesthesia, the court held that the defendants must show how this could occur in the absence of negligence.[1] However, in specific cases coming before them, the courts have not accepted that, for instance, fracture of the jaw during extraction,[1] nor dislocation of the mandible during multiple extractions,[2] were of themselves evidence of negligence, and rejected pleas of *res ipsa loquitur*.

The Law Reform (Contributory Negligence) Act (1945) formalized the concept that a plaintiff might, by his own acts or omissions, have contributed to his injury in some way, and allowed courts to reduce compensation in proportion to the extent of that contribution. However, it has not been possible to find a case of medical or dental negligence in the UK which has established such contributory negligence. It may be speculated that a patient's disinclination to follow instructions such as home care, medication or attendance for follow-up appointments might technically constitute contributory negligence. One difficulty is in assessing a reasonable standard of self-care which the patient 'owes' to himself. In medical negligence cases, it may be that the courts are unwilling to assume that a plaintiff possessed sufficient knowledge of the detail of his treatment (relative to that of the practitioner) to be held to be responsible (in part) for his injury. What of the patient who makes a sudden movement, causing a dental instrument or burr to lacerate the oral tissues? The practitioner may well, understandably, feel that the patient is at least partly to blame for his misfortune. However, in the impassive surroundings of a court of law, it might prove difficult to show that the dentist and any assistant were less well placed than the patient to take all reasonable measures to avoid harm occurring. The patient may say, for instance, that he felt pain and the movement was reflexive; it could be difficult in this case to show that the patient had failed in his duty of self-care. The area is contentious, but the point remains, that it is unwise to be tempted to an over-hasty response; 'It was your fault!'

The dentist is not only responsible for his own acts and omissions, but also for those of his employees and 'servants'. This, the legal principle of vicarious liability, will extend not only to salaried staff (except in Health Authorities, where the clinician may however have a contractual duty of supervision and direction), but also to salaried locums, hygienists and dental assistants. All dentists and hygienists should be members of defence organizations in their own right, as on occasions, the interests of individuals may be contradictory. Consider, for example, actions brought against a general practitioner, a specialist orthodontist and the orthodontist's self-employed hygienist when, on removing a patient's fixed appliance, extensive decalcification and cavitation are revealed. Each would have a part to play in rebutting the allegations, and for the purposes of their defence, they may wish to express their views independently.

The courts will not generally seek to hold a practitioner responsible for the acts or omissions of an independent contractor, such as a self-employed associate dentist. Vocational trainees in NHS general practice (employed assistant dentists, with a Nationally standardized contract) are required, currently, to hold membership of one of the three defence organizations as a condition of their contract. A separate action may be brought against the trainer practitioner, but unless it can be shown that the trainee was being unreasonably required to carry out advanced work beyond his expected abilities, the courts will generally consider that a registered practitioner assumes his own legal duty of care for patients under treatment by him. In community or hospital service, the principle of vicarious liability applies to all employees of a health authority or Trust, and although there is nothing to bar a plaintiff from additionally pursuing an action against a practitioner individually, Crown indemnity has, since January 1990, rendered such a course of action unlikely. In practice, plaintiffs have tended to direct actions against health authorities, since they may not be certain of the member, or members of staff involved. Vicarious liability does not extend from one employee to another, and a consultant, for example, is not responsible for the acts or omissions of his registrar.

Damages

Where a plaintiff has successfully shown that his injuries are due to negligence, the court can compensate in only one way – by the award of monetary damages. These are composed of two principal parts; general damages and special damages (the total being referred to as the *quantum*). Special damages are those which are awarded to compensate for specific expenses incurred by the plaintiff as a result of his injuries. In dental cases, these may commonly include the cost of remedial treatment, loss of earnings, travel costs and other incidentals. It has been established that although the treatment giving rise to the legal action was carried out under the National Health Service, a plaintiff may be entitled to recover damages for reasonable further or remedial treatment occasioned by his injuries under private contract.[10] General damages are those which are not immediately quantifiable, being usually termed as compensation for 'pain, suffering and loss of amenity'. These damages are often the subject of intense and persuasive argument by both sides in the case, and may ultimately have to be decided by the court. General damages will frequently be highly specific to the individual involved. Thus dental disfigurement or facial scarring may be assessed at a higher figure for, say, a young female fashion model than for an older, male nightclub doorman. Monetary assessment of pain and suffering are, naturally, subjective, and loss of amenity will reflect the impact of the injury on the future earnings, lifestyle or well-being of the plaintiff.

Damages in cases of tort are intended to compensate the victim, and not to punish the defendant. Courts in the UK are very reluctant to impose 'punitive' damages other than where gross malpractice or indifference on the part of individuals or institutions has been shown (and very rarely even then). In the United States, despite the introduction of tort reform measures, damages in medical malpractice cases are usually assessed by a jury, and it is difficult to escape the conclusion that punitive or exemplary (literally 'to make an example of') damages are seen as a rightful component of the restitution process of the civil law.[11]

Few UK dental cases reach courts for settlement awards to be published. Settlements reached 'out of court' are seldom publicized; for reasons such as those given above, they are rarely of general applicability. In a 1987 case, a patient who suffered four years of temporo-mandibular and facial pain following upper bridgework received £4,000 in general damages and £5,337 agreed special damages for remedial treatment.[12]

Contract law

The law of Contract is concerned with 'agreements which are binding on the parties'. Contracts may be either for goods or for services; so far as dentists are concerned, they enter into a legally binding contract to provide professional services for their patients, and may be held liable if those services do not conform to the specific or generally understood terms of such an agreement.

Although no specific dental cases have arisen, the courts have taken the view in medical claims, that patients treated under the National Health Service do not have a direct contract with the clinician, on the basis that no 'consideration' (payment) is offered directly. In a case brought against a pharmacist, when glass fragments were discovered in a medicine bottle, the Chief Justice observed; 'There will have been no sale by the chemist to the patient, the person presenting the prescription. ... The patient is not paying for the medicine or drugs, and that is so even if there is a prescription charge.'[13]

This would suggest that an NHS Dental patient is not paying for (a proportion of) his treatment cost, but is paying a statutory fee. Private patients, however, have the option of suing both in negligence and in contract, although the courts have generally ruled that the liability owed by a healthcare professional in contract is identical to that owed in negligence.[14]

One exception to this general rule is the provision of dentures, which would seem to be bound by the Supply of Goods and Services Act (1982),[15] and to be required to be 'fit for their purpose'. In one case (which, however, considerably predates this Act), a patient successfully sued her dentist for breach of contract in providing unsatisfactory dentures at a (then) considerable cost of £40.[16]

If a dentist were to make a specific promise or undertaking to a private patient, particularly in writing or before witnesses, then he might well be rendering himself liable to a future breach of contract action if the looked-for benefit failed to materialize. The lesson is plain, and 'guarantees' should not be made. As well as rendering the dentist liable at law, they may well constitute a 'misrepresentation' as interpreted by the General Dental Council (see Chapter 7).

One further area of Contract law which is of vital concern to general dental practitioners working within the NHS, is the Contractual relationship between them individually and their Family Health Service Authority. This contract, which includes their Terms of Service, is also dealt with in Chapter 7.

Criminal law

A brief mention should be made concerning the criminal law as it may apply in dental practice. Instances of criminal charges directly relating to dentistry are few, but the risks implied – arrest, deprivation of liberty, publicity, loss of reputation among them – are too great to ignore. Additional consequences (see Chapter 7) are the reporting of all criminal convictions involving dentists to the General Dental Council and the invocation of professional disciplinary proceedings.

Assault

The civil wrongs of assault and battery were distinguished in Chapter 4, in relation to consent. The parallel criminal offences are distinguished, in law, by a principal feature known as *mens rea* – intent. When a tooth is erroneously extracted, a dentist may have unwittingly damaged the patient, but his action was neither premeditated nor intentional. When a dentist whose finger was being bitten by an unruly three-year-old patient smacked him on the cheek, his action was intentional. The parents, who were sitting in the surgery, made no comment, but that was no bar to their subsequently seeking to bring criminal charges for assault.

In another case, a dentist attempted to remove a denture he had just fitted to a 'difficult' patient. The patient resisted and pulled away, unbalancing the dentist who fell on top of her onto the surgery floor. The patient called the police and preferred charges.

Whatever might be one's sympathy with the individuals concerned, a criminal assault charge is a serious matter which would undoubtedly lead to investigation by the General Dental Council. Losing one's temper and the restraint or chastisement of children are to be avoided at all costs.

The defence of dentists who face criminal charges is, in general, specifically excluded from the benefits of membership of defence organizations, although where the matter is directly concerned with the treatment of patients, discretionary assistance may be given. Assistance is also given when such changes lead to investigation by the General Dental Council and advice must be sought in all cases.

The foremost rule of risk management in all criminal cases must be; say nothing unless and until advised by a legal representative present. This advice may sound somewhat dramatic or unduly obstructive. Dentists are, after all, mostly law abiding citizens who regard the police force as reasonable and proper defenders of the public's rights. Arresting or investigating officers may be relaxed or officious, but they will be unfailingly polite – it seems only reasonable to explain the circumstances, and every television viewer knows that the words 'I must caution you that anything you say...' are spoken almost as an automatic and unthinking everyday expression. It is not so, and although the 'right to silence' is presently under legislative scrutiny, it is a right which should be exercised at all times when legal assistance is not obtainable.

An arrest may not be made; an invitation to the police station is more likely in the circumstances given in the cases cited above. Such an invitation may be accepted, but at a time of the dentist's choosing, and after contact with his lawyer, who should accompany him. If arrested, it is equally important to avoid any discussion in the vehicle on the way to the police station. A useful piece of advice is to take along a substantial bundle of work;[17] the distraction is useful, and there will probably be plenty of time to attend to it! Numerous, and mostly entirely legal, tactics will be employed to weaken the 'suspect's' nerve. Being asked to wait in a cell as there is no other space available, or suggestions that there is really no need for legal assistance (though it will virtually never be denied, given persistence), are not unusual. On completion of enquiries, release is normal in all but the most serious offences, and it may then be some time before a decision on proceedings is received from the Crown Prosecution Service.

Drugs

In the UK, dentists are permitted to supply any drug to a patient for the purposes of dental treatment – with the obvious exception of drugs (such as cannabis) which do not have medical indications and are contained in Schedule 1 to the Misuse of Drugs Act (1971). Problems can still arise. A dentist who was quite properly prescribed amphetamine-related drugs by his doctor undertook to self-prescribe to avoid the time it took him to visit his medical practice. He signed the appropriate pharmacy register, but was arrested following a routine inspection of the pharmacist's records. The knowing supply, possession or use of controlled drugs may lead to investigation and charges if they are not for legitimate use in dentistry.

Indecency

Allegations of indecent assault may occur following a quite innocent contact with a patient of either sex. Dentists' work brings them into close proximity with their patients and they must be ever watchful. It is preferable never to place or rest objects on a reclined patient's bib. It is also preferable that a dental surgery assistant remains in the surgery or X-ray room whenever patients, particularly of the opposite sex, are being treated. If for some reason this is not possible, leaving a door wide open and having staff frequently pass through is a wise precaution. Patients seen as out of hours emergencies must be accompanied into the surgery, or a staff chaperone arranged.

Recent cases have highlighted the propensity for certain intravenous benzodiazepine drugs to induce hallucinations. Especial care must be taken regarding chaperonage during their use (the presence of a 'second appropriate person' is now required by General Dental Council guidelines).[18]

Fraud

Charges of fraud against dentists usually result from incorrect claims for payment under the National Health Service. The disciplinary and investigative mechanisms are described more fully in Chapter 7. Where it is considered that a dentist may have fraudulently claimed for treatment not in fact provided, the facts may be submitted to the police by the Dental Practice Board. The matter is extremely serious, and independent legal advice should be sought at once. Custodial sentences are not uncommon in such instances of fraud involving public funds, and conviction will almost inevitably lead also to a hearing before the General Dental Council.

Dentists are also required to maintain accurate accounts, both in regard to their personal affairs and, if staff are employed, in relation to the statutory deduction of tax and National Insurance from employees. Legislation in recent years has become more stringent with regard to such matters, and it is recommended that sound and effective book-keeping procedures and a reputable accountant with experience of dental and similar professional businesses are used. Inland Revenue and Department of Social Security staff have wide powers of investigation and seizure, and full and timely co-operation with their (rather time-consuming) procedures is advised.

Areas of risk in clinical dentistry

Although the general approach advocated in this book is that risk management is a comprehensive attitude to the practice of dentistry, there is, none the less, evidence that certain clinical procedures are more inherently risky than others. This statement should not be misconstrued: the risk of litigation following a procedure is not to be confused with the risk of failing to secure a satisfactory clinical outcome, nor the incidence of unwanted side-effects. There may well be a relationship between these risks, but it is not clear cut.

Equally, it would be imprudent to regard this section as indicating certain areas in which 'special care' should be taken. The standards of care demanded in clinical practice – and in administration and professional conduct – should not be classified or prioritized. Legal standards of care take no account of the type of care provided. Procedures which have, in the past, proved to be rich sources of dental litigation may not prove to be so in the future, and new treatments, new technologies or new materials may well be the 'perennial problems' of the future. Risk management demands assiduous attention to all aspects of dental care, and places on the practitioner the onus of maintaining an awareness of contemporary issues in the development of dental science and practice as well as trends in law and jurisprudence.

In 1975, Milgrom reviewed 149 US court cases which involved dental malpractice between 1900 and 1974.[19] He used this data to evolve a classification of 'avoidable adverse dental outcomes'. In consultation with a panel of legal and dental experts, he proposed five categories; adverse outcomes from diagnosis errors, adverse outcomes from errors in treatment, adverse general medical outcomes, adverse outcomes from errors in follow-up and adverse outcomes from 'societally proscribed actions'(negligence, abandonment of patients and lack of informed consent). Whilst this paper did not attempt to ascribe quantitative incidence data to these classifications, it marked an interesting approach to the consideration of untoward clinical events which is helpful in designing means of risk prevention or minimization in practice (see Chapter 9).

Milgrom went on to discuss five criteria developed by Tancredi in the medical context and which he considered suggestive of outcomes which might lead to successful litigation.[20] These criteria were:

1. Iatrogenicity: injuries to patients due to the inadvertent actions of the dentist, or incidental to the main purpose of treatment; treatment benefits must always be weighed against possible treatment risks. (Example: possibility of gingival degeneration under removable prosthesis – but against this must be set the benefits to the patient from the treatment.)

2 Preventability: are precautions available which can reduce the possibility of a given hazard? (Example: inhaled root canal file; a highly preventable risk.)
3 Treatability: a disease or condition must be amenable to professional intervention. (Example: a longitudinal tooth fracture may not be amenable to conservation.)
4 Detectability: there must be distinct and obvious signs which alert a practitioner to the presence of the condition requiring treatment. (Example: early interproximal caries on bitewing radiographs)
5 Cost of deviation: this criterion relates to the significance of the condition or problem both in relation to other treatment requirements and to the risk:benefit ratio of the treatment required. (Example: the extraction of an asymptomatic unerupted third molar may be associated with significant operative risk.)

This qualitative approach to areas of clinical risk bears consideration in relation to the particular procedures described later.

Quantitative assessment of clinical risk – US studies

Milgrom and co-workers have recently reported findings from a major review of dental malpractice incidence. In a preliminary report they point out that there has been little empirical work carried out on dental malpractice experience, and commentaries have been largely confined to individual case reports and to discussions of the cost and availability of indemnity insurance.[21] The reasons for this have already been discussed. The preliminary report examined 194 claims relating to one dental indemnity insurer in a single US state over the period 1983–1990. Only claims which progressed beyond the original incident report and which were subsequently closed (completed) were included. Analysis of the claims by treatment type yielded the following most commonly identified prevalences:

Endodontics	18.5%
Oral surgery*	15.9%
Fixed prosthodontics	14.4%
Restorative dentistry	13.3%
Periodontics	12.3%
Removable prosthodontics	8.2%
Orthodontics	5.1%

*performed by other than oral surgeons

Pathology, paedodontics and TMJ were separately identified; these categories, together with 'other' cases together accounted for the remaining 12.3% of the sample studied.

Problems with interpretation of this data include the fact that treatment and litigation patterns for one American state may not be applicable in other areas. The insurer whose database yielded the proprietary data is not identifiable, and hence the policy details are not available. Oral surgeons and intravenous anaesthesia are not included. As the study was confined to closed claims, it may not reflect the pattern of reported incidents which did not go either to settlement or trial: it is reported that 60% were settled without issue of proceedings, almost 38% were settled after issue of proceedings, but before trial, and 2.6% proceeded to trial. No data is available on claims which were either not pursued or were withdrawn.

More substantial results from the National Dental Malpractice Survey were reported in 1994.[22] Overall incidence and trends are discussed further in Chapter 6; here the analysis of treatment types is considered. The survey involved completion of questionnaires by a representative sample of 4,278 dentists throughout the US, and considered both complaints by patients which dentists had reported to their insurers, and legal claims which had been formally filed. Complaints were not analysed by treatment type, but it was reported that 77% of claims were accounted for by five treatment areas:

Oral Surgery	21.9%
Fixed prosthodontics	19.5%
Endodontics	18.1%
Periodontics	12.6%
Restorative dentistry	5.1%

Smaller numbers of claims were reported for TMJ, orthodontics, implants, anaesthesia, removable prosthodontics and other mishaps.

Treatment errors were implicated in 55% of claims, diagnosis errors in 17%. Other categories noted included: failure to consult (8%); lack of informed consent (6%) and failure to follow-up (5%). The highest settlement figures were in endodontics ($150,000) and oral surgery ($60,000), whilst fixed prosthodontics and periodontics had the highest median settlement costs. Only three claims in the five years investigated related to implants.

This survey provides interesting and informative information on recent claim characteristics in the US, and draws attention to the fact that, in contrast to the earlier (1900–1974) dental malpractice cases examined in 1975, claims in fixed prosthodontics (bridgework), endodontics, periodontics and restorative dentistry together now account for over 50% of claims against dentists, although oral surgery remains the single treatment area most likely to give rise to litigation.

UK Dental Claims Data

Analyses of British dental malpractice data corresponding to the US surveys described above have not been available, other than by reference to the limited number of cases which reach a court. However UK defence organizations keep detailed records of all incidents and claims notified to them by their members. Such data, whilst highly confidential, is essential not only for accounting and actuarial purposes, but also to enable the organizations to pursue their aims of informing and alerting the professions to current problems and seeking to prevent avoidable mishap and injury. As part of this data collection process, the Medical Defence Union commissioned the installation of an enhanced computerized database in 1990. The author was able to access this database to review all dental claims and incidents reported to the Medical Defence Union over a 12-month period. The analyses presented below are a preliminary report of the results of this review.

The data examined consisted of all files opened between 1 August 1991 and 31 July 1992 which were initially dealt with by one member of the dental secretariat. Using the database classifications, all files not relating to indemnity matters (that is, all 'non-claim' files) were set aside. The remaining subset of new indemnity-related files numbered (n =) 317. These files were then analysed in further detail as described below. In this context, 'indemnity-related' claims are considered as those which have the potential to result in the payment of damages. Naturally, at the outset, with initial data only available, it is not possible in the great majority of cases to assess the probability of such an outcome. Of all these cases 105 (33%) arose from either informal or formal complaints within the National Health Service. Although the payment of damages to a complainant is not directly at issue in such cases, they do not preclude later civil action (See Chapter 7).

The claims and potential claims included in the data were drawn from dentists practising in the UK, both in NHS and private practice. As the time period selected was 18–30 months following the introduction of Crown indemnity, whereby health authorities and Trusts were responsible for claims incurred by employed staff on contracted duties, the majority of these files related to general dental practitioners.

Files analysis included: by practitioner and claimant characteristics; by private and NHS treatment; by treatment type and by treatment mix. Only the latter two variables are considered here. Discrimination between treatment types 'responsible' for claims is not, however, straightforward. In the first place, each claim relates to a specific incident, with individual characteristics particular to the treatment episode, and to the clinician and patient concerned. As has already been discussed, communication failure is a factor in many medico-legal claims (it was identified as a principal factor in 82 of the files reviewed here, for example). Additionally, as the data will show, analysis from the database is complex.

Although claims generally relate to an identified episode of care or treatment, there may be multiple factors involved. Initial reports or statements of claim may make reference to a sequence of events, from which the primary factor is not always, at the outset, entirely clear. For example, a patient may present with a painful tooth which is restored. Should symptoms continue, the restoration may be removed and endodontic therapy instituted. Further persistence of symptoms may lead ultimately to the extraction of the tooth, which may itself be attended by operative or post-operative complications. A claim results which might be categorized as: treatment failure; restorative care; endodontic therapy; and/or oral surgery. In order to classify such claims accurately it is essential to consider each in some detail by means of sub-analyses.

Table 5.1 shows the primary analysis of the 317 files by treatment type. This classification shows the ten most commonly identified features relating to particular treatments. Since some files contained more than one possible treatment category, as previously described, the total in the table exceeds the number of files analysed. In these categories, oral surgery/exodontia includes all surgical procedures; restoration/filling excludes endodontics and crown and bridgework, which are shown as separate categories.

Sub-analysis of the most common factor: oral surgery/exodontia is shown at Table 5.2. Whilst complications of the extraction procedure are

Table 5.1 Incidence of treatment types in 317 indemnity-related claims and complaints against dentists

Classification	No.	%
Oral surgery/exodontia	87	27.4
Restoration/filling	63	19.8
Endodontic	63	19.8
Crown/crownwork	61	19.2
Removable prosthetics/denture	53	16.7
Bridgework	25	7.8
Paedodontics	13	4.1
Orthodontics	9	2.8
Periodontal	9	2.8
Local analgesia	9	2.8

(Source: Medical Defence Union Ltd)

Table 5.2 Analysis of indemnity-related claims and complaints against dentists involving extraction

Sub-classification	No.	%
Complications of extraction	33	37.9
Unsatisfactory treatment leading to extraction	19	21.8
Lack of consent/erroneous extraction	11	12.7
Disputed fee concerning extraction	8	9.2
Unsatisfactory treatment following extraction	6	6.9
Orthodontic treatment failure involving extraction	5	5.7
Complication of general anaesthetic or sedation	3	3.5
Other	2	2.3
Total	n = 87	100.0

(Source: Medical Defence Union Ltd)

revealed as the most prevalent source of claims (37.9%), other factors are also significantly present in this sub-analysis. Treatment of the type listed in the unfortunate – but by no means rare – example given previously (restoration → endodontics → extraction) are categorized as 'unsatisfactory treatment leading to extraction'. This scenario is shown to be the next most common (21.8%) sub-category, followed by extraction carried out with alleged lack of consent or otherwise erroneous (due, for example to allegedly incorrect charting, diagnosis or referral details) (12.7%).

Remaining significant causes shown in the data include: disputed charges for treatment involving extraction; unsatisfactory treatment

Table 5.3 Further analysis of (33) indemnity-related claims and complaints against dentists involving complications of extraction. (Note: as one claim involved two allegations, totals exceed 100%.)

Sub-classification	No.	%
Retained root	17	51.5
Unspecified	5	15.2
Fracture of jaw	3	9.1
Soft tissue injury	3	9.1
Oro-antral fistula	2	6.1
Dislocated jaw	1	3.0
Crown fracture	1	3.0
Haemorrhage	1	3.0
Inhalation of fragment	1	3.0

(Source: Medical Defence Union Ltd)

following extraction; orthodontic treatment failure attributed to incorrect or unsatisfactory extraction; and complications of general anaesthesia or sedation employed for extraction.

Further sub-analysis of the most prevalent category – complications of extraction – is shown at Table 5.3. The identification of a retained root or fragment following extraction is the most commonly identified cause of claims. Such an allegation may only be made after some considerable time, for instance when acute infection occurs of the retained fragment and is identified.

In some files the precise nature of the problem cannot be identified from the initial report or statement of claim. Such cases have been noted as 'unspecified'.

Further analyses were carried out on the primary data and Tables 5.4 and 5.5 show the prevalence of principal causes of claims in the categories of 'restorative/filling' (excluding crown and bridgework) and 'endodontic' therapy. In reviewing claims submitted concerning alleged deficiencies in these categories further sources of potentially problematic classification appeared. Initial intimation of claims may be received either from the claimant in person or from solicitors. Not surprisingly, there is often considerable lay inexactitude in describing the complaint, and indeed much initial claims-handling time may be spent in clearly identifying the cause. Whilst 'extractions' are fairly well understood procedures from a lay viewpoint, more complex treatment is often wrongly identified.

Table 5.4 identifies causes of claims relating to restorations or 'fillings'. Some 22% of these claims proved to relate to endodontic

Table 5.4 Analysis of indemnity-related claims against dentists involving provision of fillings

Sub-classification	No.	%
Inadequate/unsatisfactory filling	18	29.0
Post-operative complication of filling	7	11.3
Complication of treatment: not filling itself	6	9.7
Unnecessary/erroneous filling	5	8.1
Breakdown of relationship	3	4.8
Fee dispute: filling	2	3.3
Root Canal filling	14	22.6
Cause not ascertained	4	6.4
Cause other than filling	3	4.8
Total	62	100.0

(Source: Medical Defence Union Ltd)

Table 5.5 Analysis of indemnity-related claims against dentists involving endodontic treatment

Sub-classification	No.	%
Inadequate/unsatisfactory root canal therapy	18	31.0
Post-operative complication of root canal therapy	11	19.1
Retained instrument	9	15.5
Fee dispute: root canal therapy	5	8.6
Ingested/inhaled instrument	3	5.2
Complication of treatment associated with root canal therapy	2	3.4
Claim associated with treatment prior to root canal therapy	3	5.1
Claim relating to other treatment	7	12.1
Total	58	100.0

(Source: Medical Defence Union Ltd)

therapy; a further 11% were due to treatment unrelated to the restorative work or were unspecified. Of the causes associated directly with restorations, the majority were ascribed to inadequacy of the restoration, or to post-operative complications such as pain, thermal sensitivity or recurrent replacement. Iatrogenic injuries such as laceration or haematoma occurring during restorative treatment were separately identified from failure of the restoration itself.

Claims relating to endodontic treatment were also examined for non-related causes: these most commonly arose in connection with crown and bridgework provided subsequently to otherwise satisfactory endodontics, or with treatment provided before endodontic therapy was instituted. 15% of correctly related claims cited retained endodontic instruments later identified within the tooth or periodontal tissues, and 5% inhaled or ingested instruments.

Specific risk management advice in relation to the more prevalent causes of claims identified through this review are given in the following section.

The claims experience identified from this sample was also compared with the total of indemnity-related dental claims received by the Medical Defence Union during the twelve month study period. This comparison was made using initial claims summaries, and whilst, as noted, some classifications require amendment during the claims-handling process (such as the confusion of fillings and endodontics), it is considered that these would affect the total and study claims equally. Table 5.6 shows the comparison between the UK–general practitioner study data and the worldwide data expressed as percentages of total cases reported. As in Table 5.1, all treatment categories included in the

Table 5.6 Comparison of category distribution of sample with all indemnity-related claims against dentists (worldwide) reported to the Medical Defence Union in the study period

Category	Entire claims experience %	Sample %
Oral surgery/exodontia	23.1	27.4
Restoration/filling	18.3	19.8
Endodontic	11.5	19.8
Crown/crownwork	16.5	19.2
Removable prosthetic	13.2	16.7
Bridgework	13.1	7.9
Paedodontic	5.7	4.1
Orthodontic	2.3	2.8
Periodontal	4.4	2.8
Local analgesia	2.1	2.8

(Source: Medical Defence Union Ltd)

initial intimation of the claim have been included, and more than one category may be cited in an individual case. The figures suggest that whilst the overall pattern is similar in rank order, claims relating to endodontics and removable prosthetics are proportionately more prevalent as a source of general practitioner claims in the UK, whilst periodontal problems and fixed bridgework account for greater percentages of 'all claims' reported. Certain categories of treatment, including the provision of dental implants, did not occur significantly in the UK data studied, but were represented in the worldwide data. Overall, however, implant-related claims accounted for under 2% of all dental indemnity-related claims, although numbers appear to be increasing.

All the data so far presented in this section relate to initial reports of dental claims. These initial claims, a high proportion of which will subsequently be discontinued, are none the less of interest and concern to practising dentists, since not only does their management consume considerable time and effort, but they are also indicative of problems in dental care as perceived by patients. It will be recalled that in Chapter 1, the majority of medical malpractice claims received by hospitals in the Harvard retrospective study were in fact unrelated to actual evidence of negligence;[23] patient perception of medical failure was a significant factor.

It is, however, advantageous to be able to relate 'closed claim' data to the initial indemnity-related claims received. Such information adds a further dimension to the understanding of particular problem areas. Hawkins notes from evidence submitted by the defence organizations to the Pearson Commission,[24,25] that approximately 60% of claims were abandoned, 35% settled before coming to court, and only 5% went to trial (of which 80% were successfully defended). Because of the length of time taken for cases to be pursued, it is very difficult to arrive at precise figures for dental negligence, but it must be concluded from the very small number of dental cases reported in Law Reports, and the few dental settlement figures quoted,[26] that only a very few (and probably less than the 5% quoted overall by defence organizations) dental negligence cases reach the courts.

Internal information held by the Medical Defence Union shows that in the 12 month period in which the sample data above was collected, only a small number – about 12% of the total UK dental indemnity-related new files opened – were formally considered for more advanced claims-handling procedures such as negotiation, expert reports, settlement, defence or trial preparation. Against this must be set the fact, however, that new UK dental cases received (including non-indemnity cases) had increased, on average by 12% per year, in the preceding five years. As the majority of the cases given such consideration during the study period had originated 2–4 years previously (and several more than 5 years previously), they would represent a higher percentage of those earlier years' claims. This data suggests that many putative claims against dentists are resolved or discontinued at an early stage with the expert assistance of the defence organizations. Further information on claims-handling as an integral part of risk management will be found in Chapter 9.

The cases referred during the year were analysed for treatment type. By this stage of claims-handling, a more precise identification is possible than at the inital report stage. Table 5.7 shows the breakdown by prevalence of treatment type. Individual cases may involve more than one category of treatment.

Complications or sequelae of oral surgical procedures form the largest percentage of these cases, with the extraction of third molars being the single most frequently occurring cause. The incidence of postoperative paraesthesia is a factor in many such claims. Crown and bridgework jointly account for the next most prevalent area of dentolegal problems reported in this period, aesthetics, occlusion, postoperative pain or root perforation being significant areas of concern. Alleged failure of other restorative dentistry, and of endodontic procedures are also identified in more than 5% of the cases considered.

Table 5.6 Analysis of dental cases referred for advanced claims-handling procedures 1991–1992, by principal factor

Treatment type	%
Oral surgery/extractions	30
Crown and Bridgework	24
Other restorative treatment (excluding endodontics)	9
Endodontics	7
Iatrogenic injury Paedodontics Local analgesia Medical complication of dental treatment Disciplinary Periodontal General anaesthesia/sedation Orthodontic Implant Fraud* Libel*	each < 5% of cases considered

*Such claims would only be considered where clinical care or professional principle was an integral element.

(Source: Medical Defence Union Ltd)

The identification and reduction of risk in clinical procedures

Data given in the preceding section suggests that particular causes of legal claims against dentists tend to recur in certain treatments. Notwithstanding the application of general risk management principles to dental practice as a whole, it would appear prudent to review these areas and to consider, in the light of past dento-legal experience and the recommendations of 'responsible bodies of professional opinion', what actions may be taken to avoid or to minimize litigation risks.

Diagnosis and treatment planning

Reference was made in the previous chapter to the necessity of keeping adequate records of diagnosis and treatment plans, including the importance of recording amendments and any deviations from the original proposals. Failures of diagnosis and treatment planning are implicit in many of the case analyses given above. Harris *et al.* have given an approach to diagnosis – specifically directed towards the treatment of facial pain, but in fact applicable widely in dental care – which invites the clinician to ask himself several important questions:

1 Can you establish that you were competent to diagnose and treat the condition? Can you recall the relevant training you have undergone, and your subsequent reading of relevant articles and textbooks?
2 Can you show that you have taken a proper history and carried out a proper examination? Are your notes sufficiently comprehensive to enable you to recollect what you found and did **not** find?
3 Are you able to justify your diagnosis and differentiate it from other conditions?
4 Having made your diagnosis, can you show that you were aware of the risks of proceeding with therapy, especially if the patient expressed a reluctance to undergo the treatment, or a history of an emotional disturbance which would impair a sympathetic relationship between yourself and the patient?
5 Can you show that it was proper for you to treat, rather than to refer?
6 Can you show that you monitored the effects of the treatment, and reconsidered the appropriateness of your treatment if it was proving less than successful?[27]

Whilst no-one would suggest that such a 'catechism' would be consciously recited at the outset of every routine course of treatment, awareness of these principles, and due consideration of them in proportion to the anticipated complexity, cost, or elusiveness of the diagnosis would be an ideal basis for the effective risk management of treatment planning.

In all cases, irrespective of the nature and extent of the treatment proposed, a planned approach to diagnosis is essential. Grace has suggested that this should comprise:[28]

1 Subjective information-gathering; listening to patient's presenting condition, medical, dental and social histories.
2 Objective information-gathering; intra- and extra-oral examination, radiographs, other tests
3 Assessment; integration of all findings, differential diagnosis
4 Treatment plan/consultation; discussion with patient, evolution of definitive plan
5 Education; explanation to patient of treatment, patient involvement, prognosis.

The detail of medical history required has already been discussed: opportunity should be taken routinely to record the identity of the patient's usual medical practitioner, to whom reference should be made if there is any doubt about the patient's medication or fitness to undergo treatment. Cases of subacute bacterial endocarditis, which remains a life-threatening condition, continue to occur following dental intervention without appropriate antibiotic cover.[29]

Examination, both extra-oral and intra-oral, should be conducted methodically, and with thoroughness. It is notable that many record charts do not show pre-existent restorations, but only existing lesions and intended treatment. If problems should arise later, the record chart and any diagnostic study casts may prove invaluable in confirming the pre-operative state.

Radiographs may be an essential part of the examination and diagnostic procedure. As noted in Chapter 3, good radiographic procedures balance the need to avoid unnecessary exposure of the patient against the legal requirement to obtain adequate clinical information to form a diagnosis and plan treatment. There are no 'hard and fast' rules for clinicians to work by, although recommendations for the usage and frequency of radiographic procedures for caries monitoring and detection,[30] and for periodontal assessment,[31] as well as in other specialities, are periodically updated and published. Dentists should be aware of the current recommendations. Further comments on the advisability of dental X-rays will be found in the following sections.

Shanley has commented that:

'... there is growing evidence from different sources that the quality of X-rays needs to be improved .... It is difficult to prepare a defence without the benefit of properly angled, exposed, developed and fixed X-rays.'[32]

It is not unusual for dental X-rays to be blank, stuck together, unidentified as to patient, date or view, or occasionally all of the above. In one instance where assessment of the preoperative status of an impacted mandibular third molar was vital in the defence of a claim, the panoral film had been trimmed to fit the patient's record card, neatly eliminating the one essential area.

It is also essential to review those radiographs which have been taken.[33] Obvious root perforations or inadequately obturated root canals revealed by post-operative X-rays, but noted only after a considerable time has elapsed (usually by a subsequent dentist), are not uncommon. In some such instances, it would have been possible to avert or at least diminish the consequences of the mishap; however, compounded by a failure to note the position or alert the patient at the earliest opportunity, the position may be indefensible.

Periodontal treatment

The diagnosis and treatment of periodontal disease is significant in dental litigation in two distinct ways. First, a failure to provide a timely diagnosis or therapy may be alleged as a cause of premature tooth loss;

second, the provision of other restorative treatment in the presence of identifiable periodontal disease may impair or negate the value of that treatment or, indeed, accelerate periodontal breakdown.

The UK has not, as yet, seen the growth in 'failure to diagnose and treat' litigation which has been experienced in the United States.[34] However, such actions do arise, and are gradually increasing both in number and cost of settlement. Understanding of the disease processes and appropriate treatment rationales in this field has changed greatly in recent years,[35] but certain fundamental requirements remain. The presence of periodontal pathology must be identified, recorded and monitored. The patient should be informed of the condition and prognosis and informed consent should be secured for any proposed treatment. Patient involvement in therapy is critical to success, and instructions given, together with the degree of compliance obtained, must be recorded. Finally, any concerns about competence to treat a particular condition, or the management of refractory or atypical periodontal disease would indicate a need for referral.

Accurate initial assessment of the periodontal condition is vital if subsequent changes – hopefully for the better, but even more significantly if deterioration occurs – are to be correctly interpreted. The CPITN coding has been suggested as a basic screening procedure.[38] More detailed records will be needed where the presence of pathology indicates a requirement for active treatment, and both Grace and Smales,[39] and Strahan and Waite[38] have proposed suitable systems.

The provision of further restorative treatment in the presence of periodontal disease is problematic. On the one hand, the ideal circumstance would be that periodontal health and plaque control were optimal before further treatment was instituted; on the other, the patient's condition may be apparently stable, although not perfect, and the need for further treatment may be overriding – for instance, the replacement of a fractured or missing incisor.

Smith commented:

> ... providing the [treatment] without making a reasonable attempt to treat periodontal problems would probably be construed as negligent. However, if periodontal treatment is less than 100% successful or if the patient (despite every effort by the dentist) is unable to maintain a good standard of oral hygiene, there are still occasions when it is reasonable to provide crowns or bridges and where to do so is not negligent.[39]

Needless to say, the circumstances and reasoning behind such decisions should be communicated to the patient, and recorded fully in the notes.

Restorative dentistry

As was noted in the defence organization statistical data, crowns, bridges and endodontics were the principal areas in restorative dentistry which gave rise to claims during the study period. A preponderance of crown and bridge cases were concerned with complex multiple or full arch reconstructive or aesthetic dentistry. Not unnaturally, when such cases give rise to successful claims, settlements may have to be effected at considerable cost. Care with treatment planning, discussion with the patient and establishment of the expected outcome and prognosis, together with any significant risks must therefore precede any procedure of this nature. It must be possible to show that 'reasonable care' was taken, and where extensive treatment is envisaged, it would be expected that a dentist would act with the forethought and judgement appropriate to the case.

On the other hand:

> The dentist is neither a guarantor of a favourable outcome nor an insurer of the patient. The courts recognize that, with the exercise of the best of skills, there is often no way to be sure of the outcome, and they will not permit recovery [of damages] solely because of lack of success.[40]

A review of problems arising from restorative cases highlights certain recurrent themes. Crowns and bridges which have unacceptable marginal discrepancies, giving a potential for plaque accumulation, caries, periodontal inflammation, thermal sensitivity or pulpal irritation, are a source of continual litigation. Smith has suggested guidelines for a standard of marginal fit which might be regarded as 'minimally acceptable' – that is to say, the usual standard should exceed the following:[39]

- The marginal gap should be invisible to the naked eye
- If cement has washed out, a probe tip should not be able to enter the margin
- Overhangs or deficiencies should be less than 0.5 mm, and should be capable of being adjusted or polished.

The aesthetics of fitted restorations must be entirely acceptable to the patient before permanent cementation. If any doubt exists, it will, in the long run, prove far less costly in time and laboratory fees to cement restorations provisionally. Inviting patients to be accompanied by a third party on the fitting appointment may be helpful. Avoid 'pressurising' patients at this stage.

The occlusion must be comfortable to the patient. A further indication for provisional cementation in major restorative cases is to allow time for occlusal adaptation although ideally this would not be necessary. Pre-operative and post-operative notes of occlusal contacts which hold shimstock are valuable. Extensive occlusal adjustment post-cementation may lead to unacceptable aesthetics or function, or to the presence of areas of unglazed porcelain which accelerate wear on opposing natural dentition.

Root perforations during the preparation for post crown fitting are a fairly regular medico-legal occurrence. Whilst unfavourable or unpredictable morphology may play a part, the majority of such incidents arise from mis-angulation, unsuitable instrumentation or post choice, or failure to refer to pre-operative radiographs. In the absence of any documented evidence of a known risk, explained to and accepted by the patient pre-operatively, perforations are difficult to defend, and subsequent remedial treatment, either surgical or restorative, may be prolonged.

In any major restorative case, pre-operative and working casts, laboratory notes, shade diagrams, etc. should all be retained for future reference should problems later arise.

Complications with endodontic treatment may give rise to complaints and claims for a variety of reasons. These broadly fall into two categories; those occurring during therapy, and those which arise some time later. In the former group, difficulties may be encountered due to case selection or procedures during treatment itself.

The selection of appropriate cases for treatment, referral or extraction is fundamental, and in most cases the availability of an adequate intra-oral radiograph is a prerequisite. Unfavourable or atypical morphology, partial or complete calcification of the canal, or gross apical pathology are all examples of factors which may be overlooked. If complications present, then referral or alternative treatment may need consideration.[41]

One significant source of litigation arising during endodontic treatment remains the inhaled/ingested instrument. Given that recommendations for the protection of the pharynx and airway are unequivocal,[42] such occurrences are mostly indefensible. A small but regular number of cases arise each year, usually in relation to endodontic treatment.

Failure to obtain an adequate apical seal is a further source of difficulty. It has been shown that success in endodontics is closely related to the position of the seal,[43] whilst a combination of a diagnostic radiograph and an apex locator is the ideal way to determine the correct working length, a failure to use either may significantly weaken a practitioner's case should symptoms persist.

The fracture of an endodontic instrument in a canal is not, in itself, an indication of negligence. Failure to record both the occurrence and the provision of appropriate advice to the patient, however, may well be considered negligent. It may be that a post-operative radiograph was not taken, or that it was never reviewed. It may simply be that a small fracture went unnoticed. In many cases, years, and several changes of practitioner, may have elapsed before symptoms recur.

Finally, the use of potentially irritant or toxic endodontic materials, or the trans-apical extrusion of irrigant or sealant, can give rise to permanent and distressing symptoms. The use of paraformaldehyde-containing sealants is to be avoided, and care taken with all irrigation and sealant materials; even zinc-oxide or calcium hydroxide based sealants have produced permanent paraesthesia when introduced to the mandibular canal.

Other restorative risks

Another potentially toxic material in restorative care is phosphoric acid or citric acid etchant. Despite several recent case reports, lip, facial or eye injuries continue to occur. Some patients appear to exhibit particular sensitivity to these agents, and develop seemingly disproportionate scarring in response to transitory contact. Coloured gel forms, dispensed from a disposable brush, are more identifiable and controllable. The material should never be passed over the patient, and eye-protection is mandatory. Care must be taken when washing such agents off etched enamel. to avoid blowing the material onto unprotected skin or mucosa. Facial scarring is an especially emotive topic.

Oral Surgery

Claims relating to extraction and oral surgical procedures were the most prevalent in the study population examined above. Of these, the identification of retained roots accounted for 50% of notified claims. In the 'advanced claims handling' data, third molar surgery was the single most prevalent category of treatment.

Once again, case selection and record keeping play a major role in the risk management of oral surgery. There is no legal or professional dictum which suggests that pre-operative radiographs are necessary before the routine extraction of a tooth with no significant findings in the medical or dental history of the patient. It is, however, considered inadvisable to embark on surgical treatment or the removal of impacted teeth without the benefit of good and appropriate X-rays.[24] Where tooth or root fracture occurs during extraction, there are sound and accepted bases for deciding whether removal of the fragment is justified,[45] and whether any treatment should be immediate, referred or delayed. It is not necessarily negligent that a fracture has occurred; once again, it is the failure to record the event, to advise the patient and to decide on appropriate further treatment (recording these facts too) which may lead to later difficulties.

In the case of impacted third molars, pre-operative radiographs should be regarded as essential. In the case of mandibular teeth, the radiograph(s) must show the relationship of the tooth to surrounding structures, including the inferior alveolar nerve and the lower border of the mandible.[46]

Lingual or labial paraesthesia resulting from lower third molar removal is a complication which has been shown to occur in a small but significant number of cases. Rood noted that labial sensory loss might occur in 7–8% of cases (permanent in 0.25–2.2%, dependent on technique), and lingual sensory loss in 5–13% (permanent in 0–2%),[47] and suggested that use of a bur to remove buccal and distal bone – as opposed to a chisel was statistically associated with a higher number of such complications. As previously discussed (Chapter 4), the implications of findings such as these are that patients' informed consent to the removal of impacted lower third molars should always include a warning of the possibility of paraesthesia, and this warning must be recorded.

Jaw fracture during extraction is a rarer complication, but both mandibular, and maxillary tuberosity fractures are a possible consequence of dental surgery, and occasionally give rise to claims. The courts have held that fracture occurring in the course of an extraction is not, of itself negligent where it is shown that an appropriate and orthodox technique was employed.[48] A practitioner's actions, once it was suspected or known that such an event had occurred, would properly be scrutinized, and prompt and appropriate management and referral would be expected.

Cases of mistaken extraction have been referred to in an earlier chapter. Apart from those cases which arise from a mistaken diagnosis, errors of this nature are most commonly litigated under one of two circumstances; those of referral, and general anaesthesia (frequently combined). In referral cases, it is possible that the operating dentist may not have direct knowledge of the patient's originally presenting condition, or, in orthodontic cases, may be acting on the instructions of the orthodontist. The extracting dentist is, however, the person upon whom the legal responsibility will, at least initially, fall, and he cannot abrogate that responsibility. If the referring dentist's instructions are unclear, the operating dentist has a duty to satisfy himself that the tooth or teeth to be extracted are the correct ones. If he feels in any doubt about the appropriateness of the treatment, he should make further enquiries and record that fact, deferring treatment if it is reasonable and necessary to do so. Administration of general anaesthesia should not commence until the operating dentist has had the opportunity to verify and identify the teeth for removal. Where lists of referral patients are seen, it is advisable for the patient's identity to be checked against the notes on at least two occasions, and one good example of risk management in this instance is the charting of the teeth for removal in thick felt tip on a sheet of blank paper bearing the patient's name, and attached to the notes which are placed in the surgery or theatre in such a way that the notation is visible and clear.

The growing interest in, and success of dental implantology carries with it new risks in dentistry, as well as new opportunities and benefits.

At one time, implants were regarded as experimental and patients warned that failure was likely. However, expectations have risen and failures are not so readily accepted. Implants are expensive, and so are the appliances fitted to them. There is a large amount of money at stake which means that failure is more likely to result in litigation.[39]

As with the diagnosis of facial pain, there may be psychological factors overlying requests for implants, and cases occur of their prescription and supply to patients who are ill-equipped, both mentally and physically, or ill-prepared for the degree of co-operation and persistence needed for satisfactory results to be obtained. As one leading implant surgeon has noted, the expression 'I would never have had it done if I had known' is a common expression in these unhappy instances.[49]

The use of implants requires considerable prior investment by dentists intending their use; in educational activity, in selection of a reputable and proved armamentarium, and not least in the provision of surgery facilities to the high and demanding standards required. There is no substitute for this commitment, nor for the requirement to counsel patients fully and candidly, and to secure their informed consent in writing. Implant cases are, as yet, a dento-legal minority in the UK, but worldwide information indicates that their frequency is growing.

Local analgesia

Local analgesia merits a mention as claims arising from alleged complications and side-effects of its use are frequent. The majority of these allegations are dealt with by the provision of suitable and authoritative information, but on occasions considerable time and trouble is expended on their management. Local anaesthetic agents are, of course, very extensively employed, and this very routine use, together with the high margin of safety available from modern agents can very easily induce a casual approach.[50] From the patient's viewpoint, intra-oral injections rate as one of the most-feared aspects of dentistry,[51] and any resulting complications may have a powerful effect.

Of local complications, haematoma and persistent paraesthesia are most commonly reported in claims. Whilst these unfortunate effects are mostly of short duration and can occur even with all possible attention to technique and materials, they may nevertheless result in threat of legal action. For this reason, every effort should be made to reassure and to inform the patient, and follow-up care provided. Modern disposable needles of fine gauge are more readily able to inflict damage on small vessels,[52] and the use of an aspirating technique and injection ahead of the advancing needle tip may help to minimize such trauma.

Whilst reaction or idiosyncrasy to modern anaesthetic agents is extremely rare, systemic effects from the inadvertent introduction of local anaesthetic solution are most commonly due to the accompanying vasoconstrictor. The resulting faint, particularly in a nervous patient, can be profound and even life-threatening if not observed, and if the patient is maintained in an upright position. Patients who have received local anaesthetic injections should never be left unattended, in a surgery, waiting room or elsewhere. Settlements have been effected in claims where patients have collapsed, suffering traumatic injuries, on stairways, in X-ray rooms, and even in a practice front garden, where the patient had gone (with permission from staff) to have a cigarette 'whilst the local took'. A duty of care is owed to such patients, who are technically, and actually, under treatment.

Removable prosthetics

The provision of dentures attracts a proportion of dento-legal problems. The issue of Contract Law has been raised in an earlier section of this Chapter, but allegations of negligence may also arise where a demonstrable failure to exercise a duty of care has occurred.

Much may depend, in prosthetics, on the patient's expectations, and the degree to which these are reinforced or sublimated by the dentist at initial consultation. Careful notes of all that is said at initial appointments should be maintained, and the presence of a dental surgery assistant may prove to be helpful later if disputes arise; an attentive staff member will often recall – aided by the record notes – details of such visits.

Where immediate dentures are to be provided, there is much to be said for obtaining the patient's signature on a simple declaration that explanations regarding the temporary nature of such prostheses have been given. Pre-printed forms are available for this purpose.[53] Whilst these are not legally 'fire-proof' (little is), they will often assist in dissuading a potential claimant.

Trial fittings of dentures should always permit time for the patient to make an unhurried assessment of function and appearance. The presence of a family member or friend may be helpful. The patient's acceptance of the trial set-up should be recorded. Where considerable changes to appearance or occlusion are envisaged, or forcefully requested, particular care should be taken, possibly to the extent of permitting trial dentures to be taken away (with suitable written cautions) for assessment in familiar surroundings.

Once finished dentures are inserted, the law holds that they become the patient's property, even though payment has not been made. Attempts to remove dentures in circumstances where the patient's intentions are in doubt can lead, and have done so, to criminal charges and the consequent attentions of the General Dental Council. Payment, or partial payment, in advance may be preferable to interminable fee-chasing later.

New technology or treatments

Dentists are advised to take particular care when adopting forms of treatment which are innovative. Reference has been made to the potential risks of implantology, and it has been suggested not only that considerable attention focuses on the 'hardware', but that this area is relatively poorly regulated.[39] The use of lasers in dentistry is another recent trend and caution should again be employed in securing data from the manufacturer which quotes independently refereed evidence of safety and fitness for the purposes described. Reputable makers will regard such enquiries as prudent and reasonable. Finally, in providing such cosmetic care as collagen replacement therapy, patients must be made fully aware in advance (and in writing) of the future maintenance costs involved. See also Chapter 7, concerning the definition of 'dental treatment' and its relevance to indemnity cover. Dentists undertaking any advanced or innovative treatment should ensure that they and their staff are fully and properly trained and that patients are given comprehensive advice and information concerning their intended care.

Emergency Treatment

The provision of emergency treatment may be fraught with legal hazards, although such claims are, in the event, rather less common than might be anticipated. It is certainly prudent to ask oneself:

- Is it essential to this patient's well-being that this treatment is carried out now and under these conditions (lack of staff, lack of time, lack of facilities)?
- Should a problem arise, how would my actions be interpreted in retrospect?

- Is the treatment proposed the least, reasonably speaking, that can be undertaken to resolve the problem complained of?

Should answers to these questions give rise to uncertainty, then alternative approaches might be considered. Removal of wisdom teeth or buried roots when operating alone and at night have certainly proved, in the past, to be matters of regret for all parties.

The myth persists that doctors and dentists are at risk if they render emergency assistance to, say, the victim of a road accident – the so-called 'Good Samaritan' act. Hawkins has attributed the origin of this to a survey carried out by the American Medical Association, which revealed,[54] in the 1970s that 50% of physicians would not stop to help, so fearful were they of litigation. Many US states have enacted laws specifically to protect doctors (and dentists) in these circumstances, and no known case in this category has been identified in the UK or US.

A word of caution might be offered, however, in respect of dental advice given *gratis* outside the practice. A dentist who advised a friend or acquaintance would have a duty of care in such circumstances, even though no payment or formal agreement for treatment existed.

Failure to complete treatment

It was suggested in Chapter 3 that care must be exercised in the collection of overdue accounts. Nowhere is this so important as when treatment is incomplete. It may well be that the patient has moved, gone on holiday, or been affected by illness or other trauma – and fails to respond to repeated contact. An expensive piece of laboratory work lying unfitted in a drawer can lead to vituperative letters or over-hasty County Court writs. Be certain in such cases that the patient is not in fact dissatisfied or has not suffered some complication of treatment, preferably by including, in early correspondence or communication, a request to contact the practice should there be any reason why a further appointment has not been made.

The records of patients who fail to return and whose condition may deteriorate should receive attention from the treating dentist, who should over his own signature or initials determine the appropriate action to be taken. Particularly where treatment has been instituted such as the opening of a root canal, or the initial management of an acute infection, it should be clearly documented that reasonable attempts to complete the treatment and to contact the patient have been made.

Patients who fail to attend for referral appointment should similarly be followed up. It is not sufficient to rely on the hospital consultant, or other party, to make enquiries; the duty of care does not end because a referral appointment has been made. In a parallel medical case, a doctor referred a patient to hospital for an anti-tetanus injection. The injection was not given (because the patient did not go), and the GP failed to confirm this when he saw the patient again. The patient died, and the GP was found liable.[55]

Conclusion

It should not be considered that the foregoing section amounts to a comprehensive clinical risk management strategy. The problems and events illustrated form only a small part of the many complications and hazards which attend dental practice. Their selection is solely on the basis of frequency or known dento-legal severity as reflected in the data considered earlier. Such prevalence varies continuously, and there is no substitute for continued attention to current dental and related literature, as well as the specialist advice offered by defence organizations.

The components of the dentist's legal duty of care have been summarised as; forethought, judgement, skill and care. The common problems cited above all result from a failure of one of these components, and effective risk management is a blend of them all.

References

1. *Pippin* v. *Shepherd* (1822) C Exch. 11 Price 400
2. See *Ashcroft* v. *Mersey Regional Health Authority* (1983) 2 All ER 245
3. Mason J.K. and McCall Smith R.A. (1991) *Law and Medical Ethics*. Butterworths, London, p. 211–213
4. *Bolam* v. *Friern Hospital Management Committee* (1957) 2 All ER 118
5. *Crawford* v. *Board of Governors of Charing Cross Hospital* (1953) CA *The Times*, 8 December
6. Nelson-Jones R. and Burton F. (1990) *Medical Negligence Case Law*. Fourmat, London, p. 41
7. *Garner* v. *Morrell.* CA (1953) *The Times*, 31 October
8. *Fish* v. *Kapur* (1948) 2 All ER 146
9. *Lock* v. *Scantlebury* (1963) *The Times*, 25 July
10. See: s 2(4) *Law Reform (Personal Injuries) Act* (1948)
11. Schroeder O.C. and Pollack B.R. (1987) Dental malpractice; laws for conducting professional practice, in, *Handbook of Dental Jurisprudence and Risk Management* (Pollack B. R. ed.). PSG Publishing, Littleton, Mass.
12. *Connor* v. *Fison-Clarke* (1987) QBD 9 October
13. *Appleby* v. *Sleep* (1968) CA. 2 All ER 265
14. Nelson Jones R. and Burton F. (1990) Op. cit. p. 14
15. *Supply of Goods and Services Act (1982)*, s4(5)
16. *Gordon* v. *Goldberg* (1920) 2 *The Lancet* 264
17. Ryan M. (1993) We have ways of making you talk. *Journal of the Medical Defence Union*, **9** (3), 64–65
18. General Dental Council (1993) *Professional Conduct and Fitness to Practice*. General Dental Council, London, Paragraph 21
19. Milgrom P. (1975) Quality control of end results: identifying avoidable adverse events

in dentistry. *Journal of the American Dental Association*, **90**, 1282–1290
20. Tancredi L.R. (1974) Identifying avoidable adverse events in medicine. *Medical Care*, **12**, 935–941
21. Milgrom P., Fiset L., Getz T. *et al.* (1993) Dental Malpractice Experience; A Closed Claim Study. *Medical Care*, **31** (8) 749–756
22. Milgrom P., Fiset L., Whitney C. *et al.* (1994) Malpractice claims during 1988–1992: a National survey of dentists. *Journal of the American Dental Association*, **125**, 462–469
23. Localio A.R., Lawthers A.G., Brennan T.A. *et al.* (1991) Relation Between Malpractice Claims and Adverse Events Due to Negligence. *The New England Journal of Medicine*, **325** (4), 245–251
24. Hawkins C. (1985) *Mishap or Malpractice?* Blackwell Scientific, London, p. 160
25. *Pearson Commission (1978)* Royal Commission on Civil Liability and Compensation for Personal Injury. HMSO, London
26. See, *Sweet and Maxwell, The Quantum of Damages*, Kemp and Kemp, London. This publication, updated regularly, lists all reported court settlements categorized by type of injury
27. Harris M., Feinemann C., Wise M. *et al.* (1993) Temporomandibular joint and orofacial pain: clinical and medicolegal management problems. *British Dental Journal*, **174** (4), 129–136
28. Advisory Board in General Dental Practice (1991). *Self Assessment Manual and Standards* (Grace M, ed.). Royal College of Surgeons of England, London. p. 2.1.6
29. Franklin C.D. (1992) The aetiology, epidemiology, pathogenesis and changing pattern of infective endocarditis, with a note on prophylaxis. *British Dental Journal*, **172** (10), 369–373
30. Pitts N.B. and Kidd E.A.M.(1992) The prescription and timing of bitewing radiography in the diagnosis and management of dental caries: contemporary recommendations. *British Dental Journal*, **172** (6), 225–227
31. Hirschmann P.N., Horneris K. and Rushton V..E (1994) Selection Criteria for periodontal radiography. *British Dental Journal*, **176** (9), 324–325
32. Shanley D.B. (1990) Litigation and dental defence – and Irish perspective. *Journal of the Medical Defence Union*, **6** (4), 54–58
33. Ibid
34. Anderson P.E. (1992) Are you playing Russian Roulette? *Dental Economics*, June 1992, 77–80
35. Ciancio S.G., Newman M.G. and Shafer R. (1992). Recent advances in periodontal diagnosis and treatment: exploring new treatment alternatives. *Journal of the American Dental Association*, **123** (10), 34–43
36. Croxson L.J.A. (1984) A simplified periodontal screening examination: the Community Periodontal Index of Treatment Needs (WHO) in practice. *International Dental Journal*, **34** 28–34
37. Grace A.M. and Smales F.C. (1989) *Periodontal control an effective system for diagnosis, selection, control and treatment planning in general practice*. Quintessence, London
38. Strahan J.D. and Waite I.M. (1990) *A Colour Atlas of Periodontology*. Wolfe Medical, London, Appendix 3
39. Smith B.G.N. (1991) Negligence in restorative dentistry. *Dental Update*, November 1991, 374–381
40. Warshafsky T. (1982) Plaintiff's view of malpractice litigation. *Dental Clinics of North America*, **26** (2), 333–339
41. Rosenberg R.J. and Goodis H.E. (1992) Endodontic case selection: to treat or to refer. *Journal of the American Dental Association*, **123**, 57–63
42. Harty F. (1990) *Endodontics in Clinical Practice*. Wright, Bristol

43. Stock C. (1994) Endodontics – position of the apical seal. *British Dental Journal*, **176** (9), 329
44. Shanley D. B. op. cit.
45. Caplin R.L. (1989) Oral Surgery: Assessment and Treatment. *British Dental Journal*, **166** (2), 128–131
46. Collins M.R.N. (1988) Paraesthesia following lower wisdom tooth extraction. *Journal of the Medical Defence Union*, **4** (2), 41–43
47. Rood J.P. (1992) Permanent damage to inferior alveolar and lingual nerves during the removal of impacted mandibular third molars. Comparison of two methods of bone removal. *British Dental Journal*, **172** (3), 108–110
48. *Fish* v. *Kapur* (1948) 2 All ER 176
49. Harris D. (1993) Osseointegrated implants: I would never have had it done if I had Known. *British Dental Journal*, **175** (7), 261–262
50. Moore P.A. (1992) Preventing local Anesthesia Toxicity. *Journal of the American Dental Association*, **123**, 60–64
51. Gale E.N. (1972) Fears of the dental situation. *Journal of Dental Research*, **51**, 964–966
52. Roberts D.H. and Sowray J.H. (1980) *Local Analgesia In Dentistry*. Wright, Bristol, p. 112
53. 'Admor' Ltd, Barnham, Sussex PO22 0EW
54. Hawkins C. (1985) op. cit. p. 243
55. *Coles* v. *Reading Hospital Management Committee and Another* (1963) 107 SJ 115

6
Risk transfer, insurance and indemnity

Background

In Chapter 1, it was shown that risks could not always be avoided: we cannot anticipate the occurrence of all hazards. The freak storm which removes the surgery roof, the burst water main which closes the practice for a week, a broken wrist during a skiing holiday; risks such as these can neither be foreseen nor reasonably prevented without either major or unsustainable changes in lifestyle, or unwarranted caution in working practices.

Such risks usually have two attributes. First, they are rare, or sufficiently uncommon in each individual's experience as to make the calculation of their occurrence impossible with any degree of accuracy. Second, risks of this kind may well be severe; that is, their occurrence may have a major impact on the viability of our work or business. These factors are, however, related to the nature and size of the business affected. A sole practitioner who loses a month's income from his surgery may face serious financial difficulty, whilst the same loss of a single clinician's output in a large health authority may be far less serious and indeed may be budgeted for.

Very uncommon or unforeseeable risks, particularly those which pose a serious threat to the organization, are frequently (though not always) less amenable to risk management or control. These risks are commonly transferred – most often by the effecting of insurance.

It is often said that insurance is not so much the transfer of risk – since no matter how complete the insurance, there will always be some residual loss or effect following a claim – as the financing of risk. It will be recalled that, in Chapter 1, insurance was described as the exchange of an unquantified and unexpected loss (a claim) for a known and regular loss (the premium) which could be allowed for by inclusion in the annual budget.

Also, since no risk management programme can be so effective as to eliminate all foreseeable risks (those for which the chances of incidence **can** be calculated), insurance has a role in the financing of these. It is, for example, possible to estimate the chances of a motor vehicle theft, a surgery break-in or a professional negligence claim. Whilst risk management can certainly reduce this incidence, insurance is a prudent and in some cases obligatory line of additional defence.

As has been pointed out, risk management and insurance are not alternative, but complementary strategies. The theft of a practice computer, even though the item is subsequently replaced under an insurance policy, will still cause inconvenience and financial loss; an effective security system will minimize this risk. Equally, a failure to have adequate security measures may increase the insurance premium (or even make insurance unobtainable) – the two aspects are closely intertwined. The intention, through the correct combination of risk management and insurance, is the minimization of the total cost of risk.

Insurance

Although, in Great Britain and many other countries, indemnity against medical and dental professional liability is provided chiefly by medical defence organizations which are not, legally speaking, insurance companies, most other risk financing and transfer – for third party, property and employer liabilities for instance – is transacted by means of insurance contracts. This section gives a general overview of the law relating to insurance.

An early judicial definition of insurance was given by Lord Mansfield in 1766,[1] who commented that 'Insurance is a contract upon speculation'. At this time, prior to the Life Assurance Act 1774, gambling and wagering were enforceable contracts at law. A great deal of the financial activity surrounding the workings of the City of London and other commercial centres in the early eighteenth century was little more than a lottery – the 'South Sea Bubble' being one notorious venture. The 1774 Act restricted life and other insurance business to parties who 'had an interest' in the outcome. The House of Lords later defined this as follows:

> A man is interested in a thing to whom advantage may arise or prejudice happen from the circumstances which may attend it . . .

> . . . having some relation to, or concern in the subject of the insurance, which relation or concern by the happening of the perils insured against may be so affected as to produce a damage, detriment or prejudice. . . .[2]

Further definitions of what did, or did not, constitute an insurance contract were later clarified in the courts. These included the principle of indemnity, whereby, on the occurrence of some adverse event, a benefit – usually the payment of money – would accrue to the insured person. The courts also noted that in indemnity insurance there must be some degree of uncertainty about the event occurring, together with evidence of some 'consideration' on the part of the insured, normally in the form of a periodic premium payment. These four factors, then; interest, premium, uncertainty and indemnity, form the basis of indemnity insurance.

The other chief class of insurance – contingency insurance – should be briefly mentioned here. A contingency is an event which will certainly occur, although there is uncertainty about its timing. Moreover, a contingency is not an event which will necessarily financially disadvantage the insured person. Life insurance is the principal example of contingency insurance.

Since the failure of an insurer could have grave financial consequences, insurance business is regulated by statute in most countries. In the United Kingdom, the Insurance Companies Act (1982) lays down strict controls on the carrying on of this class of business. Generally, such business may be conducted only by companies authorized by the Secretary of State for Trade, or by individual members of Lloyd's.[3]

Insurers are required to meet certain standards of probity and of financial security, including the maintenance of reserve funds which are more than adequate to discharge their likely liabilities in the event of worst case claims scenarios. They are, in effect, entitled to carry forward these funds from year to year free of taxation, and this exemption is recognition of the risks borne. Readers of the financial press will be well aware that members of Lloyd's are personally liable for the contractual losses of their 'syndicates' (the approximate Lloyd's equivalent of an insurance company) to the full extent of their personal assets.

In practice, commercial insurers will bear only a part of the risks which they underwrite (contract for), and will themselves seek insurance for the remainder, through specialist contracts of reinsurance. In a typical contract, therefore, a property owner will pay a premium to an insurer against damage to his buildings. The contract will often bear an 'excess', being the first part of the cost of any claim which will be paid by the owner himself. The insurance company will itself re-insure against losses over a certain amount, whilst 'retaining' part of the risk. In the event of a catastrophic event, such as an earthquake resulting in widespread and severe property damage, this network system ensures that the loss is widely spread, with no individual or company having to bear more than is commercially prudent.

From their earliest inception, insurers have needed to be able to calculate risks, in order to show a profit on the premiums they collect. In the early eighteenth century, Edmund Halley, the astronomer royal, produced the first reliable mortality tables for life assurance, and the profession of actuaries grew in response to the demand for more and varied insurance products. The calculation of an insurer's total risk exposure is therefore a central and essential part of its business strategy, enabling it to set premiums at a level which will both maintain its reserves and produce a dividend for its shareholders after paying operating costs.

Insured risks

Broadly, insurers use two methods of assessing risks, known as class rating and experience rating.[4] Class rating considers the claims experience of all similar policies. Thus, when setting premium levels for motor vehicle insurance, the company will review its past claim statistics for car accidents, theft, etc. The accuracy of its calculations will improve in relation to the total number of similar policies written and to the degree of similarity that can be obtained. To continue the example, the more motor policies a company writes, the more accurate should be its prediction of risk levels. It will also be able to assess, for instance, risk factors relating to driver age and address, and car type.

In contrast to class rating, experience rating considers the claims history of the insured, and by analogy with the factors determining the accuracy of class rating, risk calculation is improved with more extensive knowledge of the insured's claims record.

All of the above will be familiar to the motorist who completes an insurance proposal. The proposal form will include questions relating to both class rating and experience rating aspects of the risk. Data such as age, postal address, occupation, car type will be used for class rating, whilst driving experience, claims and conviction record will reflect experience. Similar considerations will apply in all risk insurance contracts.

Difficulties may arise where inadequate data exists, either because the insured has no 'record', or where the company is itself writing business in a new area. In the former case, the company may 'load' the initial premium to guard against possible claims. In the latter case, extensive research may be needed to assess risk factors and claims levels.

Insurance proposals

In assessing risk, the insurance company must rely, to a great extent or indeed wholly, on information given by the proposer in the insurance proposal. It has been noted that; 'There is no class of documents as to which the strictest good faith is more rigidly required in courts of law than policies of insurance.'[5]

It is therefore a basic underlying tenet of insurance that each party to an insurance contract shall abide by the principle of *uberrima fides* – utmost good faith. This legal term requires that; '... the insurer must correctly represent the period the risk will be covered, and the proposer must not only be completely honest, but also must make full disclosure of all facts material to the insurance.'[6]

This requirement, moreover, applies to the parties throughout the period of the contract. It is in distinction to the general principles of English contract law, which lays no obligation on the parties to a contract to disclose pertinent information to the other side. (It should also be noted that, in recognition of the particular nature of contracts of insurance, the provisions of the Unfair Contracts Terms Act (1977) do not apply to such contracts.)

Material information has been defined as that which would influence the insurer's judgement in setting a premium, or accepting the risk[7]. Clearly, this is a broad definition, and one which seemingly – and actually – allows insurers a good deal of latitude, since in the event of any subsequent dispute they have only to satisfy a court that, on the balance of probabilities, any information withheld at the time of the proposal or subsequently, would be likely to influence a prudent insurer. This may apply even when the relevance of the information is not apparent to the proposer, and it is therefore good advice, if in doubt, to seek the opinion of the insurance broker or company, before omitting, or failing to declare, any fact which may relate to the insurance.

It is customary for insurance proposal forms to conclude with a declaration to the effect that:

1 To the best of my knowledge and belief the answers to the questions set out in the proposal form are true and complete and contain all the material facts.
2 I will inform the company of any change to any material fact occurring before acceptance of the proposal.
3 I understand that failure to give true and complete answers to all the questions may be grounds for rejecting a claim.

There is, however, no necessity to disclose information which is either:

(a) Expressly stated by the insurer as unnecessary: for example, motor policy proposals may state that parking tickets do not count as 'previous convictions'.

(b) Not within the reasonable knowledge of the insured. A professional indemnity policy may ask whether any negligence claims are outstanding, or whether there is any reasonable cause to expect that such a claim will be forthcoming. Whilst the proposer would be required to disclose an incident such as a known recent mishap to a patient, he is not expected to have 'crystal ball' prescience.
or:
(c) Likely to diminish the risk. Thus if it is known that a new and improved burglar alarm system is to be installed in practice premises, this would not be a 'material fact' in an application for a theft policy (although the reason for such an installation, such as a recent burglary, might well be).

Recent insurance trends

Recent press reports have suggested that some insurance companies have displayed a more adversarial attitude when faced with claims, particularly with regard to property insurance. A number of factors have been cited, including the competitive nature of the insurance markets, which has acted to drive down premium levels. There has also been an increased incidence of both crimes against property, and property damage due to severe weather, flooding and subsidence. Fraudulent claims, and claims which infringe the principle of indemnity (that is to say, the insured shall not profit from his loss) are also reported to have increased.

These factors have undoubtedly led insurers to insist on strict adherence to the policy conditions. On the other hand, given that a fundamental aim of insurance companies – indeed of commerce in general – is the creation of profit, it has been argued that an increase in claims is not, of itself, a cause of detriment or concern to insurers so long as premium levels can be accurately set.[8]

The development of a more stringent approach to claims should not be a cause for undue concern to policyholders who act honestly; no such individual would wish to see premium levels raised to finance the illicit or embellished claims of others, and it is in the interests of policyholders and insurance companies to develop sound principles of risk management and also to read policy documents and proposals carefully in order to ensure that cover is adequate and appropriate.

Theft insurance provides an example of these principles. It is common for insurers to stipulate that cover will extend only to the limit of, say, £250 in cash on surgery premises, other than in a locked safe. This sum may be insufficient for a practice's needs, and yet the cost of purchasing and installing a suitable safe may be considerably more than the additional premium payable to extend the policy. If cash is taken home each evening, it may exceed home or vehicle insurance limits, and may place unacceptable security responsibilities on the staff member concerned. Against this must be balanced the increased likelihood of burglary if larger amounts are kept on the practice premises – such facts do not escape the attentions of criminally inclined visitors.

When considering the alternatives, the cost of a claim, which may include substantially increased future premiums and business interruption, may lead to the conclusion that the acquisition of a safe is in fact the less costly alternative (see Chapter 3: Security).

Types of insurance cover

Amongst the types of insurance which are most useful and relevant to the health professional are:

1. Employers' liability insurance (see Chapter 3) Employers' liability cover is a statutory requirement in the United Kingdom for all businesses employing staff. A minimum of £2 million is specified, and although it was common until recently for unlimited cover to be provided, recent industrial claims have led insurers to provide the legal minimum and no more.
2. Third party liability (see Chapter 3) Patients, their escorts and friends, students, trainees and other visitors to practice premises must be indemnified against accidents occurring on the premises.
3. Buildings insurance Where premises are freehold, this is imperative to protect against unforeseeable or catastrophic accidental damage to property. Such cover may also be a condition of the lease in leasehold premises, with either the tenant or landlord being responsible for maintaining insurance. Where the landlord obtains cover, the tenant is usually required to reimburse the cost and there should be provision in the lease for resolving disputes over this. In this case he/she should certainly request sight of the policy document and satisfy her/himself that its provisions and the extent of cover are in fact satisfactory for her/his needs.
4. Contents insurance Care must be taken, as outlined above, to ensure that cover is adequate and appropriate. External signs, walls and fences are amongst those which may be excluded from standard policies, and it is often a requirement that specialist equipment, such as computers, software, precious metals and property held on behalf of third parties (such as dentures being repaired) shall be separately itemized and endorsed on the policy.
5. Consequential loss The costs of business interruption following a claim on, for instance, property or contents insurance are frequently overlooked. Whilst specialist policies offered to the dental

profession may include such losses, more general policies will often exclude such coverage. It is necessary to review such cover at least annually, usually by reference to the most recent audited accounts. The principle of indemnity limits benefit under such a policy to the level indicated by those accounts.

6 Practice expenses policy   Consequential loss insurance will not extend to reimbursement of costs should the dentist be ill or injured. In such circumstances, sickness insurance (together with any statutory or other payments to which the dentist may be entitled) may not, under UK tax law, exceed 75% of the practitioner's net income. If disability is long-term, even the employment of a locum may not be adequate to meet expenses, and loss of 'goodwill' is a further factor to be taken into consideration in these circumstances.

7 Partnership insurance   In the event of a partner's death or disability, the partnership deed may call upon the remaining partners to purchase his or her share in the business. Cover may be effected against this eventuality.

8 Sickness and life assurance   Whilst the discussion or recommendation of contingency risks is not within the scope of this text, it would be anticipated that the prudent professional would make arrangements in this regard.

9 Professional liability insurance   This is dealt with in detail below.

Insurance – broker or direct?

The majority of insurance business in the United Kingdom is carried out through third parties. The profession of insurance broking was formerly regulated by the Insurance Brokers (Registration) Act (1977), which established a council and rules including indemnity insurance for brokers, educational requirements and a restriction of the use of the title 'insurance broker'. This failed, however, to distinguish between 'tied agents' who acted on behalf of a single insurance company, and 'independent advisers' who were free to advise their clients of any company's services and products.

The Financial Services Act (1986), and the European Commission Framework Directives (1990–91) have led to further regulation in this area. In particular the distinction between an independent broker and one who is commissioned or employed by one insurance company is more readily determined. Financial advice is increasingly provided by banks and building societies, but in the majority of cases these organizations will have 'ties' to a particular insurer, often a wholly-owned subsidiary company.

Professional liability insurance*

Professions, by their very nature, deal in a common service: the provision of expertise. Once a professional relationship has been established between a professional – whether a dentist, solicitor, stockbroker or surveyor – and a client, the law holds that a duty of care exists between that professional and that client. Such a relationship has been termed a fiduciary relationship, that is to say, one based on trust, since it will be expected that the client will not have the necessary knowledge or understanding of the professional's speciality to enable him to form a valid and rational critique of the service provided.

Jess has defined the term 'professional negligence' as:

> ... such a failure to meet the standards of care to be expected from the average competent and experienced practitioner as to render the professional person committing the act, error or omission liable in law to a client or some other third party who occasions reasonably foreseeable loss by reason of reliance on that act.[9]

Professionals are therefore uniquely exposed to a risk – failing to meet standards of care – which may render them liable, in the event of damage resulting, to substantial compensation payments and considerable costs in the defence or mitigation of the claim against them. It is primarily against this risk that professional liability insurance is undertaken.

The defence organizations

Medical professionals have faced the risk of professional liability for at least 4,000 years, since the Babylonian Code of Hammurabi proposed drastic punishments should a physician injure his patient.[10] It was not, however, until the late nineteenth century that bodies were specifically formed with the intention of assisting doctors and dentists who found themselves the subject of negligence actions. The Medical Defence Union, the oldest of these bodies, was set up in 1885, originally by a group of lay persons, including two solicitors. As a company limited by guarantee, its members were effectively its shareholders, each responsible for the contribution of a nominal one pound to meet its liabilities – a policy unchanged to the present day. The management of the Union was assumed by medically qualified individuals in 1888, and its original aims were to assist members who were libelled (a common harassment of doctors at the time), and to take action against unqualified 'quacks' (another constant source of irritation to a profession only declared

---

*The term insurance is used here to include indemnity offered by medical defence organizations (see following text).

exclusive by the 1858 Medical Act). Support for doctors (dentists were not admitted to membership until 1947) accused of negligence was confined to the payment of legal fees and costs; it was regarded as beyond the union's remit to pay damages awarded against members in unsuccessful cases. Very few negligence cases undertaken by the Medical Defence Union in its early years were, in fact, lost, and the majority were discontinued as soon as its involvement was made known to the plaintiffs.[11]

In 1892, disagreement with proposed constitutional changes in the Medical Defence Union led to the setting up, by a small group of members, of the London and Counties Medical Protection Society (now the Medical Protection Society). The Society admitted dental members from its inception, and in 1908 was the first defence organization to offer insurance – effected with an independent company, and additional to its own membership fee – against the cost of damages awarded in court. The Medical Defence Union had held that to offer such a provision would be unsound, in that it might lead to reckless practice, but soon followed suit when the society's initiative proved successful. The third defence organization, the Medical and Dental Defence Union of Scotland was founded in 1902, very much along the lines of the Medical Defence Union. The principal reasons for its formation were the considerable distance of Scottish members from the London-based organizations, and the particularities of Scottish law.

Early insurance against damages offered through the defence organizations was limited to £2,000–£3,000, and when, in 1925, the professions were startled by the award of £25,000 against two medical defendants, it became apparent that this could be woefully inadequate. The introduction of full indemnity soon followed, and subject to the discretion of the defence organizations, this remains the policy to date. This 'discretion' is only one aspect of the UK defence bodies which distinguishes them from insurance companies. In 1979 this distinction was confirmed in the judgement following the Medical Defence Union's case against the Board of Trade,[12] where it was held that the discretionary provision of an indemnity and legal advice did not amount to a contract of insurance.[13]

From time to time, this discretionary aspect of the defence organizations – that is to say, their right in a particular circumstance to decline assistance and/or support to a member – has been the subject of professional disquiet. (See also Insurance-based cover below). The British Medical Association has, for instance, been requested to introduce a contractually-based scheme of indemnity on occasions,[14] but has, on consideration, decided against taking such action, believing that the defence organizations are best fitted to perform this function. For their part, the defence organizations have defended their policy of discretionary assistance. They hold, for instance that it is no part of their remit, nor would their membership generally wish it so, that practitioners convicted of, say, fraud or theft, should be assisted from their funds, nor that a practitioner who persistently or blatantly ignored accepted professional tenets should remain in membership. Such cases are exceedingly rare.

Equally important, however, in so imprecise and personal an undertaking as medical and dental care, there must be scope for reasonable alternative approaches to diagnosis and treatment, and the defence organizations would not wish to be placed in a position of specifying that which was, or was not an acceptable teaching, method or practice. That role is properly assumed by the professional regulatory bodies, teaching institutions, Royal Colleges and professional expert advisers called upon in individual cases.

The discretionary benefits offered to members by the three defence organizations are broadly similar and may be summarized as:

Indemnity   Assistance with complaints and negligence claims arising from clinical practice. Full consultation during a claim. Payment of legal costs and damages in claims arising from clinical practice.

Advice   Access to 24 hour advisory service. Advice on medico-legal problems arising from clinical practice, e.g. ethical dilemmas, issues of consent and confidentiality.

Assistance   Assistance at hearings arising out of clinical practice including inquests and inquiries. Help with complaints procedures and responses to complaints. Assistance in proceedings brought by a patient arising from the act or omission of a member, or of a partner who is a member of another defence organization with which there is a reciprocal arrangement; a locum, whether or not a defence organization member; an assistant such as a nurse ... dental auxiliary or laboratory technician.[15]

Defence organisations will not normally accept responsibility where a claim arises as a result of the conduct of a member in an activity outside the normal range of dental practice, e.g. as a proprietor of a nursing home, laboratory or a company or firm providing services to the dental, medical or allied professions.[16]

Since the introduction of Crown Indemnity in January 1990, UK Health Authorities and NHS Trusts have assumed responsibility for the professional liability of their employees. The indemnity cover provided by defence organizations is not, therefore applicable nor available to dentists who are employed by, or have honorary appointments with, such bodies. However, Crown Indemnity applies only to NHS clinical work carried out in the normal course of such employment; it does not cover disciplinary proceedings, general advice and assistance, or 'Section 2' duties, such as the preparation of reports. Defence organizations offer cover for these aspects at a considerably reduced subscription. Additionally, if part-time work, whether NHS or private, is undertaken outside NHS employment, then full indemnity cover is required. Since subscriptions for defence organizations are broadly 'class rated' – that is to say, they reflect the risks appropriate to a member's pattern and location of practice – differential rates may be available dependant on the amount of additional part-time work undertaken.

Class rating of subscriptions will mean that, say, a dental practitioner in practice in the UK will pay a fee which will differ from a colleague in practice in Australia, due to differences in claim rates, legal costs, size of average claims payments and so on. The class ratings applied by the different defence organizations may differ; whilst one may rate an oral surgeon according to his or her registration status (i.e. on the Medical Register or the Dental Register), another will rate according to the type of work undertaken.

Until very recently, the indemnity offered by defence organizations has been on an 'occurrence' basis, but more recently, in the light of increasing membership costs, and in the interests of providing a service tailored to the differing needs within the professions, 'claims made' indemnity has been introduced. The important differences between these concepts must be understood.

First, it is necessary to point out that negligence claims against doctors and dentists are frequently brought, conducted and concluded several years, and sometimes many years, after the events which gave rise to them. Whilst the majority of dental claims are concluded 2–5 years after the causative incident (medical claims 2–7 years), it is by no means unusual for claims to be instituted after a delay of five or more years (see 'limitations on actions', Chapter 4). This in turn means that defence organizations – and insurers – must set current annual membership fees (or premiums in the case of insurance companies) at a sufficient level to cover legal costs and possible damages arising a considerable time after an incident has occurred. In the recent past there have been periods when numbers of claims, litigation costs and damages awards have risen steeply. Such increases continue, and future trends are difficult to predict. In this climate of uncertainty, the calculation of the reserve funds needed by an organization to fund this 'tail' of future expenditure is complex, yet it is this funding which part of the fees paid must be set aside to cover.

On the other hand, this – the traditional approach to medical indemnity – offers advantages to dentists or doctors, who know that following retirement, death or change to another indemnity provider, all claims which may fall due as a result of incidents which have *occurred* during the period are provided for in reserves, and the full benefits can be counted on. This, then, briefly describes the occurrence policy or membership.

As an alternative approach, the defence organization or insurer may offer cover on a 'claims made' basis. This indemnity will relate only to those claims which are actually commenced during a particular period of membership or insurance. It is usually an additional requirement of such schemes that cover must continue uninterrupted until any claims which have been made are completed (which may include appeal proceedings). For the provider of indemnity, the advantage is that membership costs or premium levels may be set to reflect the known number and size of claims actually in progress, and the need for reserve funding is greatly reduced. For the clinician, this will usually result in reduced premium costs on a year to year basis as compared to 'occurrence' based cover. However, although the death of a member can be covered by a contingency insurance (the costs of which are included in the membership or premium), retirement or change of cover will require the purchase of 'run off' cover to finance those claims which may have originated during the period of indemnity, but which have not yet been instituted. The cost of such cover may exceed the cost of the final annual premium.

Viewed over the lifetime of a – mythical – 'average' practitioner, the anticipated actual cost of meeting litigation expenses and damages will not, of course vary, whichever type of indemnity is used. Occurrence policies will be more expensive, relatively speaking, during the earlier years of practice, whilst the cost of claims made policies will be higher at retirement, since 'run off' will apply. Assuming equal administrative costs, the overall figure for premiums (or membership fees) will be the same.

Insurance-based indemnity

Following the establishment of medical defence organizations in the UK, similar bodies were formed in Australia and in Canada. In addition, many doctors and dentists in countries of the British Commonwealth have membership of the UK societies, who have branch offices in their major membership centres. However, apart from the French mutual insurer 'Le Sou Medicale', which shares many of the features of the UK organizations, medical indemnity in most other countries is secured through commercial insurers.[17]

In the UK, insurance-based indemnity remains an option: the Medical Insurance Agency extended its professional indemnity scheme for doctors, underwritten at Lloyd's of London, to the dental profession in 1992.[18] Insurance-based indemnity is normally offered on a claims-made basis (see preceding section), and being contractually based does not have the discretionary feature associated with defence organizations. As with other insurances – and indeed, the defence organizations – there is however no obligation on the insurer to renew the policy after its annual term.

In the United States, the federal system has led to a far more decentralized regulation of medical and dental practice, with licensure of practitioners devolved to State Boards. Equally, there are 53 State and Territorial legal codes in addition to Federal law. Historically, therefore, a comparatively large number of different commercial insurers have offered indemnity cover to cater for the varying needs of practitioners. In 1970, a US Government survey noted 26 major insurers active in this market,[19] and as the costs and numbers of medical malpractice cases (of which dental cases accounted for some 6.9%) continued to mount, many of these companies withdrew from the field in the following decade, leading to the 'medical malpractice crisis' in which cover became either impossible, or impracticably expensive, to obtain.

Dentistry remained to a considerable extent unaffected by this problem, until in the 1980s, it, too, saw a disproportionate increase in litigation. Major insurers withdrew, and the American Dental Association, together with some state dental associations, negotiated their own group arrangements. In the majority of these group schemes, indemnity insurance is included in an overall package covering premises, employer liability and practice interruption cover. As with most 'inclusive' packages, individual requirements are traded against convenience and comprehensiveness.[20]

Trends in dental professional liability claims

Reports produced by the medical defence organizations have shown a year on year increase in both the number and value of claims made against their members. The rate of change has, however, varied. Defence organizations and insurers work in a competitive environment, and precise numerical details of claims, membership and actuarial data are carefully guarded. Access to data on professional negligence and on untoward incidents is also subject, in the UK, to legal requirements of confidentiality, and even in the United States where more openness and accountability is traditionally accepted and required, few surveys have been carried out, particularly in dentistry.

Mention has been made earlier of the 'malpractice crisis' in North America, which is generally considered to have struck during the 1970s although statistics show that claims had been rising steadily since before the Second World War.[21] Although medical professionals were initially most affected, with less than 7% of all malpractice claims involving dentists,[22] by the mid-1980s, dental malpractice premiums were rising by as much as 600% in 16 months.[23] Some 15% of current US healthcare malpractice claims now involve dentists.[24]

In Britain, there has been a corresponding, though far less dramatic, rise in civil actions for medical and dental negligence. Membership costs for defence organizations for UK medical practitioners rose from £40 per year in 1978 to about £1,350 by 1989,[25] but Wall noted that whereas claims were being paid annually on behalf of 15 out of every 100 US physicians, the comparable British figure was 1.5 out of every 100.[26] In the corresponding period, premiums for dental practitioners rose from £20 to about £375, and whilst no direct data is available on the number of dentists involved, defence organizations confirm that they are contacted each year by around 15% of their membership. Not all such contacts relate to claims: only some 20% of all medical and dental files involve threatened or instituted proceedings (and of these, only a proportion result in settlement), but this 20% account, in legal costs and damages payments, for 40–45% of defence organizations' operational expenses.[27]

In his annual report to members in 1992, the Chief Executive of the Medical Defence Union noted that the number of files opened in response to requests for assistance had risen from around 7,800 in 1977 to about 18,500 by 1991, an increase of some 240%. These figures are for worldwide membership and integrate medical and dental members in both primary care and hospital work. Not all files relate to patient claims, but include requests for assistance on a wide range of matters relating to clinical practice and professional conduct.[28]

In the 1993 report, the Union's General Manager (Professional Services) notes that, dependent on country of practice, members' requests for assistance 'continue to rise by between 12 and 16 per cent per year'.[29] These figures are, again, composed of both medical and dental cases (Figure 6.1).[30]

Dental cases considered alone show a steeper increase in recent years. Taking 1977 cases as a base of 100, files opened per year had more than doubled to 206 by 1992. Considering UK files alone, the increase over five years was 72%, representing an average annual rise of over 15%. These figures exclude cases dealt with solely by telephone, but include both indemnity and non-indemnity related matters.

These UK figures contrast with US figures for claims by physicians reported to the St Paul Insurance Company, one of the major carriers, as cited by Dingwall (Figure 6.2).[31] The downturn in numbers of claims from 1985 onwards – although not matched by a decrease in compensation awards – may reflect an increased awareness of risk

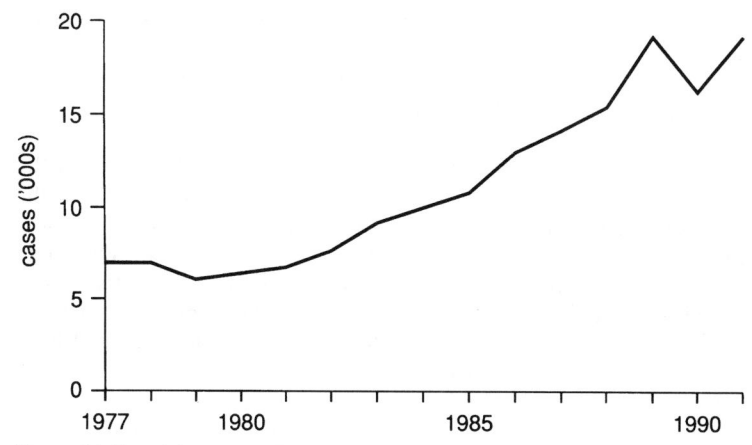

Figure 6.1 Growth in requests for assistance – number of files opened. Medical Defence Union 1977–1991. (Source: Medical Defence Union Annual Report (1992))

management, particularly in the hospital environment. At the time of the downturn, however, a number of States introduced legal reforms which may have had a significant effect on malpractice actions. These reforms included 'caps' on awards and more stringent limitation periods.[32]

In the preliminary report of the (US) National Dental Malpractice study, referred to in Chapter 5, Milgrom *et al.* reviewed completed

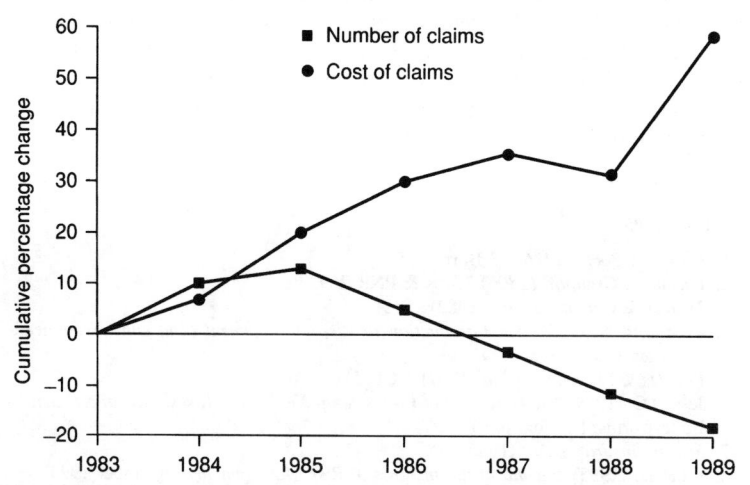

Figure 6.2 Claim experience of US physicians as reported by St Paul Insurance Company (from Dingwall R. (1992) Does Risk Management Work? *Health Service Journal*, 102, 16 April, 7 (supp.))

dental claims handled by one insurer in one American state.[33] Although the paper alludes to rising claim rates, no numerical data are presented, although it is noted that 1992 US Government figures show that dentists are cited in 15% of all malpractice claims (compared to 6.9% in 1970).

More significant trend data are presented in the fuller report of the same National survey published by Milgrom *et al.* in 1994.[34] In the previous chapter, some analysis of this data by treatment type was considered; here the annual changes noted are reviewed. The study referred to malpractice complaints and claims notified by dentists in the period 1988–1992. The results showed that the number of dentists reporting at least one complaint to their insurance carrier ranged from 2.7% in 1988, rising significantly to 8% in 1992. In all, some 24% of the sample of dentists had reported at least one complaint over the five year period. The number of dentists in the sample reporting a filed legal claim against them also increased over this period from 1.1 to 2.7%. The authors noted that the prevalence of dentists with at least one claim filed over the study period was 73 per 1,000 dentists. However, based on the data contained in the 1973 US Government survey already referred to,[19] the anticipated prevalence would have been 129 claims per 1,000 dentists. Thus, although a continuing increase in claims is borne out by the recent findings, this increase is less than would have been predicted 20 years ago. It is speculated that the tort reforms in US legislatures may have contributed to this reduction.

There is general evidence, then, that legal claims against doctors and dentists continue to increase on both sides of the Atlantic, and that although US claim rates may not be rising so quickly, the percentage of dental members contacting one British defence organization for information each year (about all matters, including indemnity) is continuing to increase.

References

1. *Carter* v. *Boehm (1766)* 3 Burr 1905
2. *Lucena* v. *Craufurd (1806)* 2 Bos & PNR 269
3. *Insurance Companies Act* (1982) s.2(2)
4. Crockford N. (1986) *An Introduction to Risk Management (2nd edn)*. Woodhead-Faulkner, Cambridge, p. 14
5. *Roberts* v. *Security Co Ltd* (1897) 1 QB 111, CA
6. Jess D.C. (1989) *The Insurance of Professional Negligence Risks: Law and Practice.* Butterworths, London, p. 103
7. *Marine Insurance Act* (1906) s18
8. Editorial (1993) *Journal of the Institute of Risk Management*, September 1993
9. Jess D.C. (1989) *The Insurance of Professional Negligence Risks: Law and Practice.* Butterworths, London, p. 1
10. Hawkins C. (1985) *Mishap or Malpractice?* Blackwell Scientific, London, p. 254

References

11. Ibid p. 17–34
12. *Medical Defence Union Ltd v. Department of Trade (1979)* 2 All ER 421; (1980) Ch. 82
13. Jess D.C. (1989) op. cit. p. 90–91
14. British Medical Association (1977). Proposed professional indemnity insurance scheme for BMA members. *British Medical Journal*, **274**, 1297–1299
15. *Medical Defence Union Annual Report* (1993)
16. Ibid
17. Hawkins C. (1986) op. cit. pp. 242–260
18. Medical Insurance Agency (1991) Press Release dated 4 September 1992
19. US Department of Health Safety and Welfare (1973) *Report of the Secretary's Commission of Medical Malpractice*
20. Schroeder O.C., Pollack B.R. and Glick M. (1987) The Insurance Contract: Professional Liabiity Insurance, in *Handbook of Dental Jurisprudence and Risk Management* (Pollack B.R. ed), 2nd edn. PSG Publishing, Littleton, Mass. p. 56–60
21. Hill G. (1991). What is Risk Management? *International Journal of Risk and Safety in Medicine*. **2**, 83–90
22. Milgrom P., Fiset L., Getz T. *et al.* (1993) Dental Malpractice Experience: A Closed Claim Study. *Medical Care*, **31**,(8), 749–756
23. Seldin L.W. (1992) Risk Management: Then and Now. *Journal of the American Dental Association*, **123**, (7), 47–50
24. US General Accounting Office (1992) *Practitioner Data Bank: Information on small medical malpractice payments*. GAO/IMTEC – 92 – 56
25. Source: Medical Defence Union Subscription Rates
26. Wall J. (1991) Is litigation bad for your health? *Journal of the Medical Defence Union*, **7**, (4), 74–75
27. Medical Defence Union (1993) *Annual Report*
28. Medical Defence Union (1992) *Annual Report to Members*, p. 7
29. Medical Defence Union (1993) *Annual Report to Members*, p. 7
30. Medical Defence Union (1993) Dental Symposium meetings for dentists
31. Dingwall R. (1992) Does Risk Management Work? *Health Service Journal*, **102** No.5298, 7(supp)
32. Schroeder O.C., Pollack B.R. and Glick M. (1987) op cit, p. 68
33. Milgrom P., Fiset L., Getz T. *et al.* (1993) Dental Malpractice Experience: A Closed Claim Study. *Medical Care*, **31**, (8), 749–756
34. Milgrom P., Fiset L., Whitney C. *et al.* (1994) Malpractice claims during 1988–1992: a National survey of dentists. *Journal of the American Dental Association*, **125**, 462–469

7
Professional risks

It might be said that to be a member of a profession is in itself a risk! A profession has autonomy, its members have specialist education and knowledge, and they enjoy positions of trust. All these attributes carry inbuilt risk. Autonomy implies self-regulation, which in turn implies rules of conduct; to risk breaking these rules is to risk incurring professional sanctions or even exclusion. To have specialist knowledge and education is to risk its misapplication. A feature of this specialism is, in the case of the medical and dental professions, to enjoy a monopoly: failure to exercise that monopoly in the public interest (as opposed to the profession's interest) is to risk losing it. And a position of trust risks betrayal of that trust; in relation to the patient, this invites not only medico-legal consequences, but possible loss of repute and of self-esteem.

This chapter examines the risks which are particular to the professional nature of dentistry. Although, in regulatory terms it concentrates on the position in the United Kingdom, other systems are briefly compared, and the principles are, in general, widely applicable.

In the United Kingdom, the profession is regulated by the General Dental Council, one of whose functions is to oversee, on behalf of the public, the conduct and ethics of dentists. The Council's role and procedures in carrying out this function are reviewed.

Many dentists are contractually involved with the National Health Service either as independent contractors – general practitioners – or as employees of health authorities or NHS Trusts. The principles of this contractual obligation are examined, and the means of investigating alleged breaches discussed.

Third, members of the profession have obligations to each other, both in ethical and in working relationships; the risks implicit in these areas are also considered.

The General Dental Council

It was not until the passing of the Dentists Act (1956) that the profession of dentistry acquired autonomy comparable to that of its sister profession of medicine. Although the Dentists Act (1878) had introduced some control over the practice of dentistry, compulsory registration was not initiated until the 1921 Dentists Act, which led to the establishment of the Dental Board of the United Kingdom. This body, however, remained ultimately answerable to the General Medical Council (which had been formed in 1858).

The 1956 Dentists Act (with further amendments since consolidated into the 1957 and 1984 Dentists Acts) vested powers of professional regulation in the General Dental Council, whose duties are defined in the preamble to the Act as; '... to promote high standards of dental education at all its stages and high standards of professional conduct among dentists...'.[1]

Amongst the Council's particular obligations under the 1984 Act are the establishment of registers – for dentists, dental hygienists and dental therapists – and the formation of five Committees; the Education Committee, the Dental Auxiliaries Committee, the Preliminary Proceedings Committee, the Professional Conduct Committee and the Health Committee.

The Council consists of forty registered dentists, one dental auxiliary, six lay members, and (for educational matters) three registered doctors. Its funding is derived from annual registration fees levied on those who are included in the registers, and it is not perhaps, therefore, surprising that dentists who 'pay for' the Council's administration and costs may overlook the fact that; 'the Council is not concerned primarily with the immediate hopes and desires of dentists, but with the provision of ever-improving dental treatment for the community as a whole...'.[3]

The over-riding concern of the Council is therefore the protection of the public in relation to the monopoly which its own existence confers on the dental profession. The exercise of professional discipline is therefore an activity which the Council undertakes on behalf of the community; it is acknowledged to be an onerous and highly responsible task. Two sanctions are open to the Council, should a dentist's professional conduct or fitness to practice be found wanting; suspension from the register (for a period up to one year), or erasure from the register (in which case application for restoration of registration may not be made for at least 10 months). Either action, in effectively depriving a dentist of his livelihood and status, is a severe penalty (possibly in addition to penalties imposed elsewhere) which, although it affects but a handful of dentists, deserves sober consideration. In risk management terms, the implications are clear: professional disciplinary action constitutes a risk of major severity.

Matters which may potentially lead to disciplinary action may be brought to the attention of the General Dental Council in various ways, including the following:

1. A complaint may be made to the Council directly by an aggrieved patient.
2. A dentist who has been found 'in breach' of his NHS Terms of Service (see later in this chapter) in a particularly serious or recurrent matter may be reported to the Council by the Secretary of State for Health.
3. A complaint against a dentist or a report which alleges serious professional misconduct may be officially lodged by a body such as a Health Authority.
4. Details of convictions of registered dentists are notified to the Council by Clerks to magistrates and Crown Courts, or by police authorities.

Additionally, dentists whose fitness to practice may be seriously impaired 'by reason of a physical or mental condition' are dealt with under a separate procedure (see 'The Health Committee' below).

The Preliminary Proceedings Committee

Complaints against dentists made under headings 1, 2, or 3 above are considered in the first instance by the President. Matters complained of may be trivial, or outside the Council's area of concern. All other cases which it is considered might relate to 'serious professional misconduct' are referred to the Preliminary Proceedings Committee, which consists normally of the President together with five Council members, one of whom is not a dentist. This committee's function is to determine which cases shall be passed to the Professional Conduct Committee for formal investigation. Complaints from individuals, including patients, must be accompanied by a sworn statement of the facts, in the form of an affidavit or statutory declaration, before formal proceedings are invoked. This procedure affords some protection to dentists against vexatious or malicious complaints. A dentist will be notified of the allegation against him and will be invited to submit his observations before a decision on referral is made.

When a dentist is reported to the Council following conviction in a court of law, the Council will accept the facts leading to that conviction as proven by the court. It is not necessary that the conviction has a direct bearing on the dentist's practice. Offences such as drunkenness, indecency, bigamy, fraud and receiving stolen property have led to erasure.[3]

The Preliminary Proceedings Committee has the power to order a dentist's immediate suspension from the register, if it considers this to be in the public interest, pending formal proceedings. In such a case, a dentist would have the opportunity to appear before the committee (legally represented if he so wishes) to state why such an order should not be made; the committee will then determine the issue; any interim suspension must be reviewed before three months elapse.[4]

In practice, any dentist receiving a personal communication from the General Dental Council (other than the annual registration renewal) should seek immediate advice from his defence organization. Even when a complaint appears petty or insignificant, no reply, other than a formal acknowledgement, should be made until expert assistance has been sought. The Council is not empowered to act on cases brought in the civil courts (unless a separate complaint or conviction is reported), nor will it usually concern itself with minor traffic offences such as parking fines.

The Preliminary Proceedings Committee meets at intervals throughout the year: it usually makes a decision on cases for referral to the Professional Conduct Committee at its meetings in March and September, for formal consideration by that committee some two months later.

The Professional Conduct Committee

This committee, unlike the Preliminary Proceedings Committee, usually sits in public session. It is composed of the President together with ten other members (none of whom concurrently serves on the Preliminary Proceedings Committee). At least five must be dentists elected to the Council by the profession itself, and at least two are non-dental, non-elected members. A legal assessor (an experienced barrister or solicitor) sits with the committee solely to guide it on points of law. Dentists appearing before it may be represented by a solicitor or counsel, whilst complainants in cases of serious professional misconduct may present their own case, or may be represented. As the Council has no power to award compensation or costs, however, and as it is considered in the public interest for serious allegations to be clearly and correctly presented, the Solicitor to the Council will usually act for the complainant.

The proceedings are judicial in nature; that is, court procedure is followed. Witnesses may be called and testify under oath; cross-examination and re-examination may take place. Hearings may last for several days in particularly complex cases. The setting and the formality are imposing, as befits the weighty and serious nature of the committee's duties; however, every opportunity is given to each party to present a full and detailed account of their case. On conclusion of the formal summing up by the parties the committee retire to consider their verdict. If a finding of serious professional misconduct is made, the dentist is afforded the opportunity, if so wished, to present evidence in mitigation, which may include character and professional witnesses.

In conviction cases, the Council's solicitor will present the facts of the conviction together with any arguments why this should lead to disciplinary action. The dentist will then have the chance to present mitigating evidence. What cannot be challenged, as already noted, are the facts as previously proven in court. A dentist who pleads guilty in court to a criminal charge (or who accepts a formal caution from the police in lieu of a court appearance) may therefore expect the Committee to regard this as acceptance of the facts as charged.

The committee has only three options: it may dismiss the case, either because it is not proved, because the facts proved do not amount to serious professional misconduct, because a dentist's conviction does not justify erasure or suspension, or (infrequently) because it believes there are exceptional reasons why erasure or suspension should not take place. If it finds serious professional misconduct has occurred, or a conviction justifies it, it may order the dentist's name to be suspended or erased from the register. Finally, it may find the dentist guilty, or convicted of a serious offence, but may postpone its decision on erasure to allow observation of the dentist's future conduct.[5]

Dentists appearing before the committee will normally be advised and represented by legal experts appointed by their defence organization. The conduct of such cases requires considerable skill and experience, and it would be unwise in the extreme for a dentist to consider self-representation.

The Health Committee

This committee meets, in private session, to consider cases where a dentist's ability to practice is impaired by reason of his physical or mental condition. This procedure was introduced in the 1984 Dentists Act in order to deal appropriately and sympathetically with dentists who, possibly through no fault of their own, may constitute a danger to their patients. Alcohol and substance abuse are no respecters of occupation or status, and physical or mental infirmity clearly have major significance when they affect practitioners of dentistry. Information may be placed before the committee from a variety of sources, including patients, fellow practitioners, family members or health authorities. On receipt of a report which appears to fall within the committee's remit, the President, or a nominated Council member, will consider the matter and if it is felt appropriate, the dentist will be invited to submit to medical examination by two nominated examiners appointed regionally by professional bodies. The dentist may in turn nominate his own examiners to submit an independent report. The committee, whose format generally mirrors that of the Professional Conduct Committee, with the addition of two Medical Assessors, will consider the evidence, and may invite the dentist to appear before it. Its proceedings are similar to those of the Professional Conduct Committee, and it may, if it finds the dentist's fitness to practice impaired, suspend his registration for up to 12 months, or impose restrictions on his practice for up to 3 years. It may also postpone its decision, requiring treatment or reports to be made.[6]

Appeals against findings of the Professional Conduct Committee, or of the Health Committee may be made to the Judicial Committee of the Privy Council. Their Lordships will consider only points of law in determining such an appeal, and will not enter into clinical matters. They have shown themselves to be generally unwilling to set aside the expert deliberations of the disciplinary committees. Prior to the passing of the Dentists Act (1984), suspension from the register was not an option open to the Disciplinary Committee (as the Professional Conduct Committee was then known) and when, in one case, their Lordships determined an appeal against the 'harsh sentence' of erasure, they noted; 'It would require a very strong case to justify the Judicial Committee of the Privy Council in interfering with a sentence that the Disciplinary Committee have thought it proper to impose.'[7]

Serious professional misconduct

The Council's central concern with the promotion of high standards in dentistry confers on it, by implication, the question of determining what 'standards' are to be applied to professional conduct and the extent to which a falling short of those standards by a dentist may constitute 'serious misconduct' in a professional sense.[8] As has been described, the Council examines each case referred to it on its individual merits, but by way of guidance to the profession at large, it has published and updated at intervals since 1957, a guidance booklet intended to illustrate to dentists the kinds of behaviour or activity which may lead to disciplinary procedures.[9] In one sense, this publication may be considered as being a guide to professional and ethical risk management. A copy is provided to each dentist on registration, and the booklet is updated periodically; its contents should be noted by all dentists.

In the Council's own words; 'The kind of conduct which may be regarded by the Professional Conduct Committee as serious professional misconduct is not defined or limited and is likely to vary with the circumstances of the time.'[10]

It goes on, therefore, to point out that the examples given in the booklet are not intended to be an exhaustive or definitive list. Amongst the topics included are the following:

General anaesthesia and sedation: The Council draws attention to recommendations for good practice which include training, personnel, monitoring equipment, techniques, record keeping, patient supervision and emergency resuscitation facilities. Many of these parallel the proposals of the 1990 Expert Working Party Report ('The Poswillo Report').[11]

Cross-infection: The importance of adhering to guidance issued by the Department of Health and by the British Dental Association is emphasized,[12,13] the ethical responsibilities of dentists who may be HIV-positive are set out, and it is made clear that it would be unethical to refuse to treat a patient solely on the grounds that he was HIV-positive.

Radiation protection: Conformity to the Ionizing Radiation Regulations (1988) is required.

Patient relationships: The Council draws attention to abuses of patients' trust, including indecency, dishonesty, failure to secure consent and breach of confidentiality. The intimidation of children, failure to refer or to provide a proper standard of care and lack of availability of emergency treatment are also highlighted.

Misrepresentation: Dentists are ethically bound to be honest and to avoid untrue or misleading statements. This applies not only in clinical situations (for instance, distinguishing between NHS and private treatment), but also in other areas such as certification (passport application counter-signature for instance) or financial and business matters.

Treatment plans, estimates: Arising from the previous paragraph, the Council considers it a dentist's responsibility to make the estimated cost and the nature of treatment clear to patients at the outset; to distinguish NHS and private treatment; to provide written estimates in costly or complex cases; and to provide itemized accounts on request.

Debt collection: The use of collecting agencies or court action should be considered only as a last resort.

Covering illegal practice: Dentists must ensure that their employees and members of their practice or staff (dentists, hygienists, therapists) maintain their registration with the Council (see later in this chapter) and that staff, including dental technicians on their premises do not contravene the provisions of the Dentists Act. Ancillary staff to whom instruction and advice on patients' oral hygiene is delegated must have received adequate training and be competent: the dentist remains personally responsible for their work.

Advertising and canvassing: Since 1985, restrictions on advertising by dentists have been considerably relaxed in the UK. Unsolicited telephone calls are considered to diminish the public's confidence in the profession. Other advertising and publicity must be legal, decent, truthful and in keeping with professional propriety. It should not compare the advertiser with other dentists or practices, 'suggest superiority', or recommend a particular product. It should not mislead nor use inflated language or claims.

Professional agreements: The Council strongly recommends that dentists sign formal written agreements when they enter into working relationships. (This area is addressed in more detail later in this chapter.)

It is instructive to compare the principal headings of the Council's current Notes for Guidance of Dentists with those issued in 1970, when examples of convictions leading to erasure included deception, forgery, indecency, drunkenness and the procuring of an illegal abortion. Of the guideline headings currently listed, the following were then absent: General anaesthesia; Cross-infection; Radiation; Treatment plans and Estimates; Debt collection and Professional agreements. The guidelines on advertising were, however, considerably more stringent and specific.[14]

The numbers of cases heard before the Professional Conduct Committee have both fallen and risen considerably since the General Dental Council was established, as the following figures show:[15]

5 year period	Conviction cases	Unprofessional conduct
1956–1960	17	21
1966–1970	9	6
1976–1980	19	13
1986–1990	24	52

In the period 1956–1960, 10 dentists were erased from the register; in 1966–1970, 6 dentists; in 1976–1980, 8 dentists and in 1986–1990, 35 dentists were erased and 14 suspensions were ordered. Prior to the Dentists Act (1984), when suspension was not an option, rather more cases were deferred by the Disciplinary Committee for observation and reporting of a dentist's continuing conduct. However, this does not explain the considerable reduction in cases heard by the committee in the 1960s and 1970s, and the more recent figures clearly show a considerable rise in the number of cases – particularly those of serious professional misconduct, which have come before the Council. A major proportion of these have arisen as a result of serious infringement of National Health Service regulations.

In his address to the 82nd Session of the General Dental Council in 1994, the President, Sir David Mason, noted however, that a 'major increase' had occurred in disciplinary cases between 1984 and 1988, as compared with ten years earlier; and this increase had not, in fact been sustained in the period 1989–1993, the total falling from 82 to 66. Despite this reduction, the Professional Conduct Committee had sat for an increasing number of days in the most recent five year period.[16] This reflects the increasing complexity of cases considered.

From this review, it would appear that the range and incidence of risks attributable to serious professional misconduct have increased markedly since the early 1980s. This is not to say, of course, that the standards of professional conduct have necessarily fallen in any way, but may rather reflect the increased pressures and complexities placed by society, and by a self-governing profession itself, on contemporary professional practice.

The United States

A note on the regulation of dentistry in the United States is relevant here, since it sheds some light on the litigation practices in that country, which have been viewed with concern over recent years. As discussed in Chapter 6, under a federal system, State law is the primary jurisdiction which affects dental practice, and there are separate legislatures for the 50 states, the District of Columbia and the US Territories.

Each state has a Dental Board, but the constitution and powers of these bodies vary. In the majority of states, the Board exercises control over dental education, registration, discipline and licence to practise. In New York, however, disciplinary and educational aspects are overseen by the State Board of Regents, which may have no dental representation, the Dental Board having an advisory role only in these aspects. Most states differ from one another in their definition of dentistry, and in the registration and permitted activities of dental ancillary workers. Reciprocal arrangements for registration between states exist in only a minority of instances.

Considerable regulatory powers are held by federal agencies such as the Occupational Safety and Health Administration (OSHA) and the Food and Drug Administration (FDA).

It may be speculated that this fragmentation of powers which is inherent in the historical development of the US may be a contributory factor in the inclination to use the civil courts for resolution of disputes and complaints. As Schroeder and Pollack note:[17]

We are emphasizing in law the payment of money to replace the dental health and well-being destroyed by poor dental care. We should emphasize in law the denial of the right of the inadequate dental practitioner to practice dentistry . . ..

Contractual relations with the National Health Service

General practice

A dentist against whom a formal complaint had been brought by a patient under National Health Service Regulations, recently complained to his advisers; 'I don't remember signing any contract with anyone – why should I have to be answerable in this way? Why can I not bring a complaint against my patient – or the Department of Health?' This observation may seem naive, but it has been voiced frequently, and it bears examining.

When the General Dental Services (the dental primary care division of the National Health Service) were established in 1948, it was determined that dental practitioners should be self-employed and should 'contract' to the NHS individually and separately for each patient they elected to treat under the NHS provisions. In exchange for this arrangement, practitioners retained clinical autonomy; the right to accept or refuse any patient for a 'course of treatment'. Practitioners who apply for inclusion in an NHS 'dental list' of any primary health care authority (Family Health Service Authority – FHSA – in England and Wales; Health Board in Scotland and Northern Ireland*) are deemed to have accepted this overall principle and to be bound by the legislation which enacts it.[18] Additionally, as each patient's treatment is recorded on an appropriate form, the practitioner's signature on this form re-affirms that care and treatment has been carried out in accordance with the 'NHS Regulations'. These regulations are currently those issued on 1 April 1992.[19] Included in the regulations are Terms of Service to which each dentist in contract with an FHSA is required to conform.

The Terms of Service indicate *inter alia*, that:

(Paragraph 20):
1 In providing general dental services, a dentist shall:
   (a)   employ a proper degree of skill and attention
   (b)   save as is provided [elsewhere] give all treatment personally
   (c)   use only materials which are suitable for the purpose for which they are used

*In this chapter, the term 'FHSA' is used inclusively for these bodies

(d) except in the case of occasional treatment and treatment on referral, provide, subject to sub-paragraph (2), care and treatment to such extent, and at such intervals, as may be necessary to secure and maintain the oral health of the patient.

2 When providing general dental services a dentist shall not provide care and treatment in excess of that which is necessary to secure and maintain oral health.

This paragraph, then, sets out the contractual equivalent of the common law duty of care, and defines the extent of the dentist's obligation to provide care and treatment for his patient. Much depends, obviously, on what interpretation is placed on the definition of 'necessary to secure and maintain oral health'. In the event of a dispute or complaint, procedures are followed as described later in this section.

In all, the regulations extend to 44 paragraphs and six schedules, and are supplied to dentists at the time of their inclusion in a dental list for the first time (and as later updates appear). Experience suggests that very few dentists are fully aware of their extensive obligations under the regulations, and, despite their dry and legal tone, they should receive a few hours careful study by any practitioner who has not recently read them. In their entirety, the dentist's Terms of Service cover most aspects of the provision of primary dental care, from the practice facilities provided to the detailed administrative procedures which must be followed.

Care and treatment provided by dentists to patients accepted under the NHS regulations is remunerated, in accordance with a nationally determined scale of fees, by the Dental Practice Board normally on a monthly basis (although there is in fact no indication in the regulations of when, or how soon, such payments shall be made). In Scotland, payments are made by the Scottish Dental Practice Board, in Northern Ireland by the Central Services Agency*. Certain other payments, for instance, for approved postgraduate education, for maternity and long-term sickness absences, and for seniority pay and vocational training, are also made under the current provisions.

The above is a – necessarily – brief account of the contractual obligations owed by general dental practitioners to the National Health Service. The emphasis here is naturally on the risks which attend such a detailed and extensive contract. The answer to the dentist's question, posed at the commencement of this section, lies in the interpretation of contract law:

*In this chapter, the term 'Dental Practice Board' is used inclusively

The courts take an objective, rather than a subjective, view of agreement, and if a person has so conducted himself that he has agreed, then he may be held to have agreed, even though, in his own mind, he has not.'[20]

If 'our' dentist has 'conducted himself', by the care and treatment of patients under the NHS Regulations, then he has, unwittingly or not, agreed to the Terms of Service. The patient, by contrast, has entered into a relatively minor contract (to pay any NHS fees prescribed) by signing the NHS treatment form. Although the practice of 'counterclaiming' in civil law against patients has become less rare recently in the United States, it has yet to appear in the UK (thankfully, many would say), and there is certainly no provision in the National Health Service for the dentist to complain about his patient.

Complaints by patients are only the first risk which a dentist may encounter under the National Health Service Regulations: a complaint may be made by the Dental Practice Board following a report by a Dental Reference Officer; or the Board may call a dentist to account as a result of its own internal administrative mechanisms. As was reported in Chapter 5, NHS complaints acccounted for about one third of all indemnity-related claims reported by dentists to one defence organization.[21]

Complaints by patients

Complaints by patients account for the majority of difficulties reported by dental practitioners under the NHS. Following recent initiatives by government,[22] and the issue of the 'Patient's Charter' for hospital care,[23] the promotion of patients' rights, including access to complaints machinery, has received increased priority. Patients who are dissatisfied with general dental treatment are recommended to first raise the matter with the dentist himself or herself. If this does not produce a satisfactory response, or the patient is unwilling to return, the FHSA may consider the matter under informal or formal procedures. The patient will also be advised of assistance available from Community Health Councils, local bodies set up under the 1974 National Health Service Act to represent the interests of Health Service patients.

A patient who chooses to pursue his or her complaint under informal procedures will be advised at the outset that if dissatisfied with the outcome, the option to pursue the matter formally will still be available.[24] It is clear from this that it will be advantageous for a practitioner to deal fully, sympathetically and promptly with any complaint received from a patient, either directly, or through an FHSA under the informal procedure. Although any comments made by the practitioner at this stage will not be 'on the record' if a formal complaint is later made, it is always important to seek the advice of a defence organization at the earliest stage of any complaint, and certainly before making any comment in writing. Comments in Chapter 4 concerning the early handling of patient complaints apply, and the patient should receive a prompt, courteous, full and personal explanation of the problem, together with an apology where applicable.

Should the patient pursue the matter informally through the FHSA, all Authorities have staff able to deal impartially with such matters and the majority of patient complaints are in fact dealt with satisfactorily in this way. The practitioner's written comments may be sought, a lay conciliator may visit the patient and practitioner separately, or a 'round table' meeting may be convened – these procedures may be combined. Meetings with patients are held in the presence of a member of FHSA staff, and the conciliator or an informal dental adviser to the Authority may also be present. Although dentists may, not unnaturally, feel apprehensive at being invited to attend such a meeting, the outcome is, more often than not, successful.

The refunding of any NHS charges paid by patients who have complained is a contentious issue, and when dentists regard a complaint as unjustified it is hardly surprising that they should resist the suggestion. It is difficult to generalize on this issue; if a complaint is clearly frivolous or vexatious, then the practitioner may feel that a refund of charges merely 'adds insult to injury'. Experience shows, however, that the treating dentist is not always in the best position to judge matters, and advice should be sought from a defence organization in such instances. Professional principles may, in some instances, have to be balanced against the prospect of considerable stress and time-consuming procedures incurred if a formal complaint subsequently follows (see 'Formal procedures' below).

It would not be reasonable for dentists to face complaints from patients when a considerable period has elapsed after treatment. Memories fade, oral conditions change and the probability of a fair and just conclusion is reduced. FHSAs are advised that informal complaints should, wherever possible, be completed within one month.[7] Formal complaints must be submitted within 13 weeks of the treatment complained of, or within 6 months of the completion of treatment, whichever is the sooner.[25] There are provisions for later complaints to be investigated formally, although the patient will have to show that there is reasonable cause.

Complaints following Dental Reference Officer report

From the inception of the National Health Service, an auditing and independent reference service has been in place. Dental Reference

Officers (DROs), appointed by the Department of Health and employed by the Dental Practice Board, periodically review patients of all practitioners. Patients are selected on a sampling basis, either from completed cases notified to the Dental Practice Board for payment, or from pre-treatment cases where the Board's consent (prior approval) for treatment – usually on the grounds of higher cost – is required. After examination of the patient, the DRO will send a copy of his clinical report to the practitioner and to the Board. In the majority of cases, satisfactory treatment (or treatment proposals) are noted. In some cases, the officer may find that treatment is unsatisfactory to a degree (or may disagree with the treatment proposed). Dental officer reports are 'coded' with an identifying number and a suffix letter – this suffix denotes the conclusion reached, the current coding being:

Suffix	Denotes
L	Treatment (or proposals) satisfactory
M	Minor degree of clinical disagreement with proposals, or, oral health not secured and maintained, but reason not significant
R	Moderate disagreement with proposals, or, oral health not secured and maintained for significant reason
S	Major disagreement with proposals, or, oral health not secured or maintained, for reason of major significance
H	Dental Officer unable to give opinion (evidence destroyed or unavailable)

Codings 'L' or 'M' will usually give the practitioner no difficulty. Codings 'R' or 'S' will generally result in a request from the Dental Practice Board for the dentist's comments. It is possible that discrepancies noted in such reports may give rise to a formal complaint from the Board, and any comments made by the practitioner may be introduced into the complaint proceedings. It is essential, therefore, that practitioners seek the advice of a defence organization before responding to such a request in these cases.

Dentists are notified in advance of patients to be examined by the Dental Reference Service and the regulations prohibit the provision of any but emergency treatment after such notification (until the report process is complete). It is advisable to review the records of such patients' treatment and to advise the Reference Service of any particular or exceptional circumstances surrounding the treatment or proposals. In the event of 'M', 'R' or 'S' coded reports it is not unusual for further patients to be sampled.

If the Dental Practice Board is not satisfied with a practitioner's comments or if it feels that the dental officer's findings indicate a *de facto* breach of the regulations, then it may institute a formal complaint through the dentist's FHSA.

Complaints arising from the administrative procedures

Since the early 1970s, the central administration of the general dental services has been computerized, since several million treatment claims are received each week by the Dental Practice Boards. For some years, such data was used to carry out some general profiling of the treatment patterns of individual dentists, and this information, as well as contributing to service planning, was also used to alert the Board to unusual treatment patterns which were usually investigated further by the Dental Reference Service. Advances in data processing have continually refined this process, and different procedures may now be followed. The Board recognise however that practitioners will have inherent differences in their patient and treatment mix, and that approaches and treatment methods will also vary.

Under current regulations, the Board has powers to require a dentist, whose treatment pattern it considers exceptional, and after allowing for any comments by the dentist concerned, to submit all treatment proposals for adult patients under the NHS (other than examination and two small X-rays) for its prior approval over a period of 3–9 months.[26] There are provisions for appeal by the dentist. Alternatively, the Board may request sight of a number of dental treatment records for patients of the dentist, and if it is concerned about aspects of the treatment recorded, may ask the dentist to comment. If the Board is dissatisfied with this reply, it may, once again, institute formal disciplinary proceedings. Whilst practitioners are always advised to co-operate fully with the Board in any enquiries, the defence organizations urge dentists who feel they are under particular scrutiny to consult them at the earliest opportunity.

The increasing degree and sophistication of computerized monitoring of dental practice undoubtedly leads some practitioners to feel that their professional autonomy is under threat. In this respect, the range of views expressed by the profession is no different to those of any citizens who view with alarm the increasing accumulation of data by police, taxation and many other authorities. The Dental Practice Board has its own risk management priorities; it is answerable for the public funds it disburses and for its own administrative expenses as a proportion of those funds. The extent and nature of its activities in monitoring and investigating unsatisfactory – and occasionally fraudulent – treatment are determined by balancing its duties to the Department of Health against the requirements of the NHS regulations which bind it as they bind each contracted dentist.

Formal complaint and disciplinary proceedings

This section heading contains within it one source of continuing problems both for dentists and their patients; if a formal procedure is instituted, it combines a disciplinary investigation of the practitioner with the consideration of any complaint. This means first that any complaint made by a patient which does not directly concern a matter regulated by the dentist's Terms of Service (for example rudeness, inefficiency or poor communication) may not be pursued. Second, although the patient's principal desire may be to have his complaint fully investigated and to receive either an explanation or an apology, none of these may result from a process which can only end in either 'dismissal' of the complaint, or a disciplinary sanction against the dentist involved. Finally, it will be apparent that the same quasi-judicial process must be followed, whether the complaint is one of serious and gross breach of the regulations, brought and pursued by officials of the Dental Practice Board, or a patient protesting at the £2 charged for dressing a tooth.

From the foregoing, the risk management implication must be that the avoidance of formal complaints procedures is, wherever possible, strongly advised. It is not the intention to describe the detailed arrangements here, other than to indicate their general format. If despite a dentist's best endeavours, formal proceedings are instituted, then assistance from the defence organization (each of whom produce literature for members outlining the process) and from the Local Dental Committee (which represents the interests of NHS practitioners) is vital.[27]

It should be added that, at the present time, moves are afoot to amend radically the procedure for patient complaints, with a view to co-ordinating arrangements for the investigation of complaints by hospital, community service and primary care patients. It is intended that the initial processes shall be instituted within a practice, clinic or department, and for simplified formal arrangements to follow if necessary. The separation of complaints investigation and disciplinary machinery is also proposed.[28]

The present format requires that a patient's complaint is reviewed by the Chairman of the FHSA Dental Service Committee who adjudges whether the matter falls within the Terms of Service. If it is 'out of time' – beyond the time limits set – the committee must consider the patient's reason, and seek either the practitioner's consent, or (if this is not forthcoming) that of the Secretary of State (through an Appeals Unit) for investigation. Complaints from the Dental Practice Board follow the same initial procedure. In the case of a patient complaint, an independent clinical report from a DRO may be commissioned. The dentist's formal written response to the complaint is required, and the complainant has an opportunity to comment further on this, again in writing. The Dental Service Committee then consider whether a hearing before the committee is required. These preliminary stages may take up to six months – not infrequently longer – to complete.

If a hearing is held, the dentist, who may be accompanied by an adviser or representative (who may not address the Committee if legally qualified), and the patient, who may be similarly accompanied, present their cases to the Service Committee, which consists of a lay chairman aided by equal numbers (two or three of each) of lay and dental practitioner members. In a Dental Practice Board complaint, a senior dentist from the Board will present its case. A senior staff member of the FHSA acts as a clerk to the hearing, and although the proceedings are confidential, FHSA secretarial support staff and observers from the Local Dental Committee, the Community Health Council, and the Council on Tribunals may be present. Thus, although strictly speaking non-judicial, the proceedings carry a considerable aura of formality.

Witnesses may be called by either side, and cross-examined, and the Dental Reference Officer may appear as an independent witness to present his findings. At the conclusion of the hearing, which may typically last from 1–4 hours dependent on the complexity of the matter, the parties withdraw, leaving the Service Committee to deliberate. The committee's report is supplied first to the FHSA itself for approval, and is then issued to the parties to the complaint, giving the decision and any recommendations. These may include:

(a) No action
(b) The issue of a formal warning to the dentist
(c) A monetary withholding from the dentist's remuneration
(d) A requirement for the dentist to submit future treatment estimates for prior approval for up to one year

Any withholding under (c) which exceeds £500, and any recommendation under (d) must receive the Secretary of State's confirmation, through the FHS Appeals Unit. The committee may direct that a sum, up to the amount paid by the patient for NHS treatment, may be repaid to the patient out of any withholding.

The sanctions listed at (b), (c) and (d) would vary in relation to the seriousness of any breach of the dentist's Terms of Service, and although there is no set 'tariff', circulars are sent, from time to time, to chairmen of Service Committees advising them of typical recommendations. As already noted, the General Dental Council may be informed by the Secretary of State of serious breaches established by Service Committees and may enquire further into the matters.

It is open to either party (against whom the decision of the committee is adverse) to appeal against a Service Committee finding. Where appeals are made by complainants, and in cases where a dentist has reasonable grounds to appeal against having been found 'in breach' of his Terms of Service, or where the recommendations are thought excessive, defence organizations may assist members in this procedure. Appeals may be determined either in writing or by a hearing, and legal representation is permitted. The procedure broadly resembles that given for Service Committee investigations, but the technicalities and legal arguments may be complex. Expert assistance is highly desirable, especially since, on appeal, a finding may be confirmed, and the severity of the original recommendation increased.

Dentists who have the misfortune to be required to appear before a Service Committee are advised to seek advice early and to keep their defence organization fully and promptly informed of progress in the initial stages, since strict time limits are applied to the exchange of documentation. At hearings it is almost invariably wise to be accompanied, both for the purposes of keeping notes of the proceedings and to have the opportunity of a colleague with whom to confer. Defence organizations and Local Dental Committees can advise on the choice of a suitable individual.

Dental Service Committee hearings have increased in number over the past decade. Between 1981 and 1991, the total number of cases heard annually rose from 304 to 472.[29] Of the cases heard in 1991, 43% resulted in findings against the practitioner (202 cases). Only in 8% of these cases was a subsequent appeal entered, and three-quarters of appeals by dentists failed.

A proportion of dentists will regard the extent and complexity of NHS regulation as being an unwarranted or unbearably onerous imposition on their clinical role, and, together with well cited financial restrictions, this may well have a bearing on the increasing number of practitioners who offer treatment only under private contract or who are moving towards this position.[30] A number of capitation or pre-payment schemes for dental treatment are now available in the UK. To protect the position of dentists and patients in this developing field, two of the schemes offer 'quality review' provisions which assess both the practice facilities and by means of clinical notes review, the standard of care provided. The General Dental Council has also proposed a scheme for resolving complaints from patients receiving private dental care which is likely to be initiated in the near future.[31]

The North American experience suggests that in the absence of a comprehensive regulatory system governing the details of the provision of dental care, increased litigation in the civil courts may result. Whilst regulation of professional ethics is largely discharged, as noted in the previous section, by state boards of dentistry, the individual insurance plan providers have widely varying procedures for arbitration of patient complaints, but these are nowhere as extensive as in the British National Health Service. Reviewing cases reported from US courts, it is notable that many civil claims result from occurrences that would more probably be dealt with under complaints procedures in the UK. Insurance companies may also file suit against dentists for breach of conditions (which are becoming increasingly complex) of insurance plans, and retain the right to exclude a practitioner from their plan. State dental societies have peer review committees whose function incorporates the investigation of dentists following patient complaints, but dentists' indemnity insurance commonly excludes assistance in these matters.[32]

In the United States, the contingency fee system has, to some extent, had the effect of making the courts more accessible to prospective litigants. In the UK, there is a tendency for patients to use the NHS complaints system for which there are no direct costs to the claimant. If a decision in their favour results, then, it is reasoned, they may go on to pursue matters in the courts to obtain financial redress. However, although the findings of a Service Committee may be taken into consideration by the courts, the disciplinary decision is based on the dentist's position in relation to his Terms of Service, whilst the courts are concerned with the legal duty of care. The two are related, but not synonymous.

Hospital and community practice

Complaints against dentists employed in the hospital and community service in the UK are dealt with under the provisions of the Hospital Complaints Act (1985), which requires all health authorities (and more recently NHS Trusts) to make provision for a system of dealing with complaints and to publicize that system. The Patients' Charter (1991) re-states this obligation. Complaints are initially dealt with on an informal basis (unless the complaint clearly indicates that a disciplinary matter or serious consequences are involved). The head of the appropriate department is usually asked to co-ordinate a response to the complaint, and will approach the individual staff involved for their comments and for details of the treatment provided. Dental staff who are required to submit comments in this way can rely on the assistance of their defence organization to assist them. Such assistance may be important, since the matter complained of may have direct implications for their Terms of Employment. Hospitals and Trusts will generally seek to respond to a complaint at the earliest opportunity, but if the complainant is dissatisfied they have the option of taking the matter to litigation, or of approaching the Health Services Commissioner (the 'Ombudsman'). The Commissioner has wide powers to order disclosure of records and to require a formal response from clinicians and administrators involved in the original treatment or the handling of the complaint. He may not, however, investigate treatment or decisions made by clinical staff, and will not normally investigate complaints where the complainant would be able to pursue a case in court. His investigations are therefore largely confined to maladministration.

Contracts for junior grades of hospital staff (i.e. up to senior registrar level) will generally follow the basic model set out by the Department of Health,[33] although there have been numerous recent reports of NHS Trusts departing from the established format. Advice on basic contractual matters should be sought in the first place from a dentist's professional association. Contracts will, again generally, contain a provision that disciplinary and grievance procedures will follow the format set out in the General Whitley Council Conditions of Service. Dentists should be aware of the provisions of these conditions, copies of which can be obtained from the Unit or Trust Administrator.

Complaints which allege a failure of clinical care may be dealt with internally, or if it is considered that litigation may result, the health authority or Trust's legal advisers may be consulted. A dentist's professional interests may not always coincide with his employer's policy on dealing with potential claims, and membership of a defence organisation will provide a source of independent advice. It will also provide discretionary indemnity support for 'Section 2' work, such as the provision of reports and opinions which is fee earning and outside the jurisdiction of Crown indemnity.

In disciplinary cases, clinical matters may be dealt with either by an internal committee, by means of two independent experts drawn from outside the authority or Trust (one should be from outside the region), or in exceptional cases by a Commission of Inquiry set up by the Secretary of State under powers granted by the 1977 National Health Service Act. If the matter is dealt with internally, the dentist should have sufficient knowledge and prior warning of the procedure and the details of the allegations against him to enable him to fully address the matter with the assistance of his defence organization and his Accredited Representative at his place of work (Community Accredited Representative in the Community Service). Legal and independent expert advice may be necessary, and the dentist should be accompanied at all meetings with those appointed to investigate the matter. At independent inquiries, legal representation is essential.

Appeals against the findings of a disciplinary investigation are provided for, either within Whitley Council Conditions, or, in the case of Independent Inquiries, to the Secretary of State.

Almost invariably, when disciplinary matters are raised against members of NHS clinical staff, it transpires that they have no specific knowledge of the disciplinary and grievance procedures operated by their employer. In the investigation of seemingly minor complaints it has happened that clinicians find themselves participating in apparently informal proceedings, only to discover that formal disciplinary action follows, typically in the form of a recorded warning. Whilst such incidents are fortunately uncommon in the salaried services, this very infrequency may lead to inadequate procedures which do not serve the interests of natural justice. As with all disciplinary matters, appealing against a decision is invariably a more complex and formal affair which 'raises the stakes' considerably. It is far better to be prepared and informed at the outset.

Relationships with professional colleagues

A survey of the subject matter of 100 consecutive telephone calls received from members on 'new matters' by a dental adviser of a defence organization revealed the following breakdown:

Concerned with NHS Regulations, disciplinary matters	31%
Concerned with actual or potential civil (indemnity) claims	31%
Concerned with contractual or employment matters	20%
Ethical, health and safety, and miscellaneous advice	18%

After disciplinary and indemnity cases, then, the third most frequent problem encountered by that organization's dental members involved their working relationships and the contracts or agreements into which they had entered. The great majority of these involved general practice.

General practice disputes

Dentists in general practice in the UK fall into one of three categories in respect of their employment status:

1. **Practice principal or partner** A practitioner who has ownership, part ownership or joint ownership of the practice property, equipment and/or 'goodwill'. The goodwill is the notional value of the patient list of the practice

2 **Associate** Customarily, a dentist who has no ownership of the practice assets, but who works as an independent and self-employed subcontractor providing clinical skills in return for agreed 'consideration' – usually but not always, a percentage of the fees earned. Strictly speaking, associateship has no precise legal definition other than that which the parties to the agreement decide

3 **Assistant** A dentist who is employed by the practice and who is paid either by a fixed salary or by a percentage of fees earned. Vocational trainees in NHS general practice are employed dentists working for an initial one year period as assistants with a standardized contract

There are, however, shades and nuances in each of the above categories, and expert legal advice may be needed to determine the rights and responsibilities of each party to a specific agreement or contract of employment. In particular, the associate's position may cause difficulty unless a prior agreement specifying the precise terms of the relationship between the parties is drawn up with appropriate independent legal advice on each side. Without the existence of such a contract, or where it exists but is ambiguous or omits important provisions, the resolution of disputes may be protracted, expensive and unsatisfactory.

In the event of disputes, defence organizations will provide advice based on the combined knowledge and experience of their professional staff. The benefits of membership do not extend to the provision of individual legal advice in contractual matters. Where both parties are members of the same organization, arrangements can be made for each side to receive impartial and confidential guidance from separate advisers, and careful precautions are taken to ensure that conflicts of interest do not arise. In this respect, the defence organizations' own ethics and procedures, overseen as they are by members of the professions they serve, are required to be of the highest standards.

The British Dental Association also offers a conciliation and arbitration service to its members. These procedures are again conditional upon both sides agreeing to take part, and, in the case of arbitration, to accept the arbitrator's decision. Conciliation involves the appointment of a dentist skilled in such matters who will attempt to bring the parties to the dispute to a mutually acceptable decision; the emphasis being on the encouragement of the protagonists to develop their own solution with assistance. Arbitration requires the appointment of a dentally-qualified arbitrator, to whom the parties submit written statements, and before whom they may appear (or be legally represented). The arbitrator then issues a written statement determining the matter. Whilst this is a more formal procedure than conciliation, and not without expense, it avoids the considerably greater costs and publicity which a court hearing will almost certainly bring.

Disputes in salaried services

Defence organizations may also be called upon for advice in cases involving members' contracts with health authorities, universities and government departments (including the armed services). Members will again be counselled to consult their own legal adviser if this is necessary. Although such legal costs in contractual cases cannot be borne by the defence organization, a number of insurance companies now offer 'legal helplines' or legal expenses insurance which may assist.

Risk management principles in general practice employment

The adage 'look before you leap' has great relevance in this context! Despite advice from defence organizations, professional associations such as the British Dental Association and bodies including the General Dental Council, dentists continue to enter into practice obligations with a potential worth of many hundreds of thousands of pounds without careful prior consideration evidenced by a formal written agreement.

A typical scenario results:

> Miss Younger completes her vocational training and responds to an advertisement for an associate in the dental press. At interview, the practice owner, Mr Elder, is charming and friendly, and the practice is reasonably equipped and looks welcoming (though, as the meeting takes place in the evening, the staff are not there). It is arranged that Miss Younger will start next month on the basis of receiving 45% of her fees (more than most of her friends). They shake hands on the deal.
>
> At first all goes well: there are plenty of patients and although her dental surgery assistant is a new recruit, she is easy to get on with, but naturally a little slow. Miss Younger understands that it will be a couple of months before her first NHS payment comes through: she signed a form on her first day to have the money paid direct to Mr Elder.
>
> The first pay statement is a surprise: she is only paid 40%, and after deductions of laboratory bills and 'bad debts' (she should have insisted on payment in advance before doing that bridge) there isn't much left. Mr Elder says that until she is producing an 'economic' turnover, 45% will not even cover his overheads.
>
> As time goes by, she works harder, but the 45% never appears. The practice has changed to a cheaper laboratory and she is not happy

with the quality. Her nurse leaves due to the poor wages and she has to train the replacement who is not really satisfactory. Also, she has realised that she is not getting her payments until three or four weeks after the NHS pays the practice.

Inevitably, there is an argument. Mr Elder now denies ever offering her 45% and says that her work is so poor that if she leaves she will have to sue him for her outstanding money and he will report her. Distressed, she telephones the local Family Health Service Authority who advise her that as an 'NHS principal' she is an independent dentist and is entitled to revoke her assignment of fees to Mr Elder.

When Mr Elder receives notice that the assignment is to be cancelled, he tells Miss Younger not to come to the surgery tomorrow, as she is 'sacked'. He will change the practice locks at once. That night Miss Elder meets a friend who tells her that no Associate has ever been paid for outstanding work after leaving Mr Elder's practice.

An exaggerated tale? Most certainly not – merely a composite of typical problems reported weekly to defence organizations. There are no magical answers, unfortunately; 'Miss Younger' may recover a part of her money by cancelling her fee assignment; lengthy legal wrangles may produce some more (probably not). She may take her list of registered NHS patients and purchase nearby premises of her own, in which case 'Mr Elder' may be deprived of some goodwill which, by neglecting to negotiate a contract, he has failed to protect. However, this may well be a recipe for many years of mutual recrimination and ill-feeling. Nor should it be considered that practice owners are necessarily the instigators of problems such as these. Associates have been known to remove patient records, circularize patients, to 'poach' practice staff and to remove equipment and materials in the process of setting up a neighbouring 'parallel' practice. No such actions on either part are professional, ethical or, ultimately, in the long-term interests of patients, or the protagonists.

The primary objective for both parties must be the negotiation of appropriate terms of agreement. The British Dental Association, which produces advice and a 'model' agreement for its members' use,[34] points out:

> The core of any associateship arrangement is a sale by a practice owner... of a licence to see patients at specified premises, the licence being bought by the associate. It is a commercial relationship between two dentists of equal professional standing, though not of equal business standing.[35]

The model agreement reflects this equal professional standing, which often receives only lip service (if that) in practice. Practice owners speak of associates 'working for' them and regard them virtually as employees. In a true associate relationship, all practical aspects of the associate's work must be regulated by the agreement; hours, staff and equipment use, laboratory arrangements, clinical freedom and so on. It is not sufficient for the practice owner to dictate such matters as though directing an employee.

Although any model agreement should be used only as a basis for negotiation, and the parties should take independent legal advice before committing themselves, experience suggests that the following items at least should receive consideration:

1. The nature of the contract should be specified; between independent parties, a licence to treat, non-assignment of goodwill, ownership of practice assets
2. Financial arrangements; are payments to be made by percentage of fees or a fixed rental? The General Dental Council frowns upon contracts which require associates to achieve a specified level of fee income.[36] If a percentage method is employed, will it apply to non-treatment fees such as capitation and continuing care payments, to postgraduate allowances and to maternity or long-term sickness payments made by the NHS? What is an appropriate percentage for the circumstances, and what evidence can either side adduce to support their views? How often are percentages or rental payments to be reviewed, and what provision is made for arbitration if the parties cannot agree? How will bad debts be treated? Hygienist fees? Laboratory fees?
3. Fee Assignments: these are a common arrangement, and a frequent source of disagreement. Some practice owners with previous experience of problems may wish to impose a form of assignment which is cancellable only with the consent of both parties. The British Dental Association recommends dentists to take legal advice before signing such a document, and to use it only in conjunction with a full written agreement.[37] The BDA has produced a Code of Practice applicable to fee assignments which should be studied and agreed
4. Hours of work and holidays; the practice owner naturally wishes to see his facilities used profitably, but cannot specify or control the working conditions of an independent associate as closely as those of an employee. Equally, the associate, as a self-employed principal, has the clinical freedom to accept or decline patients for treatment, but is usually dependent on the practice owner and his staff for arranging a supply of patients

5 Clinical provisions; the practice owner can have no automatic right to intervene in the associate's clinical work, to complain about his treatment choices or standard (unless, of course, he feels that a formal complaint is justified), nor should he restrict the associate's reasonable choice of laboratory facilities or materials. If it seems likely at the outset that problems could arise (for instance if the associate has a clinical speciality) then perhaps a fixed rental payment is preferable, with the associate paying for his own, or his share of, materials and specified equipment and laboratory costs
6 Arrangements for long-term illness of the associate; who is to arrange locum cover, after how long, on what terms and at whose expense?
7 Arrangements for termination of the agreement; these should include provisions for bankruptcy, erasure or death of either party, as well as fully specified arrangements for less dramatic termination. Notice, fee arrangements and continuity of treatment must be addressed
8 Provisions for both parties to maintain registration with the General Dental Council. The associate should produce his certificate during January of each year. Omissions do occur and can lead to disciplinary action on both parties – the practice owner is technically 'covering' an unregistered dentist. Additionally, the NHS may refuse to authorize any fees for work done in the period of non-registration. Equal attention should be paid to membership of defence organizations. In the UK, the three major defence bodies have reciprocal working arrangements, and membership of the same organization is not needed
9 Provision for arbitration; this may customarily involve the appointment of an arbitrator nominated by the Chief Executive of the British Dental Association: alternatives may be used if desired
10 'Binding out' clause; this is another perennial source of frustration, limiting an outgoing associate to practise outside a certain surrounding area to the practice for a period following termination of the agreement. Agreements stipulating a 10 mile radius are still encountered (an area of 314 square miles!), despite the courts' abhorrence of 'restrictive trade practices'. The fact is that a court would consider such clauses in the light of whether they are 'reasonable' in the circumstances. In an urban area of Britain, it is unlikely that an area in excess of half a mile radius would be so adjudged.[38] As NHS patient contracts for continuing care run for two years, it is similarly unlikely that a court would support a binding-out arrangement for longer than this. Practice owners who import unreasonable terms into an agreement may find that it is set aside by the courts if a dispute should arise.

The above list of topics should certainly not be viewed as exhaustive, but merely as an indicator of some known problem areas. The average associateship will probably exceed the value of the average detached house, but the purchase of the latter on the basis of a handshake or a brief letter would be unthinkable.

Partnerships, practice purchase

If an associateship should not be considered without a full written agreement, then an arrangement involving the purchase of all or part of the assets of a dental practice must involve very careful forethought.[39] Circumstances here can differ widely, and the involvement of possibly very large sums of money will usually act as sufficient encouragement to the prospective purchaser to take expert advice. There are occasional instances of dentists undertaking very considerable commitments on the flimsiest of evidence and the following points must always be carefully investigated.

1 All purchases must involve, from the earliest stage, discussions with an accountant and solicitor who are well-versed in the particularities of dental practice. The British Dental Association's General Practice department are able to provide lists of experienced professionals throughout the UK. The use of an experienced valuer of dental practices is almost always advisable. Other sources of essential information are the local planning authority (the practice does have planning permission, and the car parking and future expansion are feasible, of course?) and the Family Health Services Authority if an NHS practice (locations of other practices, indices of local need and area statistics for treatment)

2 If a partnership is envisaged, is there certainty that one's future partners are compatible, honest, open and diligent? It is a truism that a partnership is less easily (and more traumatically) ended than a marriage. The prospective partner must be fully conversant with the provisions of the Partnership Act (1890) and its implications for taxation. This applies especially if converting from an associateship to a partnership, and the advice of an accountant and solicitor are imperative. Is the partnership a 'full' partnership, with joint and several liability for all the firm's dealings, or an 'expense-sharing' partnership? Are the advantages and disadvantages of each clearly understood? Are there clearly set out provisions for division of profits and for termination? Has insurance been effected against the death of a partner?

In all such business dealings, dentists are apt to forget the 'opportunity costs' of any undertaking. Briefly, these are defined as the cost of not using the money or resources employed in that undertaking elsewhere. If time, savings, borrowings or securities are used in a purchase, what other opportunities for those assets are being set aside? The prudent dentist will assess such costs as an additional percentage of the purchase price, and will seek to ensure that the return – in financial, professional or personal terms – outweighs the alternatives.

Other contractual areas

It is equally important for dentists employed by health authorities, NHS Trusts or other organizations to ensure that their Terms of Employment are specified fully before accepting a post. Occasionally, even in the simplest of documents, a prospective employee may fail to appreciate the implications. A dental student who signed a binding agreement to enter into a short service commission with an armed service was made aware that his resignation before completion of the term would require repayment of his student tuition and living expenses. When, unhappily, he wished to take this step, he tried – and predictably failed – to avoid this penalty. A consultant offered a salary plus performance bonus contract found later that due to restrictions on bed and theatre availability, there was no possibility of triggering the throughput-based enhancement. Defence organizations and professional associations may advise in these instances, but unless serious matters affecting the profession at large are revealed, independent legal assistance must be sought. Risk management advice is therefore to consider all such propositions carefully before entering into binding commitments. An applicant called to interview should, if he believes an immediate offer of employment may be made, satisfy himself in advance, or by questioning during the interview itself, about the contractual conditions attaching. There is a possibility otherwise that his verbal acceptance of the post may legally bind him. If there is doubt, it is better to defer and to seek further information and advice at once.

References

1. *Dentists Act (1984)*, s1(2)
2. Hindley-Smith D. (1970) *The General Dental Council: its purpose and functions. (rev. 1992)* General Dental Council, London
3. Ibid
4. *Dentists Act (1984)*, s27, s32
5. Ibid, s27(1)(4), Schedule 3
6. Ibid, s28
7. *DuBois v. General Dental Council (1978)* PC 18
8. *Doughty v. General Dental Council (1987)* PC

9. General Dental Council (1993) *Professional Conduct and Fitness to Practice*. General Dental Council, London
10. Ibid, paragraph 16
11. Standing Dental Advisory Committee (1990) *General anaesthesia, Sedation and Resuscitation in Dentistry: Report of an Expert Working Party (Chairman Prof. D. Poswillo)*. Department of Health, London
12. Advisory Committee on Dangerous Pathogens (1990) *HIV – the causative agent of AIDS and related conditions: Second revision of guidelines*. Departments of Health, London
13. British Dental Association (1991) *The Control of Cross-Infection in Dentistry: Advice Sheet A12*. British Dental Association, London
14. General Dental Council (1970) *Notes for Guidance of Dentists*. General Dental Council, London
15. Source: Minutes of the proceedings of the General Dental Council 1956–1990. General Dental Council, London
16. Mason Sir D. (1994) President's Address to the General Dental Council, 82nd session, 10 May 1994. *British Dental Journal*, **176**, (10), 363–367
17. Schroeder O.C. and Pollack B.R. (1987) Contemporary Legal Issues Facing Dentistry, in *Handbook of Dental Jurisprudence* (Pollack B.R. ed.). PSG Publishing, Littleton, Mass. p. 162
18. See: *National Health Service Act (1974)* as amended and Statutory Instruments laid under this Act by Secretaries of State for Health
19. The National Health Service (General Dental Services) Regulations (1992), SI 1992/661. HMSO, London
20. Upex R. (1991) *Davies on Contract*. Sweet and Maxwell, London. p. 1
21. Source: internal data, Medical Defence Union Ltd
22. Departments of Health (1991) *Promoting Better Health*. HMSO, London
23. Departments of Health (1991) *The Patients' Charter*. HMSO, London
24. Department of Health (1990) Notes of Guidance to the Family Practitioner Services Complaints Procedures (Administrators' Letter)
25. *The National Health Service (Service Committees and Tribunal) Regulations (1992)* SI 1992/664. HMSO, London
26. *Regulation 29, The National Health Service (General Dental Services) Regulations (1992)*
27. See also: British Dental Association (1989) *Advice sheet B5*: Dental Service Committees
28. Wilson A. (Chairman) (1994) Proposals for Change in NHS Complaints Procedures. Department of Health, London.
29. Departments of Health (1993) *National Health Service Statistics (1993)*. HMSO London, p. 98.
30. British Dental Association (1994) New BDA NHS Survey Announced (Report). *BDA News*, **7**, (1), 7
31. Davies N. (1993) The Future of Dentistry (letter). *British Dental Journal*, **174**, (1), 14
32. Seldin L.W. (1992) Risk Management: Then and Now. *Journal of the American Dental Association*, **123**, 47–50
33. *The National Health Service (Remuneration and Conditions of Service) Regulations (1991)* SI 1991/481. HMSO, London, as amended by NHS Circular AL(MD)1/92
34. British Dental Association (1990) *Associateship Agreements. Advice Sheet A7*. British Dental Association, London
35. Ibid, p. 3
36. General Dental Council (1993) op cit. paragraph 61

37. British Dental Association (1990) *Fee Assignments. Advice Sheet A5.* British Dental Association, London
38. See for example: *Office Angels Ltd* v. *Rainer-Thomas (1991)* CA Times Law Reports 11 April
39. Abrahams R.M. (1991) Buying a Dental Practice: the Legal and Commercial Issues. *British Dental Journal*, **170**, 307–308 and 347–348

8
Occupational risk

Stress

The preceding chapters have been chiefly concerned with the identification and management of risks which are essentially external. Although their occurrence may be instigated by dentists' acts or omissions, they act principally through or on third parties; patients, staff, the profession. It is true, of course, that a dentist may himself suffer a needlestick injury or trip over a frayed waiting room carpet, but such hazards are also due to the failure of external systems (in these cases, cross-infection control or workplace safety).

This chapter concentrates, in contrast, on the intrinsic occupational risks of dentistry which originate within the dentist (or members of the dental team) and which have their adverse effects primarily on the person concerned. Although these risks are usually considered as separate, if related, topics, it is useful to think of them as different symptoms of the failure of a single internal system.

This 'system' could be called self-management or self-control, but these terms are not only inadequate but also presumptuous. The majority of individuals would assert that they were competent self-managers and were certainly 'in control' of their lives and activities – they might rightly regard failings in these capabilities as serious shortcomings. At the same time, everyone is conscious that certain aspects of life or work seem to take on a momentum of their own and that at times, even if only rarely, anger, frustration or despair can take hold.

Stress has been defined variously as both the reaction of an individual to external stimuli, and as the external events themselves which give rise to a change in the behaviour of the individual.[1] Here, the term **stressors** will be used to describe these external influences and **stress** as the individual's response. Current knowledge about the relationship between stressors, stress and body systems, including the central nervous system, endocrine system and the immune system suggest that one overall purpose of the stress response is the maintenance of homeostasis – literally the preservation of a stable state.[2] Essentially the risks being considered here are those which cause, promote or intensify an individual's instability in relation to work, lifestyle and relationships.

It has been established that mortality and morbidity are strongly linked to a 'stress-free' lifestyle. The work of Belloc and Breslow showed that six relatively accessible factors (eight hours sleep; three balanced meals daily; avoidance of smoking; moderation in alcohol consumption; regular exercise and controlled body weight) could together reduce mortality rates by 37%.[3] On the other hand there is evidence to suggest that the absence of sufficient stimulation and controlled stress may of itself have damaging consequences.[4]

Dentistry is generally considered to be a stressful occupation,[5] although overall mortality and morbidity figures for dentists have been shown to be below those for comparable professionals both in Britain, western Europe and North America.[6] However, death rates for suicide and cirrhosis are greater in British male dentists than in other male healthcare professionals,[7] which may indicate specific threats (see below). Particular stress factors identified in general dental practitioners include patient management (missed appointments, anxious patients, patient complaints); business management (financial problems, collecting patient fees); staff management and time pressures.[8] There is some evidence that dental specialists may experience lower stress levels, but this may only imply that stress-prone dental graduates tend to opt for a general practice career.[9]

Stress levels in excess of average values have also been detected in a significant proportion of dental students although interestingly, these tended to decline in the final years of study.[10] All members of the dental team have been shown to suffer from stress effects, although the stressors varied according to role.[11] Nevertheless, it is important for dentists to recognize that the problem is not exclusive to their position alone. Significantly, dental surgery assistants attributed their stress to working conditions and the management skills of the dentist, whilst hygienists regarded dentists' attitudes to their educational role and availability of support staff as particularly stressful.

Holmes and Rahe devised a scale of 'life events' to which they ascribed a points value, with 'death of spouse' (rating 100) down to 'minor violation of the law' (rating 11).[12] They showed that the annual accumulation of rating points, over a certain level, for an individual was related to their likelihood of suffering illness in the succeeding two years. This finding suggests that the 'rate of change' or degree of instability in a lifestyle may in itself induce stress-related illness. As mentioned earlier, a direct relationship between the central nervous system (which perceives stressors), the endocrine system (which may affect mood and metabolism) and the immune system (ability to combat pathogens) has been described, each system having a feedback mechanism with the others.

Dealing with stress

It has been suggested that effective stress management must begin with the identification of the stressors involved.[13] Typical stressors in dental practice include:

- payment system and level (particularly associated with NHS practice)
- negative patient perceptions of dentistry
- time pressures
- dealing with staff and management
- lack of variety or promotion prospects
- dissatisfaction with work standards

An initial approach might therefore be the keeping of a 'stress diary' in which stressors, and the response they provoke, can be recorded. If responses are graded on a scale of 1 to 5, and stressors suitably abbreviated, this need not be an overly time-consuming exercise. After a period of two or three weeks, the type, severity and incidence of stressors can be noted and evaluated.

One common response to stressors is to attempt to suppress the stress response. There is evidence that this type of 'denial' behaviour is in itself linked to chronic ill-health.[14] There are two alternative strategies which are more helpful; one is cognitive (affecting the way we understand), and one is behavioural (affecting the way we react). Either or both may be appropriate for dealing with any particualr stressor.

The cognitive approach involves a re-programming of attitude to a particular stressor. For example, every practitioner has experienced a 'sinking feeling' when a glance at the day's patient list shows a really difficult patient due to attend towards the end of a busy day. It is quite possible that the anticipation of such an event can completely overshadow the entire day's activity. Heightened stress levels not only reduce our appreciation of successfully accomplished tasks, but may actually predispose to the risk of a mishap. A cognitive approach might involve discussion with another staff member of that patient's particular management problem. Say it is a child who exhibits poor behaviour; the problem is faced squarely and a realistic goal is set – perhaps the completion of a simple procedure – and ways of accomplishing it are considered. The objective is to turn a 'negative' experience (for the dentist) into a 'positive' challenge.

The cognitive approach will not be successful for all stressors, and an alternative 'coping' or behavioural strategy may be employed. A proportion of dental practitioners working in the National Health Service have considered, for example, that their degree of work satisfaction is limited by the fees available. In setting out a programme for planned change in their practices with the objective of moving some or all of their patient care into the private sector, these dentists are essentially undertaking a behavioural change to reduce one of their stressors.

Most stressors are capable of being effectively tackled by the use of one – or commonly a blend of both – of these management approaches. What such a management system may ignore, however, is the fact that different individuals will react to an equivalent stressor (or combination of stressors) to a varying extent. There are a number of modifying factors which may determine whether one can 'ride out' or even respond positively to stressful situations, or whether they may seriously increase the risk of negative physical, emotional or behavioural outcomes. Such factors include:[15]

- Personality
- 'Significant others'
- Past exposure
- Timing
- Resistance

Several studies have shown that personality, as measured by standard psychometric testing, is a strong predictor of stress response.[16] So-called 'Type A' behavioural traits have been linked to a poor stress accommodation and to increased morbidity and mortality. Type A individuals display typically restless behaviour, difficulty in delegating tasks, perfectionism in self-analysis and 'polyphasic' activity (doing several tasks simultaneously). Such activities have been commonly observed amongst dental professionals. Whilst an hereditary element may be present in Type A behaviour patterns, recognition of these characteristics and training in their avoidance can considerably alter individuals' patterns of action and lifestyle, with a consequent improvement in their stress tolerance.

'Significant others' is a generic term used to describe those with whom we have a close relationship such as family, friends and advisers. The need for understanding, discussion and empathy at stressful times is fundamental, and in the absence of such opportunities for sharing and constructive feedback, the stress response is more likely to become a distress situation.

Past experience of stress tends to help in the development of stress tolerance. This may account for the fact that dental students in the later years of study appear to experience less stress,[17] and that dentists find the early years after qualification more stressful. It has, however, been reported that vulnerability to stress may increase in 40–60 year olds.[18] This period may be one when instabilities become more marked; children are becoming independent, career ambitions may have been fulfilled, and adaptation towards retirement must be considered. Certainly the theory that lifestyle change and stress are linked is borne out by the observation that repeated exposures to similar stressor patterns can build up a conditioning of the stress response, whereas exposure to constantly varying stressors is less well tolerated.

Timing of stressors is also significant. The coincidence of different stressors, or their occurrence at particular times of year can modify the stress response. Because both positive and negative stressors can have an equally deleterious effect, holidays and events such as Christmas can amplify the impact of work-related crises.

Resistance to stress can be acquired in ways other than repeated exposure. Belloc and Breslow's recommendations have become accepted 'sound advice' but that does not make them any less valid. A healthy diet, good sleep patterns, regular exercise and the avoidance of smoking and excess alcohol are hardly novel suggestions, but failure to accept them makes any stress management programme both more difficult and less successful.

Time pressure

It was suggested in Chapter 5 that certain medico-legal risks in clinical practice are undoubtedly associated with the dentist being rushed, and many communication faults (both written and verbal) can also be related to the failure to allow sufficient time for adequate explanation or description. Lewis has noted that lack of time planning is one of the most serious omissions in dental practice.[19] Time and stress management are closely linked in a profession such as dentistry, which is predicated on the provision of successive, individual, personal, labour-intensive services. There are numerous detailed time-management systems and a short overview only is offered here.[20,21]

It may be argued that, owing to the nature of their work, the majority of dentists already exercise more control over their use of time than most comparable professions; a dental practitioner may well have allocated the exact use of his working day, divided into segments as small as five minutes, for the foreseeable future. This by itself can be a source of stress, leading to a feeling of entrapment or what Lewis refers to as 'people poisoning' – inescapable contact with a succession of individual patients. As each dentist's approach to patient care will differ, there are correspondingly many different appointment systems, many of which work reasonably well most of the time. This is sufficient reason for the majority of dentists to claim that their time management is good, and that as emergencies or unforeseen complications are, by their nature, unpredictable, little can be done about the minority of occasions when things go wrong.

This is, on the face of it, a reasonable argument, but it ignores two facts. First, there is evidence that dentists fail to keep within their self-allotted schedule on far more occasions than they themselves believe.[11] Even though not all of those failures are major, the intensely structured nature of the day's work means that a cumulative effect occurs. Second and more fundamentally, appointment systems are only one component of time management, which has far more to do with attitudes than with mechanisms.

One of the principal internal risks of dentistry is the development of long-term attitudes to the work which can lead to frustration, boredom, depression or 'burnout'.[22] Stages in this process, which may be recognizable to many dentists, could be described as:

- Initial challenge (a new practice or department, initiating a career or project)
- Routine (immediate challenges overcome)
- Boredom (no challenge)
- Depression (inability to respond to challenge)

Douglass has suggested that the underlying reason for this trend lies in the failure to set realistic personal objectives – which effectively maintain a manageable state of challenge throughout life:[21]

> The paradox of time applies to our personal lives as well as to our work lives: we never have enough time to do everything we'd like to do, yet we have all the time there is. Furthermore, there is always enough time to do what is most important to us – if we only knew what that was.

This view is hardly new; the belief that 'the world is change – our life is what our thoughts make it' goes back nearly two millennia.[23] The links between personal goal-setting behaviour and stress or time management are fundamental. Formulating long-term objectives (and reviewing them regularly) in the work setting, in personal life, in social activities, in maintaining health and in financial matters should be a preliminary to the detailed organization of the working day, and not something to be ignored or relegated.

Once it is accepted that the management of time pressures at work form only one part of overall goals, then the collection of particular data can be undertaken. It is useful to have a staff member record the actual times which specific procedures take and the times (plus or minus relative to the appointed times) at which patients are seen and depart. Both types of data are important, since they are not necessarily the same. Merely recording patient times may not equate to the time taken for a procedure, since it may omit the time taken for activities such as patient discussion, surgery clean-up and so on. Time management is a procedure which must involve the entire dental team, and useful discussion cannot take place without objective data, since each person's perception and priorities may differ. In this context, patients are significant members of the team, and their opinions should also be sought.[24]

Time management is an amalgam of disciplines. It requires personal goal-setting, staff management ability, communication skills (hastening the departure of an over-talkative patient) and efficient procedure design. The problem is not in the fact that these abilities are lacking – quite the contrary, as most dentists can demonstrate – but that there may be unwillingness to admit that improved proficiency can be achieved in one or more areas.

Specific health risks

Modern dentistry is a sedentary occupation, and this carries with it the risks of postural and orthopaedic damage. In the days when dentists habitually stood to work, neck and spinal problems were prevalent. A hunched attitude, with one shoulder higher than the other and compensated by a contra-lateral pelvic tilt, left the weight borne unevenly on one leg.[25] The advent of virtually universal seated working – other than in operating theatres – has allowed for a less stressful posture, but has introduced new possibilities for physical stress and damage. Moreover, the rapid development of dental surgery equipment and techniques has greatly increased the range of procedures carried out by dentists. Postural risks can arise from:

- The failure to appreciate and develop correct operating positions and movement during training
- Lack of training for the integrated dental team (four- and six-handed operating)
- Insufficient attention to good and bad design features of dental equipment
- Poorly planned and co-ordinated surgery layout
- Inattention to general physical health
- Failure to take early and correct advice should postural problems occur.

Taking these points in order, there is still too little attention given to the teaching and encouragement of good postural practice in dental training. Observation of dental students for such activities and adjustment of operating stool height, positioning equipment for optimal reach and angulation and setting the dental chair position correctly for the proposed task often reveals poor understanding of the long-term consequences. Good habits must be acquired early.

Although the integrated teaching of dental students and dental surgery assistants has improved markedly, there are still many occasions when the opportunity to develop a close and complementary working technique is not available. Given the multiple department organization of the majority of dental schools, it is often not until after qualification that the possibility arises to have a stable working relationship. Ideally, newly qualified dentists should have the services of a trained, but adaptable assistant who can encourage the development of efficient, safe and healthy work practices.

Modern dental equipment is not always designed or marketed with the accent on ergonomic use. One would not normally purchase a car (especially if it were to be used daily for the length of time a dentist operates) without a test drive and assurance that a comfortable and efficient driving position was attainable. Dental equipment is often chosen without comparable care.

Overall surgery design is another area where careful planning for the individual requirements of the user must be undertaken. Analysis of the type of treatment undertaken, physical characteristics and preferences of the users, and workflow patterns must be undertaken to avoid the possibility of being 'locked into' an inefficient or damaging layout.

General physical health should not be neglected. It has been suggested that dentists in general do not take sufficient aerobic exercise,[26] and a pattern of activity should be chosen (after consultation with the medical practitioner if there are any doubts whatsoever about general fitness) which emphasizes flexibility.

Finally, professional advice should be sought promptly should symptoms of postural damage be noted, however slight. It has been suggested that the Alexander technique is an excellent preventive aid which encourages the understanding and avoidance of musculo-skeletal injury,[27] and a range of other suitable treatment options for existing problems is available.[28]

An excellent review of individual and team training in correct operating posture and management is to be found in J. Ellis Paul's 'Team Dentistry'.[29]

Alcohol and drug abuse

Statistics already referred to indicate that mortality from cirrhosis in male dentists exceeds that for males in other comparable professions. It may be speculated as to whether the insular nature of general dental practice, in particular, or the combination of clinical, financial and management responsibilities has a role to play in this problem.

Apart from mortality statistics, evidence for the extent of alcohol abuse in dentistry may be inferred from two sources: the Health Committee of the General Dental Council, and the British Dental Association 'Sick Dentist' scheme.

As noted in Chapter 7, the Health Committee of the GDC was established following the passage of the Dentists Act (1984). Prior to this time, the Council's Disciplinary Committee had no option but to deal with a dentist whose conduct was alleged to have been 'infamous in a professional respect' due to alcohol or drug-related problems in the same way as other members of the profession who appeared before it. The Committee had open to it only the sanctions of erasure or deferment pending reports, and was unable to impose conditions on a dentist's registration or a period of suspension. Broadly, the sanctions available to the committee were punitive rather than constructive and although the General Dental Council's overall concern is with the promotion of high professional standards, its procedures prior to 1984 allowed little scope for encouraging and supervising the rehabilitation or recovery of affected dentists.

As reported by the President in his address to the Council in 1994,[30] the Health Committee has heard cases involving a total of 23 dentists since its first meeting in 1985. In 19 cases, the dentist's fitness to practise was considered by the committee to be seriously impaired, with the majority having alcohol or drug-related problems or a combination of both. Five cases had been concluded with the dentist's fitness to practise having been satisfactorily re-established, whilst in a further seven cases the dentists had voluntarily sought erasure (or, in one case, had died). Five cases remained under active consideration at the time of the President's address.

In the same speech, Sir David Mason acknowledged the work of the 'Sick Dentists Scheme' in contributing to the care of dentists with dependency problems. This scheme was set up on an informal basis in April 1986, and was re-launched as an independent Trust in September 1991.[31] This fund is supported largely by donations from Local Dental Committees, the Dentists' Provident Society and the British Dental Association.[32] The present scheme, which is administered by a Board of Trustees independent of any other organization, is aimed primarily at providing a structured programme for the rehabilitation and recovery of dentists with alcohol and drug-dependency problems but is also concerned with the support of dentists with other medical problems who are not seeking professional help. Between 1986 and 1992, over 180 dentists had been assisted by the Scheme,[33] and over 40 new cases were identified in 1992/3.[32]

A colleague, family member or other person who is aware of a dentist with a dependency or related health problem can telephone a national helpline in confidence, to be provided with the names of a number of 'regional referees'. These referees are senior members of the profession who act as initial validators and as intermediaries. Chosen for their responsibility, sympathetic nature and discretion, regional referees undergo specialist training for their role. One referee is selected by the inquirer and the circumstances of the case are established. The regional referee is then able to contact, via the Trust, a 'special' referee who is a recovering alcoholic or addict and a dentist. Together the two referees will arrange a private meeting with the inquirer and obtain full details, giving an assurance that the source of their information will not be divulged.

Having fully validated the information, the referees will arrange to meet the sick dentist, with the joint objectives of offering practical support and encouraging him/her to confront the problem. The assistance of the sick dentist's own medical practitioner is enlisted in devising a structured programme of rehabilitation, including necessary treatment and attendance at support groups. The special referee will maintain active monitoring of the sick dentist and the referees can provide detailed advice on such matters as financial problems, arranging locums during in-patient treatment phase and so on.

There appears to be general agreement that cases of alcoholism and drug dependency within the profession are continuing to increase. The management of these conditions is highly specialized and although it is in the nature of such problems that those affected are unlikely or unable to seek help on their own account, the Sick Dentist Trust offers a highly confidential and understanding agency for communicating and evaluating concern about an affected colleague.

Financial risk

As noted in Chapter 1, the consideration of 'speculative risk' – where the outcome may be beneficial and not solely injurious – is not considered in this text, and investment advice and general business planning, though undoubtedly 'risk' related subjects, are more competently addressed in specialist publications and by consultation with professional advisers. However, the risk of serious financial failure in dental practice is arguably an area of 'pure risk' – the arrival at a situation whose consequences are invariably harmful to a greater or lesser extent.

Such a situation is unlikely to affect more than a small minority of dental practitioners (it is assumed here that salaried dentists benefit from a position of relative financial security). Bankruptcy rates generally have increased tenfold in a decade, with 100,000 personal bankruptcies in the three years to 1994.[34] Accurate figures for bankruptcies affecting UK dentists do not appear to be available – although subjective reports suggest that the recession of the late 1980s and early 1990s, combined with a reduction in National Health Service fees in 1992, have led to increased financial pressure on many dental practices.[35] Bankruptcy rates would in any event reflect only the most severe problems, and it is not possible to ascertain how many dentists have entered into 'Individual Voluntary Arrangements' with creditors through the Courts, or who have made formal Deeds or informal arrangements to defer repayments.

Bankruptcy is a legal formalization of the state of insolvency – when assets are insufficient to meet outstanding debts – and is arrived at by one of two means. The first is when a creditor, who is owed a sum of £750 or more petitions in the County Court or High Court for a bankruptcy order against the debtor. The debt must have been outstanding for more than 21 days following the issue of a formal demand. In the second instance, a debtor may himself apply to be adjudged bankrupt when he foresees no reasonable possibility of paying his creditors. In either event, the Court may make the bankruptcy order or it may propose an interim order to allow time for an insolvency practitioner to investigate the possibility of arriving at an arrangement with all or most of the creditors. Any creditors who do not agree to such an arrangement may subsequently present their own petition for bankruptcy.

If a bankruptcy order is made, a Trustee in bankruptcy is usually appointed, following a meeting of the creditors. In cases where there has been evidence of serious mismanagement (such as continuing to trade whilst knowingly insolvent), a public examination may be required during which the bankrupt will be questioned about his conduct. The Trustee effectively takes over the remaining assets of the bankrupt and will attempt to raise money by disposing of these in order to repay his own fees and a proportion of the monies due to the creditors. As creditors will rarely obtain any significant percentage of the sums owed, bankruptcy is a serious matter for them also, particularly as 'secured' creditors may have a prior right of acquisition of the bankrupt's major assets, such as property, vehicles or equipment.

The bankrupt is entitled to retain only certain personal possessions (and assets transferred prior to bankruptcy, to relatives for instance, at less than their value are liable to be traced and seized). Under the Bankruptcy Act (1986), the bankrupt may have difficulty in opening a bank account nor can credit of more than £50 be obtained without disclosure of his status. Any earnings must be declared to the Trustee, whose property they become. Generally, bankrupts are 'discharged' after three years, or sooner if repayment of debts and costs is made in full.

From the foregoing, it will be appreciated that bankruptcy is a most serious step to consider, and all practical means should be employed to avoid it. At the most fundamental level, this implies that all financial decisions and plans should be made with care, forethought and independent professional advice. Whilst detailed guidance is a matter for the individual and his accountant, experience suggests that the following general points should be borne in mind:

1. Professional advisers   An accountant, solicitor and other advisers should be chosen who are reputable and have experience of dental matters. They should be kept informed of material developments and their advice heeded carefully
2. Finance   Whenever practicable, competitive quotations for finance should be sought, and the conditions, interest rates and security required given careful and thorough consideration. When other factors are equal, higher interest rates may, for instance, imply a higher perceived risk to the lender, with correspondingly more stringent repayment requirements
3. Accounts   Contemporary practice demands more than a mere approximation of the continuing state of business finances. In addition to the form of accounts agreed with advisers, management accounts detailing the day by day and week by week trends should be maintained and all data should be kept updated. All sole traders or partners should be able to read accounts and balance sheets and to appreciate the positions and tendencies they reveal. If routine book-keeping is delegated, the need to regularly access and understand the completed entries is even more important
4. Communication   All businesses (bar a fortunate few) will encounter unforeseen difficulties. The maintenance of good communication with advisers and major creditors, bankers and so on is essential. They are not likely to be more sympathetic if problems are allowed to develop unchecked. Discussion at an early stage is essential
5. Statutory liabilities   Income tax, employees' tax, gas, electric, rates are all 'unsecured' creditors who do not normally enjoy the privilege of a close working relationship with a business. They are therefore the most likely creditors to take formal action in recovery of debts and should receive appropriate attention
6. Projections   Human nature being what it is, the Micawber Principle – or 'everything will turn out fine in the end' – is undeniably alluring. To resist this tendency, projected income should be (reasonably) reduced and expenditure (reasonably) over-estimated in budgets and cash-flow projections

Should these brief guidelines appear to be wholly self-evident, it may be reflected that the overwhelming majority of business failures and financial difficulties arise from lack of attention to one or more of the above.

Conclusion

Occupational risks in dentistry are susceptible to management in similar ways to other risks; identification (or awareness) being the principal factor involved. Although some of these risks are to a limited extent insurable (physical health most notably, but less so psychological impairment or 'self-inflicted' injury), monetary compensation is little gain for the loss of a professional career or its enjoyment. Risk control must therefore be the predominant feature, and to this end an occasional 'self-audit' has much to recommend it. Regular physical monitoring by the physician is but one aspect of this process. A periodic financial 'health review' is another. Perhaps most important is the consideration of progress towards personal long-term objectives and goals. A staff meeting specifically scheduled once a year to consider trends, reflect on performance generally and to project future intentions and aspirations would help to focus work-related ideals. In the areas of family, social, leisure and individual professional development, an annual review is of benefit. This must be written down if it is to be of value in comparing one year to the next, and may comprise a simple prioritized list, which can be annotated after twelve months to show progress (or lack of it) in any one area, before a new and updated list is prepared. In this regard, direction and progress are at least as important as achievement.

References

1. Kent G.G. and Blinkhorn A.S. (1991) *The Psychology of Dental Care (2nd edn)*. Butterworth-Heinemann, Oxford
2. Speirs R.L. (1993) Stress and the Immune System. *Dental Update 1993*, 20–25, Warman Publications, London
3. Belloc N.B. and Breslow L. (1972) Relationship of physical health status and health practices. *Preventive Medicine*, **1**, 409–421
4. Katz C. (1981) In search of the hardy dentist. *Nexus*, 21 December 1981
5. Kent G. (1987) Stress amongst dentists, in: *Stress in Health Professionals* (ed. Paynes P. and Firth-Cozens J.) Wiley, London
6. Scully C., Cawson R.A. and Griffiths M. (1990) *Occupational Hazards to Dental Staff*. British Dental Association, London, p. 3–7
7. Balarajan R. (1989) A survey of mortality in the health care professions. *British Medical Journal*, **299**, 822–825
8. Godwin W.C., Starks D., Green T. *et al.* (1981) Identification of sources of stress in practice by recent dental graduates. *Journal of Dental Education*, **45**, 220–221
9. Kent G.G. and Blinkhorn A.S. op. cit. p. 155

10. Newton J.T., Baghaienaini F., Goodwin S.R. *et al.* (1994) Stress in dental school: a survey of students. *Dental Update*, **21**, 162–164
11. Blinkhorn A.S. (1992) Stress and the dental team: a qualitative investigation of the causes of stress in general dental practice. *Dental Update*, **19**, 385–387
12. Holmes T.H. and Rahe R.H. (1967) The Social Readjustment Rating Scale. *Journal of Psychosomatic Research*, **11**, 213–218
13. Bosmajian C.P. and Bosmajian L. (1983) *A Personalised Guide to Stress Evaluation.* Mosby, London
14. Selye H. (1956). *The Stress of Life.* McGraw-Hill, New York
15. George J.M., Milone C.L., Block M.J. and Hollister W.G. (1986) *Stress Management for the Dental Team.* Lea and Febiger, Philadelphia
16. Friedman M. and Rosenman R. (1974) *Type A Behavior and Your Heart.* Alfred Knopf, New York
17. Newton J.T., Baghaienaini F., Goodwin S.R. *et al.* (1994) op. cit.
18. Sheehy G. (1974) *Passages: Predictable Crises of Adult Life.* E.P. Dutton, New York
19. Lewis K.J. (1989) *Practice Management for Dentists.* Wright, London.
20. McKenzie R.A. (1972). *The Time Trap.* Amacom, New York
21. Douglass M.E. and Douglass D.N. (1993) *Manage your Time, your Work, Yourself.* Amacom, New York
22. Edelwich J. and Brodsky A. (1980) *Burnout.* Human Sciences, New York
23. Marcus Aurelius
24. Howat A.P., Hammond M., Shaw L. *et al.* (1991) Quality assurance: a project on patient waiting times at appointment in an orthodontic department. *Community Dental Health*, **8**, 173–178
25. Kilpatrick H.C. (1974) *Work Simplification in Dental Practice (3rd edn).* W.B. Saunders, Philadelphia, p.792
26. Hope-Ross A. and Corcoran D. (1985) A survey of dentists' working posture. *Journal of the Irish Dental Association*, **32**, 13–20
27. Stevens C. (1987) *Alexander Technique.* Macdonald Optima, London
28. George M. (1993) Put your back problems behind you. *The Dentist*, **9** (8), 35–36
29. Paul J.E. (1991) *Team Dentistry.* Martin Dunitz, London.
30. Mason Sir D. (1994) President's Address to the eighty-second session of the General Dental Council. *British Dental Journal*, **176** (10), 363–367
31. Editorial (1991) Sick Dentists – An Escalating Problem. *British Dental Journal*, **171** (6), 151
32. Chivers A.H. (1994) The Sick Dentist Trust. *BDA News*, **7** (3), 10
33. Editorial (1992) GDSC Sick Dentist Scheme re-launched. *BDA News*, **5** (7), 1
34. McQueen J. (1994) An Association which helps bankrupts (letter). *The Probe*, **36** (3), 8
35. Lewis K. (1992) Editorial. *Dental Practice*, **30** (19), 3

9
Developing a risk management strategy

Imagine you are going to learn to drive a car, and that the recommended procedure is as follows. First you must study the history of transport and the development of modern automotive engineering. You must memorize the components of the engine, transmission and bodywork. An understanding of all the properties of the materials used is essential. Now, under close supervision you may try out some simple manoeuvres in a small car park; starting the engine, a little steering, how to work the lights and wipers. Next you study the laws relating to motoring; all the various regulations, statutes and specifications. You must understand about breakdowns, maintenance and fault-finding. Finally you may be told a little about the latest Formula One machines. You are examined on all the theory, on some simple practical exercises (in the car park) and must diagnose and repair a faulty vehicle.

*On successfully completing these arduous studies and passing the tests, you are presented with your licence – and given a job as a taxi-driver in the West End of London. The results are predictable. Out in the traffic, everything happens so fast – it is not like the car park. Other motorists obstruct you. A pedestrian steps in front of you and you just manage to brake. Pulling in for a rest, you receive a parking ticket. You are clearly heading for a major accident, but if you had one you would be hard pressed to remember what to do. You know more about how petrol is made than how to put some in the tank, and more about tyre technology than how to avoid a skid. You are a thoroughly well-informed motorist, but **you do not know how to drive safely**.*

The metaphor is exaggerated, but fundamentally apt. Professional training provides in-depth knowledge of many skills, details and subjects, the full and wise employment of which is certain to lead along the path of excellence. It does not have as its primary intention the integration and application of that knowledge to the routines and environment of safe and effective individual working practices. The introduction of risk management principles facilitates that process to occur.

The fledgling taxi-driver would certainly have benefited from a period of gentle acclimatization to the roads. In this sense, vocational training is a major contribution to risk management in dentistry. If this period of gradual adjustment and specialist learning is to achieve its full potential in this sense, it should also encourage the further development of career-long attitudes of enquiry, education and advancement, the foundations for which will hopefully have been laid by the time of graduation.

In this chapter, attention is turned towards ways in which not only the hazards, but also the opportunities which exist in dentistry can most effectively be recognised and acted upon. Techniques for risk identification are described, since it is only by identifying threats that a certain path towards opportunities can be taken. Risk analysis reviews the assessment procedures that can help in the setting of realizable goals. In conclusion, risk control will look at ways in which procedures can be improved and summarizes the ways in which the profession can most effectively work with the defence organizations and other expert advisers.

Risk identification techniques

Risks can be identified in a number of ways. It is certainly appropriate to read textbooks and journals to learn about the complications or precautions involved in a particular technique. Lectures and meetings with colleagues are another valuable source of information. These approaches are in fact the ones which the majority of professionals, including dentists, have traditionally used to improve their awareness of contemporary issues, includings risks, which they face. Additionally, dentists can read, in the publications of defence organizations or the dental press, of examples of risk (for instance professional negligence cases) which have been experienced by their fellow clinicians. As they stand, all these methods are useful and contribute to the development of safer, less risky practice.

There are two problems with this approach. First, it is not known to what extent dentists actually change their own procedures in response to such information. There have been no prospective studies on a large scale which compare the practice and risk exposure of dentists who participate in professional educational programmes to specified extents, against the practice and risk exposure of those who do not. Second, there is general acceptance that what is termed 'active learning' is more likely to result in changed behaviour than mere exposure to information.[1] For example, giving lectures on fire safety in a hospital will achieve far less in terms of staff awareness and safe practice than if the information is combined with a realistic fire drill carried out under observation and assessment.

In a study carried out with 100 dental practices in Boston, Kress carried out surveys of patient satisfaction with their dentists over a one-year period.[2] Dentists who were provided with feedback of their own patients' views at quarterly intervals reported making more changes in their practices and behaviours in response to this information than dentists who received all the feedback at the end of the year. This suggests that even information which relates to our own individual activities may have a 'shelf life', and that continual evaluation is important.

One problem with all the regulatory influences on dentists today, is that they are geared to a 'quality threshold' – a procedure is acceptable, 'up to standard' or it is not. Reviewing a major quality assurance initiative, Morris commented:[3]

> The state of the art of dental quality assurance currently focuses more on treatment techniques than on changing behavior. Such an approach leads to a preoccupation with minimally acceptable performance. The result is a 'bad apple' mentality that dominates the true purpose... namely the continuing improvement of everyone's efforts on behalf of patients.

Risk management is concerned with behavioural change; it is not enough that lectures and articles help us to identify possible threats, nor that discussion improves our ability to analyse them. Risk control must be undertaken and constantly kept under review at the personal practice level (the fire drill) – not merely as a theoretical exercise (the fire safety lecture).

Risk identification techniques which are helpful in the healthcare field include:

Checklists
Flowcharts
Organizational charts
Occurrence screening
Untoward incident reporting

There are other specialist techniques in wide use in other fields of risk management, such as Hazard and Operability Studies (HAZOPS) and Fault Trees which may for instance be applicable to hospital engineering departments or to laboratories, but which have less relevance in the clinical field.[4] Insurance risk managers tend to concentrate heavily on the consequences of risk (e.g. personal accident, property damage, business interruption), but this alone is not a particularly helpful way of viewing the problem from the dentist's viewpoint. Dentists need a means of identifying risks which is relevant to their daily tasks.

Checklists

Checklists are the most direct and basic way of approaching risk identification. All conceivable risks likely to affect the success and well-being of a particular undertaking are considered in turn, together with the appropriate preventive or controlling action which may be taken to avoid them.

There are many ways of approaching the compilation of a checklist, and these approaches, and the checklist itself should be as specific as possible to the site or undertaking in question. One approach, suggested by Crockford,[5] is to categorize a list by the various 'resources' employed – such as buildings, equipment, materials, staff, patients, laboratories, finances – and to list these on a large sheet of paper. Alongside these should be listed the various 'threats' which affect the organization, beginning with broad categories such as natural forces, human error, deliberate damage, progressive deterioration, and then breaking these down into more specific causes. Finally, the various 'consequences' of these threats could be identified and categorized; financial loss, business interruption, loss of assets, loss of reputation, legal liabilities and so on.

Such an approach would not result in a very ordered checklist, but as a preliminary measure it will help to ensure that no major area is overlooked. The usefulness of this approach is chiefly as a precursor to the development of a more detailed and logically set out list which can be combined with a site visit, or tour of the premises, together with a review of documentation.

There is certainly no such thing as a 'final' checklist, and such documents are invariably best produced in loose-leaf form, for constant additions and revisions will be called for. Some of these may be omissions, whilst others may be necessitated by changes in legislation or regulatory requirements.

One alternative approach to checklists would be to obtain a proprietary 'master' list. Developments in this field are occurring, and it is possible that such lists, applicable to different areas of dental healthcare practice, may be made available. One drawback to this approach is that there will inevitably be areas which are not relevant to specific sites, and equally there may be omissions in more specialist situations. The production of such checklists requires considerable care

230   Developing a risk management strategy

Patient Records

Is there a record system:		
(a) for every patient?	Yes	No
(b) distinct between NHS/Private?	Yes	No
Are handwritten records:		
(a) always clearly legible?	Yes	No
(b) most clearly legible?	Yes	No
(c) often not legible?	Yes	No
(d) mostly illegible?	Yes	No
Is there an accepted list of abbreviations?	Yes	No
Are personal remarks excluded from all records?	Yes	No
Are clinical entries:		
(a) too brief?	Yes	No
(b) adequate?	Yes	No
(c) too detailed?	Yes	No
Are all record entries dated?	Yes	No
Are all record entries initialled or signed?	Yes	No
Are all records written up contemporaneously?	Yes	No
Are all DNAs and Cancellations recorded?	Yes	No
Are all contacts, e.g. reviews, cases, recorded?	Yes	No
Is there a medical history summary?	Yes	No
Is the MH dated, initialled and reviewed at each course of treatment?	Yes	No
Are allergies, important MH and drug notes clearly flagged?	Yes	No
Are hospital letters, etc. filed for easy access?	Yes	No
Is correspondence always passed to the dentist with the records for review?	Yes	No
Are finanical records, receipts, lab notes, etc. retained for reference?	Yes	No
Are records culled regularly?	Yes	No
Is waste containing patient information shredded or incinerated?	Yes	No
Are records kept locked or inaccessible to unauthorized staff?	Yes	No
Are staff aware of retention periods for clinical records?	Yes	No
Are staff aware of the provisions of the Access to Health Records Act?	Yes	No
Are dentists aware of the procedures for disclosure of dental records in medico-legal cases?	Yes	No
Are copies retained of any records disclosed?	Yes	No
Is a note kept of records sent elsewhere?	Yes	No
Is a note kept of any missing records?	Yes	No
Is there a procedure for terminating a patient's care?	Yes	No

Comments:

Figure 9.1 Page from dental risk management checklist (copyright Dental Risk Management (1993) with permission)

and forethought, not least because potential documents must be tested and fully reviewed both during development and at regular intervals.

Experience with risk management checklists in widespread use in general medical practice and in hospital departments suggests that one ideal format is to frame each possible source of risk as a question, requiring either a 'yes' or 'no' answer (See Figure 9.1 for an example). Checklists which are intended for use at a number of sites may need additional 'sometimes' or 'not applicable' responses. Work with general medical practitioners has suggested that proprietary checklists may be effectively self-administered.[6]

Having established a series of responses to the questions posed in the checklists, the degree of risk (priority) and intended actions should be recorded. These aspects are dealt with in later sections.

Documentation reviews are an important aspect of checklist preparation. Such a review, in a dental practice might include:

Insurance policies (with particular reference to exclusion clauses and lists)
Equipment service schedules
Practice Manual and details of procedures
Employment information
Accounts and financial records
Health and Safety documentation:
e.g. Radiation local rules
      Mercury handling guidelines
      COSHH assessment
Staff Training records
Promotional material (patient leaflets)

One very useful checklist approach which reviews the statutory documentation requirements is provided by the Dental Practice Vade Mecum,[7] which reviews Health and Safety and other regulatory details.

There is a danger – which applies to all documented forms of risk identification – that such materials may themselves become 'regulatory'. A recent innovation in the National Health Service Regulations has been the requirement for all new NHS dental practices to be approved following a practice visit by a Dental Practice Adviser appointed by the Family Health Services Authority. It is important that risk management should be and remain essentially a tool of personal and organizational review and, like quality assurance, a means to an end rather than an end in itself. However, in health authorities or Trusts, an effective organization-wide risk management policy is increasingly becoming the norm.

Flow charts

Flow charts can be of assistance particularly in identifying risks which present as part of a procedure. They depict the flow of materials, personnel or services within a site or department, and are helpful in demonstrating vulnerabilities within the process.

For example, cross-infection control may be covered within a checklist by questions such as:

Are pre-set instrument trays in use?
Are sufficient pre-set instrument trays available?
Are instruments ultrasonically cleaned after use?
Are all instrument trays lidded and autoclaved?
Are sterilized instrument trays kept in closed closed storage cupboards or shelves?
Are all handpieces autoclaved after every use?
Are all handpieces wiped and lubricated before autoclaving?
Are disposable items used wherever possible?

– and so on, breaking down the various procedures into their various components. Drawing a flow chart for the procedure (Figure 9.2) might lead to the thought that the disposable items used (mouthwash beaker, 3-in-1 syringe tip, etc.) are similar for most procedures and, as each separate action increases the risk of contamination, perhaps all these

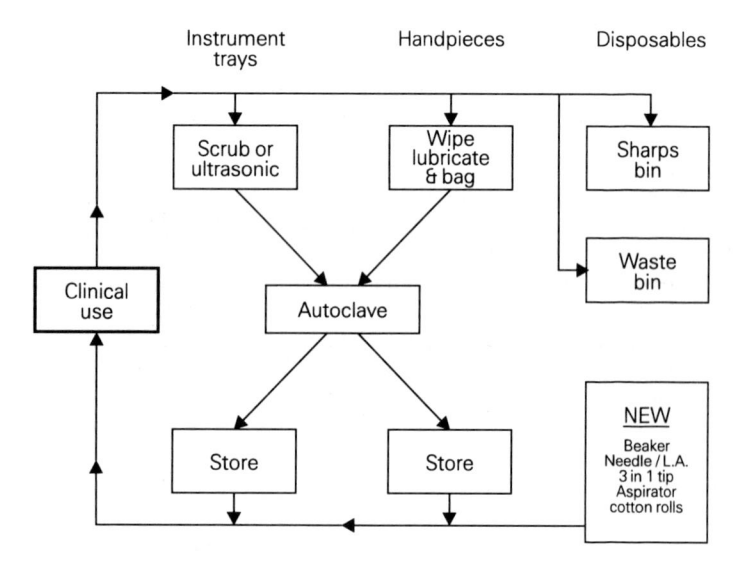

Figure 9.2 Flow chart for surgery sterilization and instrument set-up procedure

items might be enclosed in a bag and pre-packed; the bag could then serve as a waste container for that procedure and be disposed of singly. The additional cost of the bag would probably be outweighed by the time saving and potential contamination if each item were collected separately each time. Flow charting is a useful way of thinking about processes, of improving efficiency and of reducing risk. Similar applications might be found in patient record card movements, cleaning schedules or laboratory procedures.

Organizational charts

Organizational charts are of more significance in larger undertakings, but with practice and clinic sizes increasing and more centralization of services occurring, they can be a helpful adjunct in risk identification. They can be particularly useful for identifying and discussing lines of responsibility, over-dependence on one particular post or function (what if the post-holder is ill or resigns?) or duplication of effort. A sample format is shown at Figure 9.3.

Occurrence screening

Occurrence screening is a retrospective consideration of risks. A typical application is a record review for completed patients, as was described

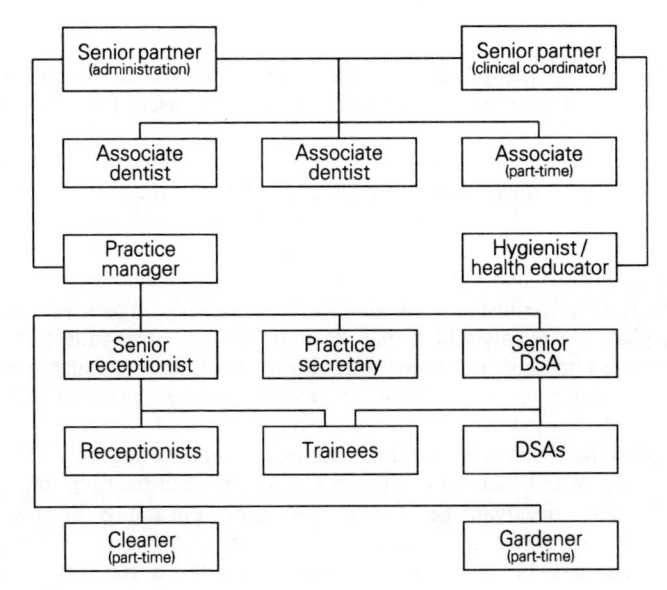

Figure 9.3 Organizational chart for a dental practice

PATIENT RECORD REVIEW CRITERIA

Positive Criteria
(Should be present)

Full personal data
Contact telephone number
Medical Alert sticker*
Medical history
Doctor's name
Treatment plan
Periodontal screening*
All visits dated
Dentist's notes legible
Dentist's notes signed
Dentist's notes dated
Post-operative instructions given and noted*
Continuation cards numbered
Orderly layout
Treatment conclusion indicated
Account details clear
Recall interval noted
Updated medical history at recall
Revised treatment plan noted*

Negative Criteria
(should be absent)

Personal comments about patient
Illegible deletions or correction fluid
Failure to return without follow-up
Repeated failure of restorations without follow-up
Illegible notes
Confidential data on outside of notes
Normal findings not recorded
Radiographic reports omitted
Untidy/unclear layout
Stains or damaged card
Evidence of re-written or summarized notes without original
Entries in pencil

* where applicable

Figure 9.4 Criteria for reviewing patient record cards

in Chapter 2. A possible checklist for a patient record card is shown at Figure 9.4. Occurrence screening can also be used for laboratory instructions, accounts books or radiographs.

The essence of occurrence screening is the identification of features which should properly have been present, as well as the review of those occurrences which should not have happened. Thus in the patient record card review, positive identification would be sought for such items as Medical History and History review, all personal details, the recording of post-operative instructions and so forth. Equally, screening should take place for events which may be indicative of some failure in the procedure undertaken; failures to return for treatment, attendance with pain or lost restoration, local anaesthetic failure, incorrect patient charge, etc.

Occurrence screening has the advantage of uncovering areas of risk or failure which are otherwise resistant to identification, but the simultaneous disadvantage of being very time-consuming. Because of this latter fact, screening tends to be infrequent, and the risks and errors identified may be long past and the opportunities for rectification consequently reduced. Additionally, occurrence screening requires that

Untoward incident reporting

Untoward incident reporting (UIR) is one of the most widely used means of risk identification in health care practice. As will be seen, UIR combines elements of risk identification with risk analysis.

An 'untoward incident' is defined as any event which causes, or has the potential to cause, damage or injury to patients, staff or resources.[8] Any such incident, wherever and whenever it occurs in the facility, is recorded on a form developed for the purpose. Reports may be made by anyone involved in the incident, and for simplicity and ease of completion, may be coded to categorize the most commonly encountered incident types.

The advantages of untoward incident reporting are that feedback is rapid, enabling prompt corrective action to be taken. Data can be provided by all members of staff. As in audit or appraisal (and UIR can feed directly into audit procedures), accurate and comprehensive information depends on an absolute assurance that UIR will not be associated with disciplinary proceedings. The only exceptions to this rule should be criminal offences, or gross negligence of a kind which could lead to summary dismissal. The introduction of UIR does require an open and non-judgemental culture to be fostered within the workplace.

One difficulty which affects UIR (and occurrence screening) is the need to have pre-existent data or standards on which to base the procedures. In practice, these problems can be overcome by pilot projects which are designed to produce the necessary information. Alternatively, since individual dental practices or departments are often small, and a representative sample of incidents may take a considerable time to be demonstrated, access to data which lists existing areas of known risk (such as that introduced in Chapter 5) may be helpful.

Figures 9.5 and 9.6 show an example of an untoward incident report form for use in a dental surgery, together with a suggested classification of codes for location, incident type and treatment type. If a pad of forms is available within a folder, instructions and a list of codes can be provided on the facing page. Forms can be designed individually to represent the particular pattern of work within a facility, or for individual departments within that facility. A reception/office area within a practice, or an orthodontic or oral surgery clinic could all adapt the basic procedures of untoward incident reporting.

UNTOWARD INCIDENT REPORT

Check Instructions before completing this form. Do not file with clinical records. Complete incident details as soon as possible after event. Ensure form is passed to practice manager at end of session.

Practice .... Patient: Surname ....
Dentist .... Forenames ....
                                                         Address ....
                                                         Practice registration No:
                                                         D o B .... Age ...... Sex M[ ] F [ ]
Time of incident: .... AM/PM
Date .... Day ....

Incident Location: Code .....   Or specify location
Incident Type   Code ...... Or specify type
Treatment type   Code ...... Or specify treatment

Details of incident   Check instructions

Reported by: ....

ACTION: FOR COMPLETION BY DENTIST OR PRACTICE MANAGER.
Severity: Minor [ ]   Medium [ ]   Serious [ ]   Dangerous [ ]
Action required to prevent recurrence   Yes [ ]   No [ ]
Dentist informed   Yes [ ]   No [ ]
Other Action

Signed ....   Date ....

Figure 9.5 Untoward incident report sheet

> **UNTOWARD INCIDENT REPORTING**
> **List of Codings: Surgery**

Location	Incident type	Treatment Type
[1] Surgery 1	[1] Complaint	[1] Diagnosis
[2] Surgery 2	[2] Diagnosis error	[2] Oral surgery
[3] Hygienist surgery	[3] Treatment error	[3] Restorative – endodontic
[4] Preventive Unit	[4] Equipment failure	[4] Restorative – crown and bridge
[5] X-ray	[5] Procedural failure	[5] Restorative – other
[6] Reception/waiting room	[6] Injury – patient	[6] Periodontology
[7] Other	[7] Injury – staff	[7] Paedodontic
	[8] Records error	[8] Orthodontic
	[9] Communication breakdown	[9] Prosthetic
	[10] Other	[10] Other

Figure 9.6 Untoward incident report – list of codings

Once the basic data have been entered, a brief description of the incident is provided by the reporter. It is important that this is completed as soon after the event as possible, and thought should be given to designing forms which require the least time to complete, whilst capturing essential data. Thus a patient registration number might render address details unnecessary. It is important that UIR forms are not stored with patient notes, first because the completion of the form in no way excepts the normal requirement to document individual patient records with details of any occurrences which affect that patient's care, and second because the inclusion of administrative UIR data with records may breach confidentiality or may be prejudicial to a subsequent legal defence if disclosed.

Summary

Risk identification is the essential first step in developing a risk management programme. Risk awareness is not, in itself, sufficient, since it may suggest only a passive or reactive attitude. An active and 'personalized' approach is necessary in order to properly identify hazards and to encourage a forward-looking policy of containment or elimination. Checklists and untoward incident reporting techniques are probably the most useful tools in dental risk identification, although occurrence screening and other analyses may be applied.

Risk Analysis

Risk analysis is chiefly concerned with two dimensions: incidence and severity. The attitude taken towards a particular risk must be influenced by the likelihood of its occurrence, and by the consequences which follow. These two factors are linked: studies show that that a 'risk hierarchy' exists.[9] Risks of low severity tend to occur more often than those of high severity. This distribution, noted in Chapter 3, is often portrayed in the form of a risk pyramid, indicating the ratio of 'severe' risks to 'medium' and 'minor' risks.

This principle applies generally throughout the field of risk management. Thus in an analysis of 1,232 accidents occurring in a general hospital, Le Guen found that for each 'severe' accident (one which resulted in more than three days absence from work),[10] there were 10 'minor' accidents and 195 'non-injury' accidents. Klein, reviewing complaints against general medical practitioners,[11] noted that for every formal complaint investigated by Executive Councils (the forerunners of Family Health Service Authorities), about 100 'grumbles' were dealt with informally, and there were about 400 reported instances of minor 'friction'. These risk distributions are depicted in Figure 9.7

The importance of such classifications is obvious in that the cost:benefit ratio of taking major preventive action to avoid a risk of insignificant consequence is clearly uneconomic. Conversely, the 'catastrophic' risk which occurs only very rarely may be resistant to any sensible local measures, and so it is insured against. At the one extreme, magazines may disappear from the waiting area but the cost of this is so low it is easily absorbed; at the other extreme, a lorry may drive into the premises, but because this is so unlikely, it can be economically insured against. Difficulties may however still arise in classifying risks into separate categories. An insurance company can simply define a 'severe'

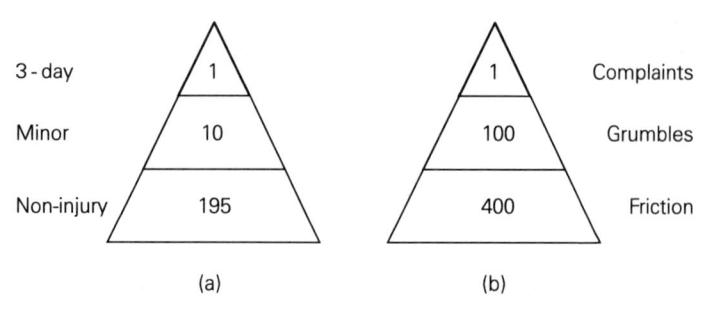

Figure 9.7 Risk triangles: (a) Hospital accidents (after Le Guen): (b) Complaints against family doctors (after Klein)

Developing a risk management strategy 239

Cost £ ↑						
10,000	£10,000	£20,000	£40,000	£80,000	£160,000	£320,000
1,000	£1,000	£2,000	£4,000	£8,000	£16,000	£32,000
100	£100	£200	£400	£800	£1,600	£3,200
50	£50	£100	£200	£400	£800	£1,600
10	£10	£20	£40	£80	£160	£320
1	£1	£2	£4	£8	£16	£32
	1	2	4	8	16	32

Incidence →

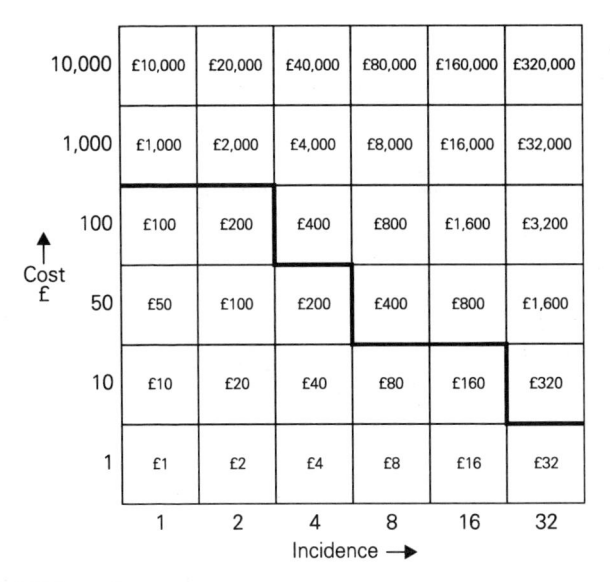

Figure 9.8 Risk matrix

risk as, say one over £100,000, and a minor risk as one below £1,000. In clinical care, one would categorize any risk of permanent harm to a patient, the risk of a formal complaint or a breach of a statutory liability as 'severe', but the classification of hazards of medium severity is problematic.

One approach is the use of a 'risk matrix' as recommended by Roberts.[12] Here the probable incidence of a risk is plotted against its severity (which may be expressed as cost). The point at which an occurrence, or numbers of occurrences, is unacceptable is then portrayed by the heavy outline on the matrix grid (Figure 9.8). In the example shown, the tolerance line has been set at £200. An incident with a consequential cost of £10 would be 'acceptable' if it were to occur 16 times a year, whereas a loss of £50 would be acceptable no more than four times a year. In larger clinics or departments, the use of such matrices, together with untoward incident reporting systems which assign a financial value to each occurrence, has proved valuable in containing costs and in training programmes.

In smaller practices or units, prioritization of identified risks tends to take place according to more or less subjective criteria. This can lead to unfortunate consequences, in that attention may be diverted away from apparently insignificant risks with potentially severe outcomes. Factor rating should be applied to all identified deficiencies and hazards, and

RISK ASSESSMENT FOR WARD/DEPT		DATE		TASK			
Probability of exposure to/contact with hazard		Frequency of exposure to hazard		Maximum probable loss		Persons at risk	
Exposure/ contact	P.E. value	Frequency	F.E. value	Loss	M.P.L. value	Number	N.P. value
Impossible	0	Infrequently	0.1	Fatality	15	(1–2)	1
Unlikely	1	Annually	0.2	Loss of limbs/eyes	8	(3–7)	2
Possible	2	Monthly	1.0	Loss of limb/eye	4	(8–15)	4
Even chance	5	Weekly	1.5	Break (major)	2	(16–50)	8
Probably	8	Daily	2.5	Break (minor)	1	(50>)	12
Likely	10	Hourly	4.0	Laceration	0.5		
Certain	15	Constantly	5.0	Scratch/bruise	0.1		

1 Please circle level at which risk is assessed in each of the four "value" columns – for each task.

2 Please calculate hazard rating number (H.R.N.) using the following equation:–

Probability of exposure × frequency of exposure × maximum probable loss × number of persons = hazard rating number

P.E. × F.E. × M.P.L. × N.P. = H.R.N.

H.R.N.	Risk	Action Requirment
(0–1)	Acceptable	Accept risk/Consider action
(1–5)	Very low	Action within 1 year
(5–10)	Low	Action within 3 months
(10–50)	Significant	Action within 1 month
(50–100)	High	Action within 1 week
(100–500)	Very high	Action within 1 day
(500–1000)	Extreme	Immediate action
(>1000)	Unacceptable	Stop the activity

Figure 9.9 Risk analysis by factor rating – Assessment sheet (courtesy of Mr. P. Harris, Risk Manager, Homerton Hospital)

this should include; the probability of exposure, the frequency of exposure, the maximum probable loss and the number of personnel at risk.

An example of factor rating used by an NHS Trust is shown in Figure 9.9.[13] Such an approach would be helpful in the complex risk assessment of larger units, but can be simplified and modified for application in smaller facilities.

Summary

Risk analysis is concerned with the incidence and severity of a known hazard. These factors can be determined from existing research, or from untoward incident analysis/occurrence screening. A prioritized approach should be taken to risks which have been identified and analysed, leading into risk control measures.

Risk Control

Once risks have been identified and some understanding of their incidence and potential severity has been gained, there are four alternative strategies which can be employed in risk control:

- avoidance
- reduction
- retention
- transfer

Risk avoidance implies the complete elimination of the risk. For instance, a dentist may choose to avoid providing a particular form of treatment which is associated with known risks. Alternatively, it may be possible to take preventive action which eliminates the risk, although complete avoidance may be difficult to achieve, and may only have the effect of introducing an alternative risk. An example was considered under 'security measures', when it was suggested that removing all cash from the reception area at night might increase the likelihood of 'revenge' damage by an intruder, or the theft of some other item of value. If a dentist elects to refer all impacted third molar extractions, there may be a risk that delayed or inconvenient arrangements for treatment on referral may adversely affect patient relationships or precipitate acute symptoms.

Risk reduction is a more feasible aim in the majority of circumstances. Installing fire safety equipment and having a fire drill will not eliminate the risk of fire, but will reduce the severity of its impact. These measures alone, however, will not necessarily reduce the frequency of fires; that would require a different, though parallel approach, involving checking wiring, ensuring equipment is switched off, careful storage and use of flammable substances and so on. In some instances, it may be relatively difficult to reduce frequency and measures must be concentrated on severity (for example the availability of emergency resuscitation drugs and equipment); in other instances, reduction of frequency will be the chief aim (for example, reducing needlestick injuries).

Where measures to avoid or reduce risk are either not worthwhile (because the consequences are trivial) or not feasible (because the risk is unpredictable and potentially severe), then risk retention and transfer are the appropriate strategy. Mention has been made of trivial risks, but it is important to keep them under review. A cluster of individually minor problems may reveal an underlying fault which may require attention. If one capsule of local anaesthetic leaks or is cracked, it may simply be discarded. If two or more from the same batch are faulty, then the failings should be acted on. Risk retention is essentially a matter of decision about what can economically be absorbed, relative to the cost of taking action. However, it should not be an excuse for failing to attend to details.

Risk transfer has come to be synonymous with insurance in the fields of commerce and industry – it is also known as risk financing, since the cost of insurance premiums must be weighed against the probability of the insured risk occurring. In healthcare, risk transfer might also be considered to include such instances as the referral of patients, but as noted above, this may increase other risks in proportion. Some examples of insurance were considered in Chapter 6.

Risk transfer by means of insurance cannot, however, be considered as a 'clean break'. The terms and conditions of an insurance policy may require, for instance, that the insured person uses any reasonable endeavours to reduce the risk, and explicit actions or exceptions may be cited. A theft policy may require the fitment of suitable security measures, and may exclude items above a certain value. A sickness policy may exclude pre-existing and certain other conditions, and a consequential loss (business interruption) policy may require that accurate and up to date accounts are kept to assess the loss.

Professional indemnity insurance, or the benefits of defence organization membership, may be similarly affected by the terms and conditions of the policy (or membership). In common with most other insurances, cover may be conditional on the prompt and accurate submission of claims or potential claims. The cost of legal advice sought independently before a claim is reported is specifically excluded, and although, as described in Chapter 4, a sincere expression of regret is generally regarded as beneficial, any admission of liability before seeking expert advice, is most unwise – and where commercial insurance is involved, may well invalidate the cover.

Complaints and claims management

The importance of good communication and the maintenance, whenever possible, of a continuing relationship with a complainant has been stressed earlier. It is important that a complaints policy be discussed, agreed and accepted by all staff. Training courses are available for reception staff especially in dealing with angry, argumentative or just plain 'difficult' patients.[14] A complaints policy should include:

The opportunity for patients to express their views without interruption or argument

The availability and accessibility of clinical staff involved to discuss their care in person

Reasonable, objective and prompt consideration of complaints brought

The provision of a detailed and polite reply to complaints

It is assumed that in all but the most straightforward of cases, expert advice will be sought by the dentist at the earliest opportunity. To repeat the suggestion offered in Chapter 4, patients who complain should be allowed to voice their problem, no matter how compelling the urge to cut them short (by any means!). The clinician involved must be advised at once of the matter, and should be personally available. Notes should be kept of all that is said, and expert advice sought. The patient should receive a full and courteous reply – either in writing, or backed up in writing (and a copy kept). If it is believed that the matter can be resolved by a refund of fees, or an offer of review or continued treatment by another dentist, then such an option should receive serious consideration. Fee refunds should always be accompanied by a note in writing to the effect that the refund is offered 'entirely as a gesture of goodwill and without any admission of liability'. Specific and detailed advice on such wording should be sought.

Care must be taken to distinguish complaints from putative legal claims. This distinction is not always entirely clear, but one or more of the following characteristics may be identified:

- the complainant demands 'compensation' over and above the treatment costs
- the complainant indicates (and it seems possible) that legal advice has been sought
- complaints are phrased in terms which are uncharacteristic of the complainant, suggesting legal 'coaching' or 'ghost writing'
- it is clear that the complainant has suffered injury or permanent damage

Obvious claims are signified by the receipt of a solicitor's 'letter before action' – that is, a letter which alleges negligence, breach of contract or other wrong. Alternatively, a writ of summons may be served, either by registered post or via a 'writ server' who delivers the writ in person. This is a rare occurrence in dental negligence cases, since the plaintiff's solicitors will usually want to have some indication of their client's course of action by requesting disclosure of the patient's notes as described in Chapter 4. Needless to say, the arrival of a County Court or High Court writ is a matter of some concern, and is usually the result of either ignoring previous correspondence from solicitors (unwise), or the fact that the limitation period for the proposed action is nearly expired. The issue, or anticipated issue, of a writ should be notified to the defence organization or insurer without delay, and will normally be forwarded to their solicitors who will formally 'accept service' on the dentist's behalf. This must be done within a very limited period of time if a defence to the action is to be entered.

Summary

Risk control is the ultimate aim of risk management. All risks must ultimately be dealt with either by avoidance, reduction, retention or transfer; the object of an efficient risk management strategy is to determine the most efficient (in terms of cost:benefit ratio) and effective (in terms of providing good quality healthcare) mix of these alternatives. Responsibility does not end with risk transfer; a clear understanding of insurers' and defence organizations' conditions and requirements – including sound claims handling procedures – is essential.

Full circle

It will be recalled that risk management was introduced as a 'cycle', and there can therefore be no conclusion, as such, to the process. Dental procedures, personnel and technology change constantly. Public perception of risk, and the regulatory frameworks, both professional and legislative, are continually shifting. Risk management must therefore involve continual re-identification, re-assessment and reinforcement of control measures.

Anthony Giddens has suggested that we adapt to the presence of risk in one of four ways;[15] pragmatic acceptance, sustained optimism, cynical pessimism and radical engagement. Pragmatic acceptance is not without psychological risks of its own, since it implies deep anxieties. Sustained optimism suggests a rather foolhardy lack of concern with the realities of life. Cynical pessimism cannot be all bad, since we derive from it a certain amount of black humour without which life would be dull indeed. Radical engagement sounds rather like a political rallying cry, but that aside it does suggest that the solutions to the problems of daily life and work are in our own hands. Risk management offers one approach to those problems.

References

1. Carrotte P.V. (1993) Active Learning in the United Kingdom Undergraduate Dental Course. *British Dental Journal*, **175** (6), 204–208
2. Kress G. (1987) Improving Patient Satisfaction. *International Dental Journal*, **37**, 117–122
3. Morris A.L., Vito A.A., Bomba M.R. *et al.* (1989) The impact of a quality assessment program on the practice behavior of general practitioners: a follow-up study. *Journal of the American Dental Association*, **119**, 705–709
4. Dickson C.G.A. (1991) *Risk Analysis (2nd edn)*. Witherby, London
5. Crockford N. (1986) *An Introduction to Risk Management (2nd edn)*. Woodhead-Faulkner, Cambridge, p. 19 *et seq.*
6. Roberts G. (1993) Healthcare Risk Management Ltd. Personal Communication
7. Sheffield Dental Consortium (1994) *The Dental Practice Vade Mecum (2nd edn)*. Sheffield FHSA
8. Roberts G. (1992) *Criterion based untoward incident analysis*. Healthcare Risk Management Ltd, London
9. Crockford N. (1986) *An Introduction to Risk Management (2nd edn)*. Woodhead-Faulkner, Cambridge, p. 12
10. Le Guen, J-M. (1993) Making Risk Management Better Informed and Less Intuitive. *Journal of the Institute of Risk Management*, January 1994
11. Klein R.E. (1973) *Complaints against Doctors*. Charles Knight, London, p. 106
12. Roberts G. (1992) Planned Risk Management and Patient Care. *Healthcare Risk Management Bulletin*, September 1992, No 4, 5–7
13. Harris P. (1994) Risk Management Strategy. Seminar presented to the Institute of Risk Management, London. 22 February
14. Details of the British Dental Association/AMSPAR dental receptionist courses are available from the BDA or from Radcliffe Medical Press
15. Giddens A. (1990) The Consequences of Modernity. Stanford University Press, Stanford, California, p. 134 *et seq*

Appendix

Sources of further information
Audit and peer review
Self Assessment Manual and Standards
(Clinical Standards in General Dental Practice)
Published 1991 by:

Faculty of Dental Surgery,
The Royal College of Surgeons of England,
35–43 Lincoln's Inn Fields,
London WC2A 3PN
Tel: 0171-831 9438

Clinical Audit – A Workbook
Published 1993

British Dental Association,
64 Wimpole Street,
London W1M 8AL
Tel: 0171–935 9875

Health and safety
Detailed and authoritative guidance on matters relating to health and safety can be obtained from the Health and Safety Executive (HSE) Information Services: Tel: (Sheffield) 01142 892345

Details of HSE books and publications can be obtained from:

HSE Books,
PO Box 1999,
Sudbury,
Suffolk CO10 6FS
Tel: 01787 881165 (free leaflet line)
   01787 313995
– or from Dillons and Rymans bookshops

HSE 'Autofax' services

If a fax machine is available, updated health and safety information and leaflets can be faxed back to an enquirer by return. Calls are charged at 36p/minute or 48p/minute at peak times (1994 prices)

For details of Autofax services:	01483 811 822
HSE Autofax index page: (1 page)	01839 060606
Monthly list of HSE publications: (5 pages)	01839 060600

Employment medical advisory services

See local telephone directory or contact HSE area offices:

England South west:	01179 290681
England South:	01256 473181
England South east:	01342 326922
London North:	0181 594 5522
London South:	0171 407 8911
East Anglia:	01245 284661
Home Counties North:	01582 34121
East Midlands:	01604 21233
West Midlands:	0121 200 2299
Wales:	01222 473777
Marches:	01782 717181
North Midlands:	01159 470712
Yorkshire South:	01142 739081
Yorkshire West and North:	01132 446191
Greater Manchester:	0161 831 7111
Merseyside:	0151 922 7211
North West:	01772 59321
North East:	0191 284 8448
Scotland East:	0131 225 1313
Scotland West:	0141 204 2646

National radiological protection board

Dental Monitoring Service,
Hospital Lane,
Cookridge,
Leeds LS16 RW
Tel: 01132 300232

Autoclave/Pressure vessel certification

Strovers (Insurance Brokers) Ltd,
9 Gayfere Street,
London SW1P 3HN
Tel: 0171 982 6335

The Associated Offices Technical Committee,
and
Council of Independent Inspection Authorities,
St Mary's Parsonage,
Manchester M60 9AP
Tel: 0161 839 7038

The Independent Engineering Insurers' Committee,
57 Ladymead,
Guildford GU1 1DB
Tel: 01483 68161

First aid

British Red Cross Society, St John Ambulance, St Andrew's Ambulance Association: consult local telephone directory for details or contact:

British Red Cross Society,
9 Grosvenor Crescent,
London SW1X 7EF
Tel: 0171 235 5454

St John Ambulance,
1 Grosvenor Crescent,
London SW1X 7EF
Tel: 0171 235 5231

St Andrew's Ambulance Association,
St Andrew's House,
Milton Street,
Glasgow G4 0HR
Tel: 0141 332 4031

Mercury analysis

Details obtainable from:

Dr P. Warren,
Department of Biochemistry,
Basic Medical Sciences,
Queen Mary and Westfield College,
Mile End Road,
London E1 4NS
Tel: 0171 982 6335

Index

Accidents, 48–50
Account(s), 138
Accounting system, adequate, 3
Apical surgery, 110
Acts of Parliament
    Access to Health Records Act (1990), 120
    Access to Medical Reports Act (1988), 120
    Age of Legal Capacity (Scotland) Act (1991), 112
    Children Act (1989), 112
    Civil Evidence Act (1968), 119
    Control of Pollution Act (1974), 84
    Data Protection Act (1984), 89, 119, 120
    Dentists Acts (1878, 1956, 1957, 1984), 183
    Employers' Liability (Compulsory Insurance) Act (1969), 45
    Employment Protection (Consolidation) Act (1978), 77
    Environmental Protection Act (1989), 84–5
    Environmental Protection Act (1990), 64
    Factories Act (1961), 39
    Factories Act (1971), 69
    Family Law Reform Act (1969), 112
    Financial Services Act (1986), 171
    Fire Precautions Act (1971), 54
    Health and Safety at Work etc. Act (1974), 9, 39, 52, 85
        autoclaves/pressure vessels, 69
        training, 79
        waste disposal, 64
    Hospital Complaints Act (1985), 200

Acts of Parliament – *continued*
    Insurance Brokers (Registration) Act (1977), 171
    Insurance Companies Act (1982), 166
    Law Reform (Contributory Negligence) Act (1945), 133
    Life Insurance Act (1974), 165
    Misuse of Drugs Act (1971), 88
    Occupier's Liability Act (1957), 55
    Occupier's Liability Act (1984), 45, 84
    Offices, Shops and Railway Premises Act (1963), 39
    Police and Criminal Evidence Act (1984), 122
    Prevention of Terrorism (Temporary Provisions) Act (1984), 122
    Reporting of Accidents Act (1894), 48
    Road Traffic Act (1988), 122
    Sex Discrimination Acts (1975, 1986), 77
    Supply of Goods and Services Act (1982), 135–6
    Supreme Court Act (1981), 123–4
    Trade Union Reform and Employment Rights Act (1992), 77
    Unfair Contract Terms Act (1977), 103, 168
Advisory, Conciliation and Arbitration Service (ACAS), 78
Alcohol abuse, 219–21
Alternative treatments, 110–11
American Dental Association's Principles of Ethics, quoted, 111
Amphetamine-related drugs, 137
Appraisal, 26–9
Armed service, short service commission, 209

Assault, 108, 136–7
Audit, 24–5
Audit and press review, 246
Autoclaves, 69–70
  certification, 248
Autofax, 247

Bankruptcy, 221–3
Battery, 108, 112
Benzodiazepines, 138
Body language, 96
British Dental Association's advice sheets, 37 (fig.)
Burnout, 217

Canada
  litigation in civil courts, 200
  professional liability risks, 106
  state regulation of health care institutions, 8
Cannabis, 137
Cardio-pulmonary resuscitation, 3
Cases
  Bolam v. Friern Hospital Management Committee (1957), 108, 131
  Canterbury v. Spence, 109
  F. v. West Berkshire Health Authority, 113
  Gillick (1985), 112
  Sidaway (1985), 108, 109, 110
Central Services Agency (Northern Ireland), 192
Charts
  flow, 232–3
  organizational, 233
Checklists, 229–31
Citric acid etchant, 155
Claims management, 242–4
Clinical notes (records), 114–27
  abbreviations, 116–17
  access to, 119–21
  accuracy, 118
  adequacy, 115–17
  computerized, 119
  confidentiality, 121–4
  contemporaneity, 119
  disclosure, 121–4
  legibility, 117–18
  periodontal disease, 116
  retention, 124–7
  updating, 116
Clinical practice organisation, 15–34

Common law duty, 46
Communication, 94–108
  apology (saying 'sorry'), 105–6
  breakdown avoided/minimized, 98–106
  effective, 95–9
    achievement, 97–8
    definition, 95–6
  exaggerated behavioural patterns, 101–2
  manipulative behavioural patterns, 102–3
  post-traumatic behavioural patterns, 103–4
  suppressed behavioural patterns, 102
  sympathy, 105
  time pressures, 100–1, 216–18
  timeliness, 104–5
  trust, 94
  unexpected treatment complications, 104
  written instructions to laboratories, 98
Community Periodontal Index of Treatment Need (CPITN), 116
Complaints management, 242–4
Computers, 53, 119
Consent, 106–14
  alternative treatments, 110–11
  children, 112–13
  consequences of refusal, 111
  effect of treatment, 108
  financial cost, 111
  forms, 113
  future of, 113–14
  legal actions, 112
  material risks, 108–10
  nature of treatment, 108
  'special cases', 112–13
Contract law, 135
Criminal law, 136
Cross-infection control, 55–64
  model, 58 (fig.)
Crown Immunity (UK), 9, 174–5

Damages, 134–5
Declaration of Geneva (1968), 121
Defence organizations, 172–6
Dental claims data, 142–8, 149 (table)
Dental health education facility, 19 (fig.)
Dental Practice Board, 192
Dental Reference Officer, 193
  complaints following report, 194–8
Dental surgery assistant, tasks/standards, 28 (fig.)

Dentists
  complaints against (England), 13
  insurance payments, 12
  number, 12
  professional training, 15–16
Dentures, provision of, 135–6
Disputes, in:
  general practice, 202–4
  salaried service, 204
Drug abuse, 219–21
Drugs, 137–8

Effluent, 65–6
Electrical appliances, 70
Emergency treatment, 159–60
Employees welfare, 45–7
Employment, 75–82
  contracts, 77–8
  disciplinary procedures, 80–1
  dismissal, 81–2
  grievances, 80
Employment
  inadequate procedures, 3
  recruitment, 76–7
  training, 79–80
Employment Medical Advisory Service, 52, 247
Environmental risks, 36–90
European Commission Framework Directives (1990–91), 171
European Union harmonization, 40–1
Experts systems, 6

Failure to complete treatment, 160–1
'Failure to diagnose and treat' litigation (periodontal disease), 152
Family Health Service Authority, 191
Financial risks, 221–4
Fire precautions, 54–5, 56 (fig.)
First aid, 47–8, 248
Flow charts, 232–3
Fluoridation of water supplies, 8
Fraud, 138

General Dental Council, 182, 183–90
  advice on estimates, 112
  Health Committee, 186–7, 220
  Preliminary Proceedings Committee, 184–5
  Professional Conduct Committee, 185–6
  serious professional misconduct, 187–90

General practice
  disputes, 202–4
  partnerships, 208–9
  practice purchase, 208–9
  risk management principles, 204–8
Good Samaritan, 160
Griffiths Report (UK, 1983), 25

Hand dermatitis, 52
Hazardous substances, 71–4
Health Boards (Sotland; Northern Ireland), 191
Health risks, 218–19
Health and safety, 39–75
  policy, 42 (fig.), 43
Health and Safety Executive Information Services, 246
Hepatitis B, 59–60
  vaccination, 52
Herpes viruses, 60
Hepetic whitlow, 60
Hippocratic Oath, 121
Human immunodeficiency virus (HIV), 58–9, 61–2
  Florida outbreak, 63–4

Impacted third molar, 156
Implants, 157
Indecency, 138
Industrial Tribunals, 78
Infections, 55–64
  hazards in dentistry, 60 (fig.)
  risk analysis, 61–2
  risk control, 62–4
  risk identification, 59
Information to patients, unclear/misleading, 4
Informed consent, see Consent
Injuries, 48–50
Insurance, 164–80
  broker or direct?, 171
  class rating, 167
  contingency, 166
  experience rating, 167
  indemnity, 166
  insured risks, 167
  professional liability, 172
  proposals, 167–9
  recent trends, 169–70
  transfer of risk, 164
  trends in dental claims, 177–80
  type of cover, 170–1
  United States, 177
Insurance-based indemnity, 176–7

Jaw fracture, 156
Joint Commission on Accreditation of Healthcare Organizations (JCAHO), 8

Labial sensory loss, 110, 156
Lasers, 68–9
Learning disabilities, patients with, 121
Legionella infection of air-conditioning towers, 85
Life events scale, 213
Lingual paraesthesia, 156
Local analgesia, 157–8
London and Counties Medical Protection Society (Medical Protection Society), 173

Management
  decision-making processes, 10
  definition, 16
Manual handling, 54
Medical Defence Union, 172–3, 178, 179 (fig.)
  dental claims data, 142–8, 149 (table)
Medical Insurance Agency, 176–7
Mens rea, 136
Mercury, 73–4
  analysis, 249
  screening, 52
Mistaken extraction, 156–7
Mortality rate reduction, 213

National Health Service (UK), 9, 191–209
  complaints, 193–4
    against dentists in hospital/community services, 200–2
    arising from administrative procedures, 196–7
    following Dental Reference Officer's report, 194–6
    formal/disciplinary procedures, 197–200
    general practice, 191–3
  Terms of Service, 191–2
National Radiological Protection Board, 247
Negligence, 82–3, 130–4
Nerve damage following extraction, 109–10
New technology/treatment, 159

Non-insurance based indemnity, 106
Nuisance, 84

Occupier's liability, 82–5
  negligence, 82–3
  nuisance, 84
  pollution, 84–5
  trespass, 84
Oral surgery risks, 155–7
Organization/procedures, 17–32
  aims/objectives, 17–21
  procedure planning, 21–2
Organizational charts, 233

Paraformaldehyde-containing sealants, 155
Patients' Charter (1991), 200
Patient record review criteria, 234
'People poisoning', 216
Performance measurement, 23–4
Periodontal disease, 116, 151–2
Personal protective equipment, 50, 51 (fig.)
Phosphoric acid etchant, 155
Pollution, 84–5
Practice manual, 22–3
Pressure vessels, 69–70
  certification, 248
Procedures, *see* Organization/procedures
Professional indemnity insurance, 242
Professional negligence, definition of, 172
Proximate cause, 132
Pseudomonas sp., water supply contamination, 66
Psychological damage, 131

Quality assurance, 29–34
  in health care, 30
  risk management and, 31–4
  standards, 31

Records, *see* Clinical notes
Regulations
  Control of Substances Hazardous to Health Regulations (1988), 52, 71
  Electricity at Work Regulations (1989), 70
  Health and Safety (Display Screen Equipment) Regulations (1992), 53–4

Regulations – *continued*
  Health and Safety (First-Aid) Regulations (1981), 48
  Health and Safety (Personal Protective Equipment) Regulations (1992), 50
  Health and Safety (Reporting of Injuries, Diseases, and Dangerous Occurrences) Regulations (1985), 49
  Ionizing Radiation Regulations (1985), 66
  Ionizing Radiation (Protection of Persons Undergoing Medical Examination and Treatment) Regulations, 66
  Management of Health and Safety at Work (1992), 41–5
  Manual Handling Operations Regulations (1992), 54
  Nursing Homes (Laser) Regulations (1984), 68
  Pressure Systems and Transportable Containers Regulations (1989), 69
  Provision and Use of Work Equipment Regulations (1992), 53
  Workplace (Health Safety and Welfare) Regulations (1992), 46
Relationships with professional colleagues, 202
Removable prostheses, 158–9
Res ipsa loquitor, 132
Respected body of opinion, 109
Restorative dentistry, 153
Risks, 4–13, 130–61, 182–209
  analysis, 238–41
    by factor rating, 240 (fig.)
  areas in clinical dentistry, 139–41
  assessment, 10–11
  citric acid etchant, 155
  control, 11, 241–2
  cost, 12
  criteria, 4 (table)
  dental claims data, 142–8, 149 (table)
  endodontic treatment, 154–5
  financial, 221–4
  fracture of endodontic instrument, 154–5
  failure to obtain adequate apical seal, 154
  identification/risk reduction, 149–59
    diagnosis, 149–51
    endodontic treatment, 154
    periodontal treatment, 151–2

Risks – *continued*
  identification/risk reduction – *continued*
    restorative dentistry, 153–5
    treatment planning, 149–51
    X-rays, 151
  identification techniques, 227–9
  impacted third molar, 156
  implants, 157
  jaw fracture, 156
  labial paraesthesia, 110, 156
  lingual paraesthesia, 156
  local analgesia, 157–8
  management cycle, 11 (table)
  management strategy development, 226–44
  management principles in general practice employment, 204–8
  matrix, 239
  mistaken extraction, 156–7
  oral surgery, 155–7
  occurrence screening, 233–5
  phosphoric acid etchant, 155
  political, 4
  professional, 182–209
  public perception of, 7 (table)
  pyramid, 74
  quantitative assessment (US), 140–1
  removable prostheses, 158–9
  responsibility for employees, 133
  root perforation, 154
  sealant, 155
  speculative, 4, 5
  transfer, 242
  triangles, 238 (fig.)
  workplace, 36–90
Risk assessment, 43, 44 (fig.)
Risk management, 2–3
  relevance to healthcare, 3–5
Risk manager, 7
Root perforation, 154
RUMBA, 20

Safety, *see* Health and safety
Safety precautions/regulations, 8
Salaried services, disputes in, 204
Scottish Dental Practice Board, 192
Security, 85–90
  computer data, 89
  drugs, 88
  equipment, 87–8
  money, 88–90
  personnel, 87
  premises, 86
  records, 89

Serious professional misconduct, 187–90
Sick Dentists Scheme, 220–1
Sou Medicale, Le, 176
Stress, 212–16
  dealing with, 214–16
Subacute bacterial endocarditis, 150
Subject Access Modification Order (1987), 120
Surgery design, 3
Systems theory, 39

Time pressure, 100–1, 216–18
Trespass, 84
Triumph of professionals, 6
Tuberculosis, 60
Type A behaviour, 215

United States
  contingency fee system, 200
  dental malpractice crisis, 17, 190
  insurance, 177
  litigation in civil court, 200
  medical malpractice crisis, 177
  National Dental Malpractice study, 141, 179–80

United States – *continued*
  professional liability risks, 106
  quantitative assessment of risk, 140–1
  regulation of dentistry, 190–1
  state regulation of healthcare institutions, 8
Untoward incident reporting, 235–7

Vaccination, 52
VDU users, 53–4
Vicarious liability, 79–80, 134
Vocational trainees, 134

Waste disposal, 64
Water
  fluoridation, 8
  pollution, 65–6
'Working for Patients' (White Paper, UK, 1989), 31
Workplace risks, 36–90
Workplace safety, 52–4

X-rays, 66–8, 151